the precise

you the territor

Heide

quanti

ers thrive

at Cranbrook can

act as a validation of

ct. The di

or from L

deas, and

in a studio plat-

form that supports

designer. The

studio is a host

their own

visions of

conflic

and oc

the precise

om Heide

technologi

technical

in a m

precise

m Heide

the new

CRANBROOK DESIGN

discourse

First published in the United States of America in 1990 by
Rizzoli International Publications, Inc.
300 Park Avenue South, New York, NY 10010

Library of Congress
Cataloging-in-Publication Data

Cranbrook design: the new discourse: essays / by Hugh Aldersey-Williams... [et al.].
p. cm.
ISBN 0-8478-1252-9.
ISBN 0-8478-1253-7 (pbk.)
1. Design — Study and teaching — Michigan — Bloomfield Hills.
2. Cranbrook Academy of Art — Curricula.
I. Aldersey-Williams, Hugh.
NK 1170.C7 1990 90-34704 CIP
745.4'071'177439 — dc20

This book is published to accompany the exhibition
Cranbrook Design: The New Discourse

Cranbrook Academy of Art Museum
Bloomfield Hills, Michigan
November 1990

Steelcase Design Partnership
New York, NY
January 1991

Designed by Katherine McCoy, P. Scott Makela, and Mary Lou Kroh
Editorial assistance by Mary Lou Kroh
Photographic assistance by Allen Hori
Endpaper and divider images by P. Scott Makela
Typesetting by Key-tech, Birmingham, Michigan
Printed by Dai Nippon, Tokyo, Japan

the new CRANBROOK DESIGN discourse

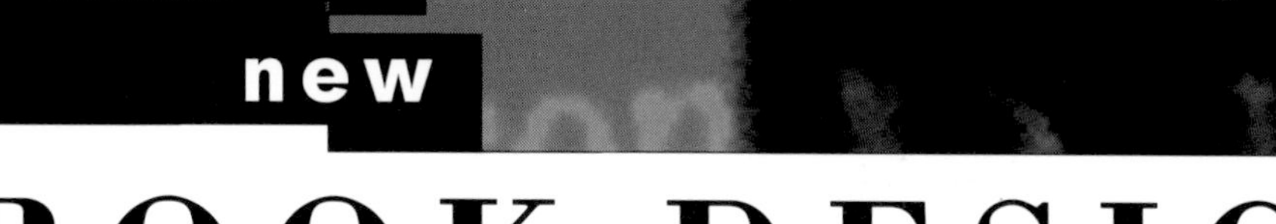

Hugh Aldersey-Williams
Lorraine Wild
Daralice Boles
Katherine & Michael McCoy
Roy Slade
Niels Diffrient

RIZZOLI
NEW YORK

Acknowledgments

This book is a testament to the power of the educational theories of Eliel Saarinen. He strongly believed that the best learning situation was a supportive studio environment where a great diversity of philosophies and ideas could flourish. And they certainly have flourished in the last decade at Cranbrook. Many people have played a role in this remarkable creative output. First of course are the students, who enter Cranbrook with some trepidation but soon gain their vision and their own voice in design and contribute to the very rich discourse that is the lifeblood of the studios. Everyone contributes to the strata of ideas and projects that make up the body of work of the Design Department. Equally important are the alumni - the students who after leaving the protective environment of the Cranbrook studios test their ideas in the sometimes hostile environment of the world. They often see that their ideas can make a difference in the course of the profession.

This is a visual book about ten years of design by Cranbrook students, faculty, and alumni. What it cannot show are the equally important but non-visual areas of design, where Cranbrook designers have made significant contributions to design history, theory, methodology, criticism, and education. It should be stressed that these areas are highly valued components of the Cranbrook design project though they are not dealt with here.

We could not progress without the dedicated group of patrons, clients, and critics who have supported the work over the past ten years by offering projects, grants, and other kinds of funding, and critical advice to help shape and project these ideas into the world. They include Robert Blaich, Managing Director of Design for Philips in The Netherlands; Jeffrey Osborne, former Vice President of Design at Knoll International and now Executive Director of the International Design Conference in Aspen; Susan Grant Lewin, Director of Publicity for Formica Corporation; Nathan Felde, Director of Media Research at NYNEX; Niels Diffrient; design critic Steven Holt; Beverly Russell, Editorial Director of *Interiors*; Gert Dumbar of Studio Dumbar in The Hague, Netherlands; and many others.

We would like to thank Lorraine Wild, Hugh Aldersey-Williams, Daralice Boles, Niels Diffrient, and Roy Slade for their insightful essays on the nature of this work. In as much as the environment and people here at Cranbrook have supported, critiqued, and inspired this work we would like also to thank again Roy Slade, President of the Cranbrook Academy of Art and the artists -in- residence of the Academy.

Katherine and Michael McCoy

Bloomfield Hills, Michigan

March 1990

Contents

ROY slade

Tradition and Vision

From its founding, Cranbrook has nurtured design and designers. The Cranbrook community embodies the generosity and vision of George G. Booth, Detroit newspaper publisher and patron of the arts, and the genius of architect Eliel Saarinen, who came to the United States from his native Finland after winning second place in the Chicago Tribune Tower competition of 1922. Saarinen and Booth shared a concern for the role of art and design in daily life, and in 1924 the publisher invited the architect to prepare a master plan for an art academy. Over a period of almost two decades, they transformed Booth's farm estate on the outskirts of Detroit into a community devoted to education and the arts. Their interest in the Arts and Crafts movement and design is evident from the initial concept of Cranbrook. George Booth was a great supporter of the Arts and Crafts movement and was interested in design in many ways, drawing in his sketchbook daily — a habit from his early days as a coppersmith. Of course, Eliel Saarinen was a phenomenal architect and designer, and Cranbrook is his masterwork.

Booth envisioned Cranbrook Academy of Art as a school that would train artists, an atelier that would produce handsome objects to embellish and improve the American environment, and a community where art would be integrated with daily life to the benefit of all. In practice, the Academy was born of the Arts and Crafts movement of the late nineteenth and early twentieth centuries and developed to meet the demands of industrial design that dominated the mid-twentieth century. As early as 1927, master craftsmen were invited to establish studios at Cranbrook. They supplied works for the Cranbrook institutions under construction, taught at Cranbrook School and Kingswood School Cranbrook, and, in addition, accepted outside commissions and took on student apprentices. The Academy of Art was formally established in 1932 with Eliel Saarinen as President.

Saarinen's philosophy was the integration of art, architecture, and nature. As a designer, he felt that no item was too small and no task too large for

The Cranbrook approach was evolutionary. Its artists and craftsmen created new designs not with dogmas or preconceived notions but by enthusiastic, almost playful experimentation with traditional craftsmanship and styles. Wolf Von Eckardt, **Time,** May 7, 1984, p. 118.

A flowering of genius, prosperity and vision, Cranbrook was created by George and Ellen Booth, wealthy philanthropists, with Eliel Saarinen, a Finnish architect of prodigious talent, in one of the most felicitous of collaborations. It is unlikely that there was another patron-artist combination in our history that worked better: In outlook and temperament, the Booths and Saarinen fitted each other perfectly. And together they created a masterpiece. George Nelson, **Signature,** July 1983, p. 51.

his concern, be it the design of a spoon or the planning of a city. His work covers that full spectrum. Accordingly, the founding of the Design Department at Cranbrook came out of the interests of the founder and the genius of the architect. The department was established in 1936 with William W. Comstock as the instructor. However, the course was conducted under the direct supervision of Saarinen.

In 1939 Charles Eames was appointed Instructor in Design. A statement of the objectives of the course, found in the 1940-41 announcement, reflects the impact of his concepts on the nature of the course as offered at the time and the direction that the department has since largely followed. It read, "This course forms a preliminary training in design for all branches of work. Its object is to produce in the student an attitude toward design, by having him become creatively familiar with the characteristics of materials and by having him experience the relation between the structure of the object and the purpose it is to serve. Time is divided to allow work in the shop and drafting room and individual activity combined with group projects to allow the student to coordinate his work with that of others." Students from the early days recall games and parties, as well as the intensity of work in the studio. Florence Knoll recalls, "We used to work from early morning...'til ten o'clock" and talks of taking time off for a late-afternoon touch football game.

Saarinen's stately, romantic brick buildings, with their web of walkways, courts, terraces, stairs and walls, all highlighted with sculptures and other objects by the outstanding artists Saarinen attracted to Cranbrook, probably represent this century's most successful integration of architecture, landscape design and works of art. Every brick, shrub, fountain, gate and ornament contributes to the delight of the whole. The Saarinen architectural vision soon left its mark on other parts of the U.S. as well. Wolf Von Eckardt, **Time,** May 7, 1984, pp. 118-119.

Art science
pulls you into the ter
sign. It is the borderline wh
tifiable and the poetic. It i
rive in those conditions, mo
ranbrook can easily move in a

The Design Department always embraced an interdisciplinary philosophy. Today, the Department is divided into two fields of design: two-dimensional visual communications design and the three-dimensional design of furniture, interiors, and products. Although many students focus upon one area of design, others combine the two fields. Frequently, students find that new theories apply to both two- and three-dimensional design problems. Since its inception, the Design Department has attracted an international group of graduate students. Their backgrounds have ranged from graphic, industrial, and interior design to architecture, engineering, crafts, and fine arts. Katherine and Michael McCoy cochair the Design Department and, through their teaching and their work as designers of national and international repute, extend the finest traditions of design at the Academy.

Confirmation of the ongoing effectiveness of their teaching and the influence of the Academy on its students is evident in the writing of

The story of interior and furniture design at Cranbrook is one of the most important chapters in the history of twentieth-century American design.... First and foremost, it chronicles the struggle for a reconciliation between the ideals of the Arts and Crafts movement and the demands of industrial design. Moreover, it affirms the paramount role played by architects in the battle for modern design. The story also involves an assessment of the impact of European emigres who came to the States around the first World War and in the thirties. Most importantly, it entails the work of a brilliant generation of American designers that emerged after World War II as leaders of western design for some two decades. It is a remarkable story that concurred with the founding of one of the most influential design schools in America, the Cranbrook Academy of Art.

Craig Miller, "Interior Design and Furniture," **Design in America: The Cranbrook Vision 1925-1950,** New York: Harry N. Abrams, Inc., 1983, p. 91.

a 1987 graduate, Jim Hill, who in an Italian magazine, *Modo*, stated, "Cranbrook Academy of Art has kept a high profile in contributing to America's history of twentieth century art and design. Eliel Saarinen as architect has imbued the physicality of the place with a quality that inspires and it is a tribute to his instincts as an educator that his philosophical vision survives, challenging creative individuals to become significant artists."

The importance of the historic influence of Cranbrook Academy of Art in design is best realized in the exhibition and publication *Design in America: The Cranbrook Vision 1925-1950.* The exhibition was named by scholars and curators and was organized by the Metropolitan Museum of Art and the Detroit Institute of Arts in collaboration with Cranbrook Academy of Art. The title for this tribute to the first twenty-five years of Cranbrook underscores the fact that Cranbrook is synonymous with design in America.

As a result of the Academy's focus on the individual, its design alumni tend to work independently. Distinguished Cranbrook alumni such as David Rowland, Niels Diffrient, and Don Albinson practice furniture design independently; and Mark Harrison and the late Robert Gersin have headed consulting firms for many years; Cooper Woodring recently founded an independent design office; and Florence Knoll's design vision for Knoll International shaped the course of postwar modern American furniture design. In addition, recent graduates of the Academy have founded a number of influential young design firms. Over the years there has been a trend for design graduates to go into partnerships together, which is an effective way of extending the experience gained in graduate school. Perhaps the best example of this was the lifelong collaboration of Ray and Charles Eames. Currently we have the Doublespace team of Jane Kosstrin and David Sterling as well as Nancy Skolos and Tom Wedell of Skolos/Wedell.

The Academy continues with a faculty of working artists-in-residence in the disciplines of architecture, ceramics, design, fiber, metalsmithing, painting, photography, printmaking, and sculpture. The students are inspired in their own processes of discovery by having the faculty and the President working in their own studios near the student studios. There is a mutual atmosphere of investigation and experimentation that infuses the studios with energy and a common purpose. As you will see in the following pages, personal effort and innovation go on as they have since the beginning of the Academy.

The Cranbrook Academy of Art, in Bloomfield Hills is, in fact, our equivalent of the Bauhaus, and it has had an equally profound influence on our contemporary design.

Wolf Von Eckardt, **Time,** May 7, 1984, p. 118.

Cranbrook is like no other institution in the United States. It is part artists' colony, part school, part museum and part design laboratory, and it has never allowed its students to be bound by the narrow lines separating the various design disciplines...the effect of Cranbrook and its graduates and faculty on the physical environment of this country has been profound. . . . For Cranbrook, surely more than any other institution, has the right to think of itself as synonymous with contemporary American design.

gn. It is the borderline
ifiable and the poetic.
ve in those conditions,
anbrook can easily move
validation of being to the

Paul Goldberger, **The New York Times Magazine,** April 8, 1984, p. 49.

NIELS diffrient

Grounds for Discovery

One of the most delicious walks to be had in civilized America is around the grounds of Cranbrook. One can amble, as I did while a student, through a glorious park of rolling hills, ponds, and mature trees, encountering on the way a highly eclectic but breathtaking collection of structures, landscaping, and artifacts. At one moment there is a stone re-creation of an English manor house, and at the next, world-class sculpture gardens. Through a delightful processional of small courts and programmed vistas, one arrives in a piazza that would vie on a reduced scale with Siena or San Marco. The architecture one sees is not at all modern in the Bauhaus sense, but rather, intense with detail, material mix, and decoration that recalls the Gothic or Louis Sullivan. It's impossible to roam these grounds without a sensual bombardment of the gentlest sort that leaves one aware of the power of design to reach the more profound levels of being.

Oddly enough, when I was there in the early fifties, it never occurred to me what a contradiction this situation presented. My cohorts and I were rabid modernists distilling our designs to the barest, pristine essentials. Our manifesto was "rebuild, remake," in the pure functional mold, all of the outdated, artificial world. But at the same time, I would have been horrified to think of taking down the Cranbrook complex and replacing it with anything else, however pure and functional. Time and gray hairs have allowed me to understand this contradiction better. If the walls of Cranbrook could speak they would also tell us, perhaps in the voices of Saarinen, Milles, Eames, Bertoia, and a chorus of others, that many design themes have gestated in this glorious crucible. An innovative attitude is nurtured by a presence and stature entrapped in earth, stone, and mortar that enlarges the human spirit and supports the creative urge.

The spirit and creative urge are once again alive and at work on the Cranbrook grounds. There are waves of design novelty emanating in ever-expanding circles, rocking many complacent boats and drawing curious eyes to the epicenter. It's a bittersweet pleasure to see new and exciting work coming from the design studios I once roamed without being an intimate part of them. One cannot avoid a moment of panic at being left out of something vital, while at the same time being stimulated by the freshness of the view.

The view, as it were, is of something referred to as design semantics. Design theoreticians have transformed the science of semantics and linguistic meaning to include, in this case, form and pattern. The postulation is that symbols and metaphors retained in the subconscious, which affect conscious linguistic attitudes, also have a parallel response in design. Without dwelling further on this theory, since it will be more energetically illuminated in the pages to follow, it is interesting to recall that, aside from the novelty and charm of the new, such movements, which summarize and define an attitude in art or design, always find ready adherents and proselytes. This is only natural, because any codification or adaptive theory that provides even partial relief from the agony of achieving virgin novelty in each and every design will be warmly embraced.

Actually, to consider design semantics as entirely new is not quite accurate. Design infused with meaning has been around for centuries. The decorative arts have long been saturated with visual cues to enhance themes from mysticism to whimsy. Some design has resulted in deeper meaning even though functionality was the primary intent. The functional needs in these cases have been met so exquisitely that the designs become root metaphors, providing references for future recall and visual replay.

Perhaps it is no accident that a design movement at Cranbrook should break away from Modernism as couched in the International Style and Bauhaus tenets. That is, after all, exactly what happened in the first place. Eliel Saarinen steadfastly eschewed the rigid discipline of the Bauhaus and followed his own natural, Scandinavian tendencies toward a more complex, eclectic, and anthropomorphic plan. And now, history repeats itself: Mike and Kathy McCoy are catalysts of another departure from formalism and minimal orderliness. What is new about their direction is the infusion of meaning into the production of a plethora of objects and graphics that have become mundane and boring. It can perhaps be argued that Modernism, as represented by the Bauhaus, also had meaning. And indeed it did, but the meaning most often was in expressing the materials, function, and process rather than the subtleties of human interaction. This often resulted in a kind of dry neatness, devoid of the essential messiness and ambiguity of the human condition.

At first glance it might appear that messiness and ambiguity is the object of some of the graphic design work. Elements seem to float at random, and type styles are varied and contradictory. This may grate on the nerves of those who admire the orderliness of graphic elements aligning with a preordained grid. The discipline of the grid does appear to have been thrown to the winds. Yet, content and meaning cannot be as freely expressed if the organizing geometry is too restrictive. The obvious challenge, in both graphic design and product design, is to enhance the meaning while not totally abandoning the framework that unites the whole. In short, it is a simple matter of priorities: which has primary call on the design elements, relationship to the person involved or expression of the structural components? It is a question that can be debated in various forms indefinitely.

As in most art and design movements, debate on the merits is a natural by-product. In the product designs, the debate will, in part, revolve around whether it is a passing trend or, indeed, represents the infusion of deeper meaning in the forms of the objects. If it is the latter it will alter the design of artifacts in our culture. Interestingly enough, the artifacts graced with the semantic touch are not as yet that broad in type. To date, the examples are largely in furniture and electronics. Furniture is a natural because of its rich history as a purveyor of design movements. And it is perhaps also predictable that much of the semantic design explorations are practiced on electronic devices. For one thing, there is great latitude to arrange electronics into almost any form one might desire. As a result of miniaturization and a lack of the constraints inherent in mechanical products, electronic devices have a flexibility of arrangement that permits unusual freedom of design. Given this latitude, it is an easy step to turn one's notion of function from the "gearbox" to the "service" being performed. The "service" in this sense is, of course, the interaction with the user. What we have, then, is a rather interesting case of human engineering resulting from semantic intent, in which the product is expected to explain itself to the user: an exercise in self-evidency, one could say. In addition, electronics, being the quintessential product type of our time, with its potential as a modifier of lives and experience, needs a counterbalancing limiter. It is only reasonable that a counteractive, humanizing force should rise up to balance the social equation.

All this is not to say that the McCoys and their progeny have their direction wrapped up in a package complete with instructions ready to be applied, as this season's latest trend. Indeed not: the process of innovation is never so prim and clear-cut. One must hang out the philosophical wash for the neighbors to view. Fortunately, enough of the neighbors are intrigued to ask for more — myself among them. I want to see if this notion of visual semantics will wash, will hold up to time. Will it build the basic lexicon of design practice? Will it, indeed, better the human condition? But it is presumptuous and premature to place such stringent measures on what is still in a formative stage. The designs are still experiments, most being trials, models, and prototypes, not in ongoing production with popular consumption by the masses. They are, however, some rather grand experiments.

Since America's halls of commerce do not see the wisdom in supporting research and development in the areas of aesthetics and amenities, this chore must be accomplished in other ways. *Cranbrook Design: The New Discourse* is a glimpse at another way. It is aesthetic R & D being put together and tried without a checklist or ready audience. It is an experiment in very classy ambiguity carried to an elegant extreme by a small number of enlightened individuals. What follows, dear reader, is a treat, and a treatment. It is not a thrill without a price. You must involve yourself because the designs you see will haunt you and tug at your subconscious. You will find yourself asking, even while you may disagree with the direction, why do I find these things so compelling? I'd like to think this work has class because it was done in such a classy place. Has this plot of earth called Cranbrook worked its magic one more time? I suggest **you turn the pages and feel the magic that is Cranbrook.**

the
new
discourse

KATHERINE McCOY
MICHAEL McCOY

the new discourse

ART science

Nothing pulls you into the territory between art and science quite so quickly as design. It is the borderline where contradictions and tensions exist between the quantifiable and the poetic. It is the field between desire and necessity. Designers thrive in those conditions, moving between land and water. A typical critique at Cranbrook can easily move in a matter of minutes between

MATHEMATIC poetic

a discussion of the object as a validation of being to the precise mechanical proposal for actuating the object. The discussion moves from Heidegger to the "strange material of the week" or from Lyotard to printing technologies without missing a beat. The free flow of ideas, and the leaps from the technical to the mythical, stem from the attempt to maintain a studio platform that supports each student's search to

DESIRE necessity

find his or her own voice as a designer. The studio is a hothouse that enables students and faculty to encounter their own visions of the world and act on them — a process that is at times chaotic, conflicting, and occasionally inspiring.

Watching the process of students absorbing new ideas and influences, and the incredible range of interpretations of those ideas into design, is

MYTHOLOGY technology

an annual experience that is always amazing. In recent years, for example, the department has had the experience of watching wood craftsmen metamorphose into high technologists, and graphic designers into software humanists. Yet it all seems consistent. They are bringing a very personal vision to an area that desperately needs it. The messiness of human experience

Purist pluralist

ence is warming up the cold precision of technology to make it livable, and lived in.

Unlike the Bauhaus, Cranbrook never embraced a singular teaching method or philosophy, other than Saarinen's exhortation to each student to find his or her own way, in the company of other artists and designers who were engaged in the same search. The energy at Cranbrook seems to come from the fact of

Individual communal

the mutual search, although not the mutual conclusion. If design is about life, why shouldn't it have all the complexity, variety, contradiction, and sublimity of life?

Much of the work done at Cranbrook has been dedicated to changing the status quo. It is polemical, calculated to ruffle designers' feathers. And

DANGEROUS rigorous

Personal **universal**

it has done that. Cranbrook has been called "the most dangerous design school in the world." Perhaps. But the profession of design in the 1970s had fallen into a state of stasis that was suffocating. This new generation of students, some of them now

Systematic **idiosyncratic**

working in their own very successful studios, has challenged the sterility of "universal design" and is emerging with highly personal interpretations.

Philosophies and forms constantly flow and evolve as successive waves of students respond to new ideas, changing audiences, and the professional status quo. The past ten years of Cranbrook graphic design have seen a pronounced shift in emphasis. To understand this, one must look back to the

Objective **subjective**

Cranbrook graphic design of the early seventies, which was based on a rational, systematic approach to visual-communications problem solving and a minimalist vocabulary of forms heavily influenced by Swiss Modernist graphic design. The late seventies and early eighties brought a questioning of the severe expressive limitations of this vocabulary. Design students pursued a great deal of formal experimen-

Complexity **contradiction**

tation during these years, consciously breaking virtually all the rules of the deadly seriousness and antiseptic discipline of objective Swiss rationalism. Complexity, layering, syntactical playfulness, irony, vernacular forms, and classical pre-Modern typography and composition were explored in an outburst of energy. But for all its rule breaking, this dissecting and recombining of the grammar of graphic design was a logical outgrowth of the Modernist emphasis on structural expressionism.

Ferndale Street Signs Project
1981
Kenneth Windsor, designer; Cranbrook Studio assignment.
A block of a suburban commercial main street is recorded photographically and recombined in collage form in an interpretive graphic essay. *detail*

These experiments at Cranbrook and a few other American schools rapidly overcame the professional field's initial resistance and began to be

Classical **vernacular**

enthusiastically adopted across the United States, codified into a formalistic style so predictable it could be described as a sort of beaux arts academy of graphic design. In response to this stylistic assimilation, students began to search beyond this largely formal experimentation by the early 1980s.

New influences rapidly began to appear in the Design

Visual **verbal**

Department, centered around readings in post- Structuralist French literary theory and post-Modern art criticism. The emerging ideas emphasized the construction of meaning between the audience and the graphic design piece, a visual transaction that parallels verbal communication. Building on the linguistic theories of semiotics

Signifier **signified**

SEEING reading

but rejecting the faith in the scientifically predictable transmission of meaning, these ideas began to have an impact on the students' graphic design work. New experiments explored the relationships of text and image and the processes of reading and seeing, with texts and images meant to be read in detail, their meanings de-

TEXT image

coded. Students began to deconstruct the dynamics of visual language and understand it as a filter that inescapably manipulates the audience's response.

An interest in the vernacular has continued, with a great deal of appropriated imagery and typography evident in recent work. Personally generated original "design" forms and highly personal graphic vocabularies are

SENDER receiver

often rejected. Sometimes the presence of the designer seems so invisible that the piece seems to spring directly from our popular culture, encouraging a dialogue between the piece and its audience. Reflecting current literary theory's suspicion of "authorship" and its potential for manipulation, graphic pieces are no longer one-way statements from the designer to the receiver. Many pieces have explored

PROVOCATION information

the possibilities of destabilized "open" meaning, which provokes the audience to actively consider multiple interpretations of the piece's meaning. Design becomes a provocation to the audience to construct meaning, consider new ideas, and reconsider preconceptions.

Much of this new work shares the earlier Cranbrook interest in

FORM content

formal layering of collaged elements, but with a critical difference — content. Layers of form are now used to reveal successive layers of content. Often the most immediately readable layer carries the most stabilized objective message, while successively imbedded layers carry more open, critical, or personal content with subtexts, deferred meanings, hidden stories, and alternative interpretations.

DISCOURSE dialogue

This new interest in text-image relationships uses images and symbols as "words" that interact through juxtaposition with verbal language elements. Verbal wordplay, a literary influence, links with typographic play, inherited from the earlier Cranbrook experiments, producing verbal/visual puns, jokes, and ironies that critique or subvert content and create a critical discourse. Much of this work is

CONCEPTUAL aesthetic

very self-critical and self-conscious. The pieces talk about themselves and expose their own mechanics, holding a discourse or dialogue about their own constructs.

Formal refinement and elegance are no longer primary objectives. Much of the work is "aformal" and sometimes defiantly antiformal, perhaps

WRONG right

STYLE expression

in reaction to the technical perfection and stylistic mannerism of the professional mainstream of graphic design. But also, the trend is for Cranbrook graduate students to have had a number of years of professional experience. For these experienced designers, refinement and mastery are no revelation and are frequently rejected in

CRITICAL lyrical

favor of the directness of unmannered, hand-drawn, or vernacular forms.

“Correct” form and the univalent “universal” criteria of Modernism are often rejected, reflecting the pluralistic cultural fragmentation of our post-Modern, post-industrial milieu. The look and structure of graphic form is underplayed in favor of verbal signification, valuing semantic expression over

SEMANTIC syntactic

syntactic style. Cranbrook graphic work has moved from the lyrical celebration of form to a critical exploration and discourse on the meaning of form.

In the 3D side of the program it is perhaps most useful to take a tour of the ideas and projects of the past decade, to see how they have grown and metamorphosed over the years. The early part of the decade saw the beginning of

LANGUAGE life

work in product, furniture, and interior design that referred to the life around it through its form, in an attempt to make connections and move away from the hermetic, self-referential work of the previous decade. The first place we looked was language — the world of semiotics and structural linguistics, and the use of analogy and metaphor to lift the meaning of the design beyond its immediate circumstance. In recent years, insights about design have been gained by looking at post-Structuralism and phenomenology.

Stereo Receiver Model 1984
Robert Nakata, designer;
Cranbrook Studio assignment.
This wall-hung electronic audio component communicates its function and operation through semantic forms that relate to music and sound. The volume control communicates nonverbally through the use of an indexical sign. *detail*

In furniture design, that often meant pointing out the relationships between furniture, the figure, and architecture. Some of the projects pointed to the

FIGURE space

role of furniture as the mediator between the figure and space. Some dealt with furniture as smaller-scale architecture, and some looked at the history of furniture, a memory that had been denied by the previous decade of design. It was clear that it was time for furniture to assert its traditional cultural role as a carrier of ideas about imagery, decoration, craft, art, and design. The so-called art-furniture movement grew

CULTURAL natural

in this decade, and some of our students have continued to grow in that milieu, usually working out of their personal studios and showing their work in galleries like Art et Industrie. Others have moved into the furniture industry, dealing with issues of mass production and the quality of the workplace as defined by furniture.

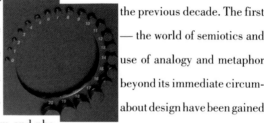

INDUSTRY gallery

PARTICULAR general

In the realm of interior design we began a series of experiments reflecting the internal activities of the space in the actual design of the interior. The first project was the Office of the Year for *Interiors* magazine, in which the forms of aircraft were used to signify an aerospace executive's office. It was a denial of the beige-on-beige anonymity of typical corporate office design and later led to

MINIMAL metaphorical

faculty and student projects at Cranbrook that explored the possibilities for an *architecture parlante* of interior space design — spaces that speak about the lives within them. Much of this, of course, was inspired by the work of an earlier Cranbrook personage, Eero Saarinen, and his highly metaphorical works like the TWA Terminal at Kennedy Airport, Dulles Airport, and the St. Louis Arch. But, like Saarinen,

ABSTRACT referential

we also recognized that design problems did not always call for highly articulated metaphorical solutions (Saarinen had his minimalist projects like the CBS Building and the GM Technical Center as well), and you will find elegant, subdued works among the projects presented here.

It was in product design that the greatest changes occurred in the eighties.

FUNCTION expression

Dissatisfied with the narrow channel of expression to which industrial design had confined itself in the seventies (with the exception of the Italians, of course), we began to investigate the possibilities for products to reflect their place in our lives through their form. Along with some like-minded experimenters around the world, we first used semiotics to look at the meaning of the form of products. The products

GEOMETRIC biomorphic

that emerged from those first experiments were sometimes too obvious in the relationships they were trying to make, but they served their purpose in showing the possibility for product form to clarify its use and to locate itself in one's life. These were aspects of industrial design that had not been focused on for some time. The earlier work gradually shifted through the decade toward design that undertook to "conceal

CONCEAL reveal

and reveal." We are now deeply concerned with the essences or archetypal qualities of objects, looking for the spirit in the artifact. The discussion in critiques now is less about the linguistic construction of meaning and more about the experience of using the object. We are looking for design that is connective but that does not require decoding to make the connection. The sense running through all the work, from the

CODE essence

beginning of the decade to now, is the awareness of the responsibility of the designer to act as the interpreter of our increasingly pervasive technology.

The need to connect theory with practice has always been an important aspect of the program. The energy is in the encounter between a con-

THEORY practice

Need want

ceptual idea and the program of use. While the definition of *necessity* has been broadened to encompass psychological, social, and even spiritual desires, it is still the resolution of the personal vision with the needs of the audience that drives the work of the design studio.

On one hand, applied projects that address enlightened

Experimentation application

clients' programs provide the opportunity for the challenge of professional practice. Over the years a number of supportive clients and patrons have been crucial to the development of sponsored projects and critiques that have given the students the necessary link to real-world projects, allowing the students to engage their ideas with rigorous programs of use and technology. On the other hand, it is equally important

Support critique

for the experimentation to continue beyond the protective environment of the Cranbrook studios and enter the larger cultural milieu. The work of alumni shown here bears witness to their continuing growth and the application of experiment in the world. Alumni often return to Cranbrook to share work and ideas with current students, with mutual influence.

Change continue

The essays in this book contain both praise and criticism of past and present projects and philosophies. Criticism is specifically included because that most closely approximates how the design studio and the critiques at Cranbrook work. Nothing is sacred; everything is available for questioning and criticism. This occasionally makes for uncomfortable moments, but it also ensures that

Vision voice

the Design Department continues to grow, to resist formulas and dogma. Each new group of students has to question, criticize, and ultimately posit its own positions, which in turn, and in time, will be criticized by succeeding groups of students. It is this continual dialectic that renews the studio Zeitgeist and ensures that everyone keeps pushing outward. Projects emerge that are sometimes insightful, sometimes answer

Questions answers

important questions, and sometimes create more questions than they answer.

The Design students are exhorted, above all, to take risks that they might not take in the outside professional world, to get used to questioning and growing by doing polemical work that could well fail, but in failing teach everyone something. In these pages are the results of that risk taking, experimentation, investigation,

Failing finding

and growth. What you will see here is just a trace of each student's sustaining vision in his or her work. For most, their time at Cranbrook is just the beginning of a **lifetime of exploration.**

Endings beginnings

Hugh aldersey-williams

The Mannerists *of* microElectronics

In the middle years of the sixteenth century, Benvenuto Cellini was at his drawing board trying to come up with a design for the saltcellar that Francis I, the king of France, had commissioned from him. He thought to make Neptune the principal feature of the elaborate metalwork piece. Neptune, god of the sea, signified that the product contained salt. It made the cellar easier for its user to understand. This way, Francis wouldn't make a fool of himself in front of the courtiers by thinking it contained sugar and ladling salt onto his cornflakes by mistake.

Cellini's imagery was not original. He copied a sculpture of Michelangelo's, done on a rather larger scale a while back for some Medici tombs. Nonetheless, as time passed, Cellini's design, too, came to be regarded as art alongside the Michelangelo.

During the 1980s, students and graduates of Cranbrook have been approaching design in a similar manner. They have been trying consciously to imbue their designs with extra significance for today's consumers by drawing upon familiar symbols, sometimes, like Cellini, from art, sometimes from everyday life.

The result is a gallery of designs, always startling and frequently beautiful, that challenge the rule of anonymous minimalism in mass-made products. At Cranbrook, complex geometries took the place of boring boxes. Seductive curves appeared where straight lines, right angles, and uniform radii used to be. Three-dimensional signs and symbols blended into the form, combining function and decoration in place of banal decal graphics. A toaster by Van Hong Tsai stood upright like two slices of bread placed side by side. Wavy vertical lines were molded into the design's exterior, signifying the heat that would turn bread into toast. A telephone-answering machine by the Cranbrook alumnus David Gresham's Chicago firm Design Logic looked like a U.S. mailbox, indicating that its electronic job was analogous to that of a mailbox for printed messages.

This was *product semantics* or *metaphorical design*. Many found it an attractive proposition, and for a while it looked as if "semantic products" would provide a welcome escape for designers trapped within the boundaries of expected form giving. Before long some design directors were beginning naively to think of product semantics as something they could consciously choose to incorporate into or leave out of their products. One firm even advertised for a designer "with product semantics experience." All this very soon began to suggest that semantics was simply another style, to be applied and discarded at will.

But product semantics is not a style, nor even a design language. It is a device whereby designers try to indicate through more thorough and more clever means than ergonomics and decal graphics how to use a product and what it might mean to you and how it plays a role in your life. It is a system within which a variety of design languages can flourish. Unlike some of the system's admirers, Cranbrook has recognized this and has pushed the debate forward. The school has extended its exploration and is now addressing the deeper philosophical questions that are raised when a designer *consciously* attempts to build "meaning" into a product.

It was product semantics, an old idea arrived at along a new route, signposted by the French post-Structuralists, that gave Cranbrook its recent mark of distinction. Stated not in terms of literary theory but in language designers are used to, this approach aims to extend human factors from the physical and psychophysical into the cultural, psychological, and social domains. It aims to provide a vocabulary for a reaction against what Gresham calls the "Euclidean vernacular," the generic European product Modernism refined by the Bauhaus and Ulm schools and endorsed and canonized by the Museum of Modern Art. This "pretend functionalism" has been a dubious grail for "good design" ever since America's rejection of its very own style of streamlined, exuberant excess. In the Cranbrook view, form may still follow function. It's just that psychology and culture are admitted as part of function.

Art science
pulls you into the ter
sign. It is the borderline wh
tifiable and the poetic. It i
ive in those conditions, mo
anbrook can easily move in a

The United States has never truly shared the European obsession with function. There is another functionalism, not the serious deductive sort, but an inventive sort which in the United States is sometimes called "yankee ingenuity." An American patent from the 1890s for a "Combined Shoebrush and Hipflask for Travelling Gentlemen" is typical of this functionalism. Such useless utilities, such nonessential essentials, are an important ingredient in the American product culture. Read any airline's in-flight catalogue and you will find their successors today.

Many Cranbrook projects are unashamedly in this vein. As Victorian ingenuity was inspired by the mechanical revolution to devise all sorts of new conveniences, so the electronic revolution inspires Cranbrook, not so much to devise the gadgets themselves as to present them in new and more useful combinations and place them in new and more approachable packages. For these designers, the crisis of form giving centers on the ubiquitous commodities of the electronic era — the telephone-answering and fax machines, the televisions and computers, the microwave ovens. Their creativity feeds upon the perceived demands of a population of gadget-crazy consumers, which, in its turn, is fed a strict diet of limited expectations by the manufacturers.

It is curious, then, to find their philosophy informed by Marxist critique. For example, it has been fashionable among some at Cranbrook to quote Jean Baudrillard on "object culture" and the "sign function" of objects in an attempt to explain how their designs abet the creation of their eventual owners' domestic myths. Cranbrook thinking soon parts company with Baudrillard, however. His philosophy rejects the whole capitalist manufacturing system. Most designers can't afford to do that and wouldn't want to. Their future success lies in alliance with the forces of commerce. Cranbrook graduates should recognize (and accept?) that they are using "object culture" to fulfill new capitalist fantasies.

To see this, it is only necessary to look at the finesse and realism with which students' work is often executed. Unlike many schools, Cranbrook places great emphasis on final-appearance models over sketches and conceptual presentation. These three-dimensional little masterpieces serve to persuade people of the potential power of the mythic product and thus of the validity of the underlying philosophy. But, complete with everything except a price tag, they also serve as propaganda to broaden consumers' expectations. Manufacturers may at first find the Cranbrook polemic mildly irritating, as they do all prospects of change that are not of their making. But they will soon see that the new design serves to stimulate demand.

More pertinent is the thinking of Jean-Francois Lyotard, whose 1985 exhibition and publication "Les Immateriaux" highlighted the ever-greater degree to which people find it hard to relate to current technology. He argues that, far from alienating people, the complex workings of the latest gadgets can free them from former cares. Where understanding how to operate a product was once the priority, there is now the scope, instead, to develop a feeling for it.

For this to become possible, design and technology must collaborate to make products self-instructing. The "Phonebook," a telephone-answering machine designed by Cranbrook student Lisa Krohn and Tucker Viemeister of Smart Design, shows how it can be done. It looks like a book and so immediately belongs to its desktop setting. It also *works* like a book. Each double-page spread is devoted to a different function, with electrical connections in the "spine" providing the necessary switching between them as the pages are turned. The few instructions needed are displayed on the relevant page.

Several large corporations currently producing the sort of "neutral" designs that the Cranbrook philosophy opposes are showing interest in these new ideas. Krohn's design was admired by the European electronics company Philips. Design Logic designed its telephone-answering machines at the request of Dictaphone. The design-led Danish hi-fi manufacturer Bang & Olufsen commissioned Design Logic to devise alternative products that could lift the firm out of its minimalist rut. With similar intent, the California consultancy frogdesign hired another Cranbrook graduate, Paul Montgomery, and put him to work designing concepts for their best-known client, Apple Computer.

Cranbrook designers are offering consumers a choice between the "neutral" standard product and their own value-added expressive object. Leaving aside for a moment the doubtful assertion that the former is really neutral, the new content is a gift to manufacturers and their advertising agents. Soon it will no longer be sufficient to have a simple, working telephone or toaster. You'll have to have one that fits your life's ritual. But the choice is not so simple. By the very fact of its existence in opposition, does not the lackluster "neutral" product of old now fit the life ritual of another person, a dullard maybe, but someone's valued customer nonetheless? The important thing here is not to make a value judgment between the "neutral" and the "expressive" design. It is to recognize the addition of choice. And real choice at that, not the false choice between today's virtually indistinguishable black or brown boxes, whose major distinguishing characteristics are the labels of their rival complacent manufacturers.

The uneasy collision of Baudrillard's political philosophy and the Cranbrook designers' commercial environment does not only raise an ideological conundrum. In some of these projects, the symbolism, the cultural and ritual concerns, begin to outweigh practical aspects.

Commodity and firmness are occasionally diminished in favor of delight and "meaning." Some designs are impractical when measured against current criteria of manufacturability or patterns of usage. This is forgivable for student work and is even praiseworthy where it leads to legitimate questioning of existing tenets. There is no reason, for example, that acknowledgment of the constraints of plastics molding should automatically restrict the form of the products to that of a rectangular box. Yet it happens routinely today because it is the easy course to take. Cranbrook is doing much to break the vicious circle of lazy design that excuses itself by claiming ease of fabrication.

There are social as well as political questions inherent in the new Cranbrook projects. In the supposedly classless United States, what are these designers doing raiding the manual worker's vernacular? When Montgomery designs a portable microwave oven that resembles and even serves as an analogue to the workman's lunchbox, or when Krohn designs a personal computer that looks and unpacks like a tool kit, they are trying to link the labor culture of the manual era to that of the electronic. There is social awareness, a certain wit, and utility here, but there are also risks in adopting vernacular motifs. It runs the risk of patronizing workers in old patterns of labor; and it might also patronize the more sensitive users of the new equipment, plucking at their guilty consciences. After all, theirs, in a roundabout way, are the jobs that have supplanted the old manual ones.

Consider one of Design Logic's Dictaphone machines. It adopts that American icon, the mailbox, as its simile. Is this merely a precious quote from popular Americana? Or is it valid social commentary of the sort that fine artists in all fields are expected to produce? The consultancy's two alternative prototypes for Dictaphone use a different source of imagery, quoting from Cubist and Abstract modern art. Is this sort of quotation any different from that employed by architects, composers, and painters in pursuit of their art? Is it any different from Cellini's appropriation of Michelangelo?

And whether the source of the image is life or art, how durable will the image prove? How long would you want it in your home? Any answer must take into account the likely longevity of the technology the product contains. Perhaps the lifetime of the ideas expressed on the exterior of a product should match that of the technology within. But with the shape of a product no longer constrained by its internal layout, there is no need for this to be so. You probably could not stand a "Garfield" telephone over its full working life. Thus, its casing signifies disposability. Conversely, one could imagine a design of such artistic merit that it would be kept long after its electronics had become defunct or obsolete. Technology is changing fast, but not so fast that this is not a tall order for the designer.

Cranbrook graduates present a timely and challenging theory of design. But the ideas they express so forcefully and eloquently in prototypes may not prove transferable in undiluted form into actual products. There is a risk in trying to create products that are also symbols, signifying the importance to each of us of our daily chores or recreations. By enshrining them permanently in plastic, designers may inadvertently demean those very rituals they seek to celebrate.

Here, the designer's consciousness is the crux. Is it possible, for example, to quote consciously from the vernacular and make a product of lasting value? The designer and critic George Nelson wrote: "Objects are the fingerprints left by a culture on the walls of its particular cell in time and space." It is a remark fondly repeated by Cranbrook alumni. Nelson chose his words well. He was referring not to deliberately made finger marks, but to those that a sleuth might find left as an *unintentional* record of a thief's visit. As fingerprints inform the sleuth, so today's objects might tell a future archaeologist something of the values our culture holds dear. A time capsule provides one very deliberate record of a culture. Scattered artifacts found on a dig provide another, unconscious, record. To the archaeologist, both are useful in their way. So there remains the question of intent.

Cranbrook students' adding of "meaning" to the products of complex modern technology during the 1980s has been conscious. Now, in an attempt to judge the degree to which meaning can or should be introduced as a deliberate act of design, they have turned for help to the philosophy known as *phenomenology*.

Maurice Merleau-Ponty holds that any attempt to investigate consciousness (or, by extension, the products of consciousness - the Apollonian dimension in design) will fail if it overlooks the contribution of the self (the Dionysian, intuitive dimension). The designer's *intention* in creating a product, by the very fact of his or her creation of it, finds expression in that product.

The phenomenologists prefer that we should confront the immediate reality of things as they appear to us rather than the complex truths of their underlying nature. As technologies become more unfathomable, this is good advice for consumers. It also provides a respectable intellectual underpinning for designers who wish to humanize the products of technology. However, the difficulty phenomenology has in accepting current scientific knowledge does not augur well for its use as a basis for a design theory if designers must still assimilate the technologies that new science makes possible. In addition, phenomenology's insistence on the primacy of our experience of the lived world appears to run counter to the previous train of thought at Cranbrook, which sought to reinforce the myth of the everyday.

Despite the difficulty of the choice of philosophical foundations, the evolution of Cranbrook design during the 1980s has been a logical one. The progression from the iconographic (Design Logic's mailbox answering machine) to the metaphoric (Paul Montgomery's ornate picture frames placed around screen images on videophones and computers) to the phenomenal is a pleasing one.

It is now possible for Cranbrook students to produce elegant objects once more. Hung about with signs of their "meaning," the projects of a few years ago were often unconventionally resolved compositions. The shift from a philosophy developed to describe verbal and visual language toward something more holistic is evident in the most recent student projects.

Peter Stathis's bedside television is pivotal. The black, cloth-covered articulated monitor and stand lie curled like a cat; it is brought to life by a stroking action; it raises its head when in use. The metaphor of domesticity is obvious, but no longer intrusive. There is an echo of Brancusi in the overall shape, but again, this does not detract from the utility or practicality of the appliance. There is, in other words, no detail on this product that, if you do not catch the reference, leaves you wondering what it's for.

And that's more than can be said for Cellini's saltcellar.

DARALICE boles

Given the relative ease with which early 1980s Cranbrook graduates in graphic design, and to a lesser extent, product design, could be identified by their work, the first question to be asked of former students in the furniture and interior design division is whether or not their work, too, betrays a "house style." The answer depends on who's answering. Outsiders tend to believe there is indeed a "Cranbrook School,"one that has evolved over the years in a pattern roughly parallel to that taken by the McCoys themselves. Thus, for example, when they began in the early 1980s to explore the use of metaphor in design, the department, too, turned in that direction. Michael's design for an aerospace executive's office with its airfoil room dividers and runway desk, which was typical of that "style" in their work, is echoed in numerous student projects that followed its completion and, perhaps more significantly, publication.

Yet what appears from the outside to be more or less monolithic is revealed from within as a welter of diversity. The McCoys are famous for the way in which they select the students for each class so as to provide a full spectrum of personality types. "There were people interested in digitals, and then there were the people who welded and ate sawdust — sort of the Bronze Age meets the Information Age," says former student Lisa Krohn. Any given class is likely to have a mix of "woodchucks," to use McCoy's term for the more handicraft-oriented students, classic fine- arts graduates in painting or sculpture, a healthy helping of techies, and a few wild-cards with degrees in biology, journalism, or other nondesign subjects.

Life AFTER CRANBROOK: furniture and interior design

These students are for the most part usually directed individuals who come to Cranbrook with definite and distinct agendas. They have to do so, as the department offers no conventional class schedule. In the 3-D area, a minimum of projects are assigned; most are the result of individual initiative, and readings are also tailored to the individual. In this way, says Michael McCoy, the department has remained true to Eliel Saarinen's intentions. "Analogies to the Bauhaus or the Weiner Werkstätte are fairly inaccurate," says McCoy. "The Bauhaus was about a specific methodology. Saarinen wanted simply to set up a studio where personal directions would be encouraged." That process continues. "Cranbrook provided an opportunity to nurture individual language. That was the principal focus for all work, be it interiors or product design," says Tom Lehn. "Everyone develops their personalities through their work," says Ken Krayer.

These diverse directions are most easily identified when all students address the same design problem - a rare occurence at Cranbrook.

The NYNEX projects, for example, reveal a considerable array of answers to the same problem. Asked to design a work station, Mike Scott produced an anthropomorphic table whose legs are complete with knee-caps and translucent "skin." Peter Stathis, on the other hand, focused on the task itself, designing a movable writing pad that can be "docked" on a computer in the desk. Tod Lawrence designed a high-tech version of the traditional wing chair. These designs reflect the idiosyncracies of the designers more than they do a common Cranbrook ideology.

Students and graduates tend naturally to stress these differences. To the 3-D students, there is a world of difference between a Lisa Krohn, who describes her main interest as the "interpretation of technology," and a Jonathan Teasdale or Terry Main, whose work tends more toward the art end of the spectrum. At the same time, both students and graduates may have more in common than they care to admit - with similarities defined as much by what they are not as by what they are. Thus, there are no pure product engineers at Cranbrook. There is little craft for craft's sake. As for art furniture, "I would hope there isn't any at Cranbrook," says Krohn. "It seems to me a pursuit that lacks discipline. If it's furniture, why is it art and vice versa?" Teasdale may represent an art approach to his classmates, but he himself draws a finer distinction. "I don't do art furniture," he says. "The stuff I do is usable; it's just not intended to be produced in mass quantities."

Furthermore, if the furniture and interior design graduates deny the notion of a house style, they will own up to a common Cranbrook approach. "It seems to me to be a well-read approach to design," says Michael Scott.

"They are trying to tie thinking about design to thinking in other disciplines. People will say, 'That looks like Cranbrook,' " says Krayer. "My interpretation of that comment is that the work looks thoughtful, that it tends more to the theoretical end of the spectrum. I wouldn't call it a style, but a way of working."

This working mode draws heavily from the mix of disciplines at Cranbrook. Interior design students especially, working as they do in a discipline that is still in the process of defining itself, seem to have benefited from exposure to other Cranbrook departments, from fibers to architecture. "There is a more all-encompassing vision of design taught at Cranbrook than most interior designers have," says Lynn Barnhouse. Lehn agrees. "Most other interior design schools are too involved in developing the professional end; they don't give enough energy to developing a conceptual framework," he comments. Moreover, the McCoy's emphasis on the study of rituals and how they affect interiors is borne out by the environment itself. Perhaps more than any other students in the design department, interior designers learn directly from Eliel Saarinen. "If you walk the campus on a daily basis, you can't help but be the recipient of subliminal teaching,"says Lehn.

The interior design students seem also to have been less affected by “product semantics” than were the furniture designers, who at first enthusiastically embraced this theory, which came to identify the Cranbrook design department in the mid-1980s. Characteristically, “product semantics” is itself not a “look” or style but a philosophy of design. The notion that, as Michael McCoy puts it, “products should look like what they do” was readily adapted to furniture and, in a looser sense, to interior design. “Furniture has always had a tradition of metaphor,” says McCoy. “The idea of giving meaning through form was transferred from architecture and interiors to technological products.” Yet, equally characteristically, many Cranbrook graduates are now highly critical of this approach, which would seem to outsiders to bind them all together, and some of the most outspoken skeptics are former students in furniture and interior design. “The whole semiotic gimmick became a bandwagon,” says Teasdale. Even Krohn, whose Phonebook is perhaps the quintessential example of product semantics (“It’s a book, get it?”), questions the approach. “You can end up with really prosaic solutions that lack mystery — one-liners,” she says.

Responding to these criticisms, the department, and in particular the 3-D division, has already begun to shift directions. “There is less ‘make the design speak’ and more ‘what are we asking it to say?’ ” says Stathis. “It was ‘clarity clarity clarity’ for years; now ambiguity has moved in. It’s a shift from a structuralist approach to a phenomenological one.” “Mike himself was very encouraging of other approaches. He saw it getting formulaic,” says Scott. “In the last three to five years, all our work has moved away from too-direct connections, while still remaining referential,” says McCoy himself. “A lot of the current thinking holds that we should allow the viewer to judge. There’s a new interest in sensuality, materiality. Experience is emphasized.”

In these remarks, McCoy echoes one of his own students. “Design has rarely transcended being an object of gaze, apprehended through one sense only — the eye,” says Stathis. “Once in a while there’s touch — but we have five senses. What other essential qualities of objects can be used?” Krohn asks a similarly comprehensive question in her design for a wrist computer: “How close does a person want to be to their own information?” she speculates. “Information is so evanescent; so why are computers so cumbersome?”

The very fact that they are asking these kinds of questions is, finally, the one thing all Cranbrook graduates have in common. “What you get at Cranbrook may be only the idea of looking at things slightly askew — taking a whimsical, oddball approach,” says Stathis.

“We just sow the seeds in the studio,” says McCoy.

LORRAINE **wild**

"That CRANBROOK stuff" How many times has this author heard that phrase, uttered suspiciously by any number of otherwise sophisticated East Coast graphic designers, in an attempt to dismiss student work that seems demanding in a way that well-behaved student work ought not to be? Those who have not visited Cranbrook, or who only know the work through reproduction, or through acquaintance with alumni (a small group, who tend to act like the brethren of some obscurely passionate cult), often regard Cranbrook graphic design as a stylistically monolithic mystery. Or worse, graphic design from Cranbrook has been accused of being nothing more than formalist polemic, attacking the most hallowed shibboleths of design practice: that graphic design is *problem solving*, that *self-expression is irrelevant* to graphic design, that design is *value-free*, *universal*, obliged to reveal elemental *truths*, etc., etc..

The geographic isolation of Cranbrook adds to its inscrutability; just how much credence can be given to design theory emanating from the Rustbelt? The fact that Cranbrook has had a history of experimentation and production dealing with design and design theory was re-established in the collective memory by the 1984 exhibition *Design in America: The Cranbrook Vision 1925 - 1950* (organized by the Metropolitan Museum of Art, New York, and the Detroit Institute of Arts). Though contemporary work was not included in that exhibition, it was displayed at the same time that, after fifteen years of direction under the McCoys, work produced in the design department achieved a sort of formal and theoretical cohesion; since that time it has been difficult for the critics to ignore the production of Cranbrook students and alumni.

TRANSGRESSION AND DELIGHT: Graphic design AT CRANBROOK

A truly inventive and coherent design curriculum cannot be created overnight, and the student work of the 1980s reproduced in this volume has its roots in the work produced by Michael and Katherine McCoy and their students in the first decade of their interdisciplinary program. Like many other young and serious designers of the late sixties, the McCoys combined a fascination with methodology, sociology, and process with the visual vocabulary of "International Style" late Modernism (in both two- and three-dimensional work), influenced particularly by the Bauhaus, Ulm, Swiss design, and radical Italian industrial design of the sixties. The general feeling among many contemporary designers and architects was that formal issues had been identified and resolved through the work of the early Modernists and that the future of design advancement would result from work on the methodology and analysis of problem solving in design. This "hippie Modernism" of the early seventies reflected a generation's commitment to a utopian dream of design working for the public good, with form being secondary to process. The McCoy's first poster announcing the formation of an interdisciplinary design program at Cranbrook mentioned nothing about the actual product of the students' work, only the process. It stated: "We are a newly reorganized community of twenty designers in the various environmental disciplines concerned with hardware solutions to human needs.... In complex design problems multiple relationships are often obscured. For this reason graphic methods such as process networking and non-linear charting are used to clarify and communicate...."

There are factions of design educators who abide by this idea to this day — but the McCoys were affected by and involved in other ideas which moved the work in their programs away from the formally banal outcome of much methodology-obsessed seventies design. Responding to a Cranbrook tradition (most visible in the work of Charles and Ray Eames and Eero Saarinen), they favored a more pragmatic (midwestern?) synthesis of ideas from many sources — and Cranbrook's distance from Europe and the East Coast freed them from the extremes of polemicism and professionalism to formulate a truly independent program. Of particular relevance to the graphic designers was Katherine McCoy's professional background, which encompassed two distinctly different — some would say contradictory — approaches to design: the American corporate International Style of Unimark, where she worked in 1967-68, and the American advertising style of Designers & Partners, a Detroit studio where she worked before 1971. Through the work of several designers at Designers & Partners (but particularly in the work of Edward Fella, a designer who convincingly deployed highly personal art-based imagery and typography in his design for the public), the McCoys and their students were exposed to the extremely knowledgeable eclecticism of commercial graphic design (and the ability — and willingness — to see the entire high-to-low art spectrum as grist for one's visual mill). Early Cranbrook graphic-design projects combined a rather straightforward exposition of typographic principles (Tschichold and Ruder) with the more anarchic tendencies of pop imagery from illustration-based commercial art and the ironic strategies of conceptual/pop art (Ruscha and Warhol).

in those condition
rook can easily mo
MATIC POETI
dation of being to t
iscussion moves fro

Though serious designers were not supposed to be paying attention to form, some were definitely bothered by the universal use of

"Helvetica-on-a-grid" for everything from corporate communications to the covers of avant-garde jazz albums. Serious doubts about the function of the International Style as a means of visual communication led to a great deal of ironic experimentation and violation of the style. Intellectual fuel for these experiments was provided by Robert Venturi and Denise Scott Brown's *Complexity and Contradiction in Architecture* and more importantly, *Learning from Las Vegas*. Venturi and Scott Brown's radical analysis of architectural style as a language capable of communicating to its audience on many levels inspired the McCoys and their students to explore form as a language and reinforced their interest in the vernacular, the impure, the incorrect, and all the other forbidden excesses that were already familiar to them through the art business.

If this sounds like a recipe for a post-Modern soup, that is exactly what it is — but one must emphasize that it took on very homemade flavors at Cranbrook. The trickle of information about graphic-design history that began to be available to students in the mid-seventies became another enormously important influence on the graphic work at Cranbrook as well. There was simply too little information to encourage scholarly work (and no art history department at the Academy), but, taking their cues from architects, graphic-design students began to use historical forms as referents in their compositions. The historically eclectic, "incorrect" Modernism of Saarinen's *gesamtkunstwerk*, the Cranbrook campus, supplied incontrovertible evidence that interesting and humane design could be achieved without formulas for form.

"Form WITHOUT guilt"

Thus, Cranbrook students turned to form with a vengeance by the mid-seventies. "Type 'n Stripe" was the irreverent local nickname for the exaggerated, neo-Constructivist violations of proper Swiss typography, grids, and rule lines. The work bore some resemblance to Wolfgang Weingart's typographic experimentation at the Kunstgewerbeschule in Basle, but Cranbrook students were not immediately exposed to that work; independent analysis (based on analysis of function, not form) simply led them to similar, but more eclectic, attempts to mold a richer graphic language out of the stiff grammar of Swiss graphic design.

What was eventually developed through the student work at Cranbrook was a third path, a way of generating form out of neither formal nor sociological extremes, but through a synthesis of elements from both sides, plus the addition of ideas from philosophy, linguistics, and critical theory. The path was not particularly linear or scholarly, but instead reflected the improvisatory "garage-mechanic" (or "garage-band," depending on one's generation) energy empowering the work. An example of this was the group project by graphic-design students in 1977-78 to design an issue of *Visible Language* (vol.7, #3 Summer 1978). Titled "French Currents of the Letter," the journal contained eight very difficult essays on post-Structuralist French *ecriture*. With the help of Daniel Libeskind, the head of Cranbrook's architecture department, the students were provided with a crash course on the theoretical background of the work and created a design for the journal that was a visual analogue for the disruption and self-consciousness that post-Structuralism traces in texts. The first few pages of the issue were designed in a standard format for a scholarly journal. After the first two essays, elements of the page (footnotes and word and letter spacing, in particular) move in ways that are distinctly aggressive. The design of the journal attacks the visual "transparency" of the text (the naturalistic assumptions behind traditional book design) in the same manner in which the authors attack the notion of "transparency" of meaning behind language. By the end of the journal, all typographic conventions have been jettisoned — but in a manner which is actually quite obedient to the text!

Ten years later, the Cranbrook student work on "French Currents of the Letter" is still held up, by certain critics of design education, as an example of design transgressing its moral duty to deliver seamless communication. This criticism ignores the obvious correlation between the form of the journal and its particular contents, and that neither one was being promoted as a replacement for normative design or language. One can, of course, revive the boring arguments against the value of any experiment that does not somehow deliver applicable advancement, but that would ignore how useful the experiment was for the students, for it really began their forays into applying theory from other fields to enrich their own development of form.

After "French Currents of the Letter," linguistically based, Structuralist/post-Structuralist/semiotic research and analysis of design began to be applied, more readily to 2D rather than 3D projects, but interdepartmental critiques and theoretical discussions eventually led to the development of "product semantics" as a direction for 3D projects as well. The "research" that students engaged in to develop projects was simply expanded beyond data-gathering (or the endless production of sketches) to include ideas about the production of meaning. There are many who oppose the use of critical theory (especially *French* critical theory) as a source for design discourse, and the more knowledgeable will point out that some texts (those of Roland Barthes, for example) "went out of vogue" with literary critics a long time ago. It may well be that critical theory, which approaches all verbal and visual phenomena, indiscriminately and synthetically, as *text*, is most precisely relevant and empowering to design criticism and theory; whether it is still chic in comparative literature seems beside the point.

By the late seventies, the graphic-design program had coalesced into its present form, and the work presented in this book represents the maturing of the curriculum established by Katherine McCoy. The curriculum is no more than a changing sequence of projects (the history poster, the "label" sequence, the science project, and a few others) that demonstrate contemporary principles of graphic design. The projects have become more complex over the years as the students that attend the program arrive with more education and experience. While students are working on the projects, they are expected to carry out their own investigations; they also collaborate on experimental and "real" freelance projects. The department operates like a very democratic R&D lab, where all are expected to contribute to the common passion for design, particularly in the critiques. The entire department takes a trip once a year (an antidote to the isolation of Detroit); students are encouraged to ask tough questions of the design establishments that they visit, and, nurtured by their own independence at Cranbrook, they do.

The "label" sequence project, now referred to as the "vernacular message" project, is worthy of close attention because it demonstrates the transformation of a classic modern problem into a problem more responsive to current thinking in design. The project, with its roots in didactic exercises illustrated in Emil Ruder's book, *Typography* (1967), involved the typographic layout of a simple, "objective" message, such as a recipe, a weather report, or a set of directions, on a gridded field. Following a prescribed set of steps, the student composed the message on the grid repeatedly, using the Helvetica or Univers type families. Each version allowed one variation in the typography — for instance, size or weight — which was used to organize and clarify the message. This project provided an efficient demonstration of typographic syntax — the formal means by which a message could be communicated, within the limited set of options permitted in the International (Swiss) Style.

Katherine McCoy assigned this project in the early seventies, as did many other typographically driven design programs (notably, Yale, Rhode Island School of Design, and Philadelphia College of Art). Responding to other ideas in the program, she continued to manipulate the rules of the project, away from its original form. The first steps of the project are now covered rather quickly. The type from the original — an example of the vernacular such as a Yellow Pages ad or a product label — is applied to the grid, and then in its own arrangement, breaking down the distinctions between designed and nondesigned typography (and demonstrating how vernacular type stubbornly retains its character even when pulled out of context onto the grid). An abstracted visual analysis of the typographic composition is created, which feeds back into the typographic arrangement. Images are added, and the student discovers that a hierarchy of meanings and interpretations is within his or her control. In the final, most controversial step, students create a subjective visual interpretation of the entire process — which attempts an essential interpretation of the object or ad that they started with.

It is this last step that violates all of the premises of "graphic design" but that in fact reverberates most accurately with the richness of design thinking at Cranbrook. High and low visual culture are synthesized; the late-Modernist pretense of universality and objectivity in communication is rejected; the graphic designer becomes a participant in the delivery of the message, not just a translator. Breaking the taboo against "self-expression" becomes an enormously liberating stage for the students; notions of "correctness" are negated, and a way of generating imagery without rules suddenly becomes viable. The challenge to objectivity represented by the use of material outside the realm of "correct" graphic design, such as the vernacular, was largely due to the influence of Edward Fella. A frequent guest critic during the mid-seventies and a Cranbrook degree candidate in the mid-eighties, Fella produced numerous sketch books and collages ("art about design") that were a rich resource for Cranbrook, inspiring visual rule breaking.

studio plat- form that supp
signer. The studio is a ho
their own visions of the
chaotic, conflicting,
process of student.

From TYPE that talks to TYPE that reads

This process is also carried out in the other projects — for instance, in the science concept project — where the main criterion, to make invisible processes intelligible, is reached in a variety of ways that admit a great intuitive responsiveness on the part of the designer, and account for the participation of an intelligent audience; or the history posters, which are fueled by a subjective interpretation of history that is certainly more in line with advanced trends in historical thought of the last few years than with the proper graphic design obsession with objectivity and the elusive "truth." Katherine McCoy and David Frej discussed this process in their article "Typography as Discourse" (*ID*, March/April 1988):

> **Reflecting current linguistic theory, the notion of 'authorship' as a personal, formal vocabulary is less important than the dialogue between the graphic object and its audience: no longer are there one-way statements from designer to receiver.... Objective communication is enhanced by deferred meanings, hidden stories and alternative interpretations.... It is an interactive process that — as art always anticipates social evolution — heralds our emerging information economy, in which meanings are as important as materials.**

The power of the search conducted with such freedom (what better definition of graduate school?) reveals itself in the existence of the independent "editions" — unassigned projects that the students do among themselves. These projects have always existed at Cranbrook; they are taken seriously and they create a kind of feedback that ends up influencing the faculty and other students, and influencing the course of the program. A series of posters produced by students during 1986-87 are particularly important, because they focused on the problem of the instability of meaning concocted out of words and images and the possibility of multitudinous meanings created in the mind of the audience, as well as the intention of the designer. This thought, which really came out of readings and discussions based on reception theory, post-Structuralism, and deconstruction, inspired students to spend the next few years visualizing these literary concepts and has led to a body of work which, despite its relentlessly verbal base, is visually quite inventive. There is an obvious uniformity of style in prescribed projects such as the "label" project, but the independent work displays a much wider formal range, from delicately layered, high-production refinement to bold imagery crudely juxtaposed in an exploration of "antimastery" — signifying the persistence of Cranbrook's pragmatic/imaginative ideal of a design language created out of the coexistence and tension between high style and low vernacular.

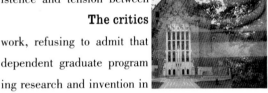

The critics continue to howl about this work, refusing to admit that maybe, just maybe, a small, independent graduate program is precisely where such daunting research and invention in graphic design should occur. The program and the work that it has produced are demanding, and there is undoubtedly some resistance to that; there also continues to be some confusion over the appropriateness of design education that is not based on a replication of professional practice. What is not widely understood is the honesty and unpretentiousness of the questions raised by the students in their work; they do not pretend to revolutionize graphic design but seek to participate in it as deeply as possible. The projects are a process (back to that original passion of twenty years ago); you derive great pleasure in the struggle, then you move on. Alumni go on to all sorts of practices — design offices, corporate offices, their own studios, academia. A look at their work attests to three obvious facts: that this tiny program has turned out a disproportionate share of smart and talented designers; that despite their pursuit of different directions after Cranbrook, common passions and ideals motivate them years beyond Bloomfield Hills; **and that American graphic design has been enormously enriched by their efforts.**

Projects

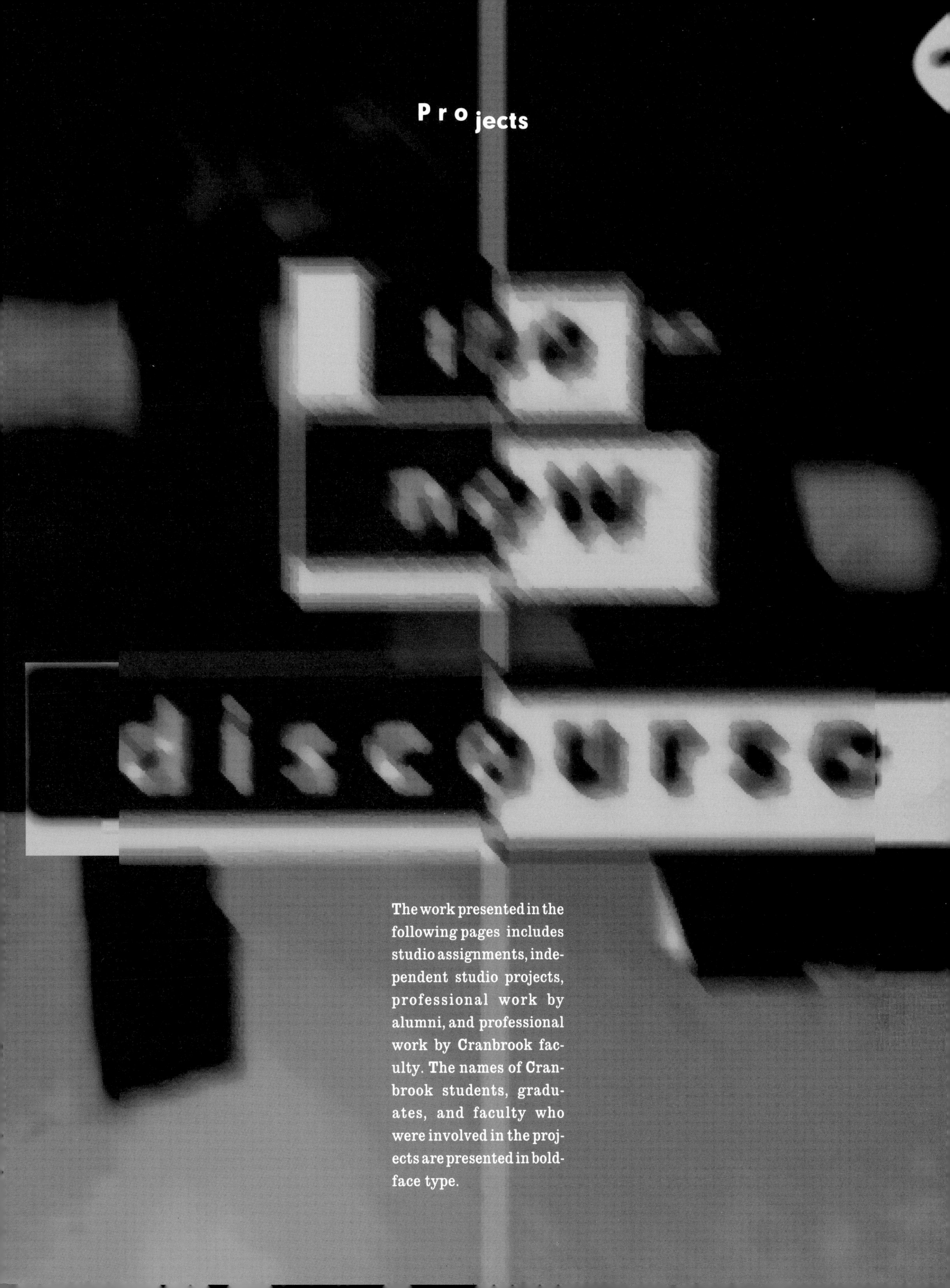

The work presented in the following pages includes studio assignments, independent studio projects, professional work by alumni, and professional work by Cranbrook faculty. The names of Cranbrook students, graduates, and faculty who were involved in the projects are presented in boldface type.

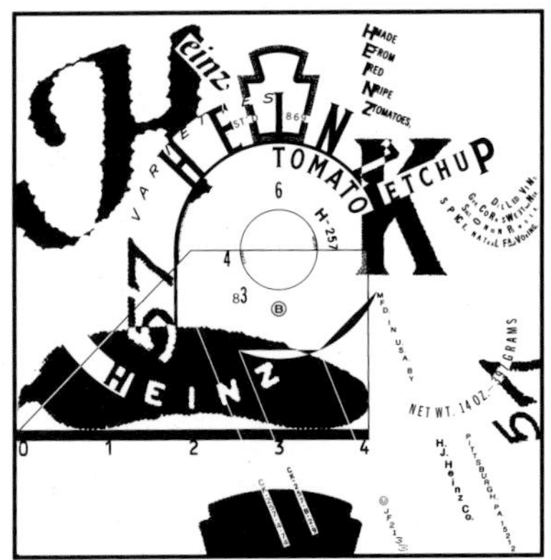
TOMATO
KETCHUP
HEINZ

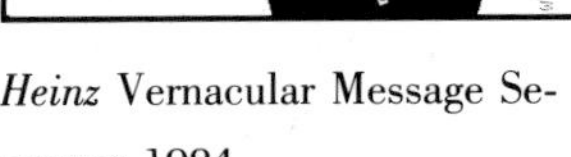

Heinz Vernacular Message Sequence 1984
Robert Nakata, designer; Cranbrook Studio assignment.
Four steps of a progressive sequence in which a ketchup-bottle text is progressively reinterpreted to build a personal mythology. Ketchup becomes the icon for fast food and the shopping-strip street, with visual references to commercial signage viewed from a speeding car at night.

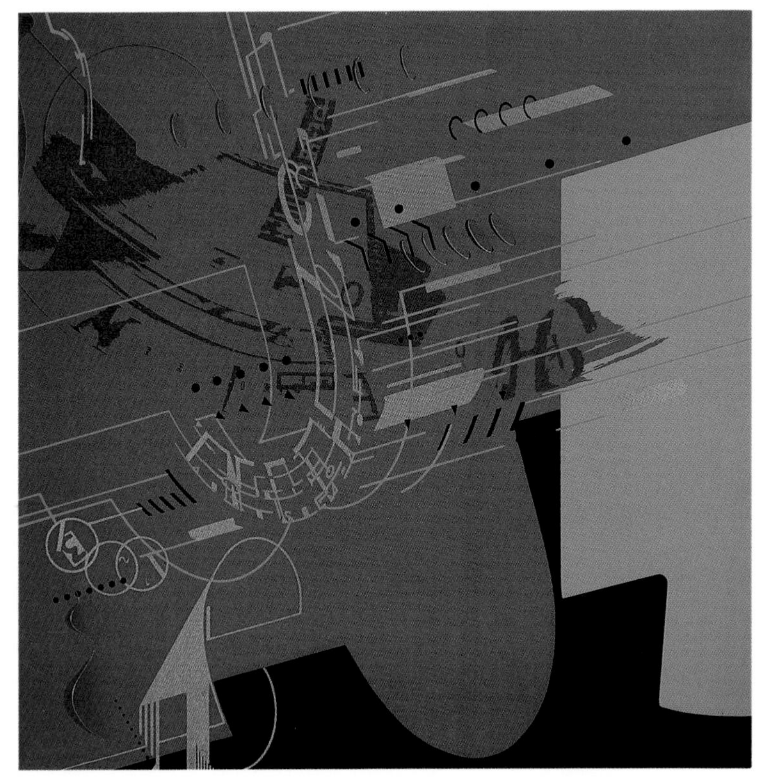

Heinz Vernacular Message Degree Project Model 1984
Robert Nakata, designer; Cranbrook Studio project.
The imagery developed in the two-dimensional sequence is materialized in a three-dimensional "sign" for Heinz as it might appear on a commercial street at night.

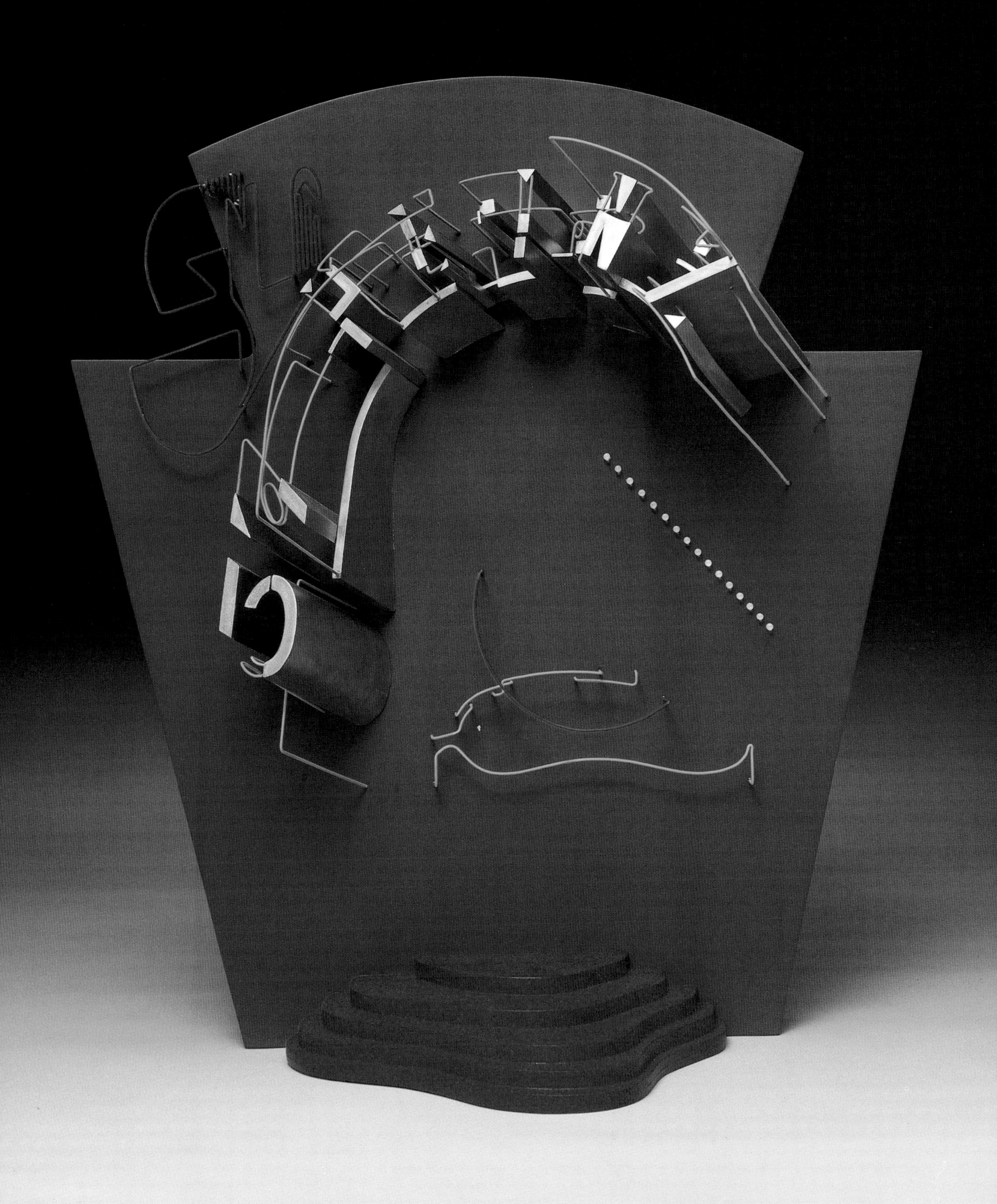

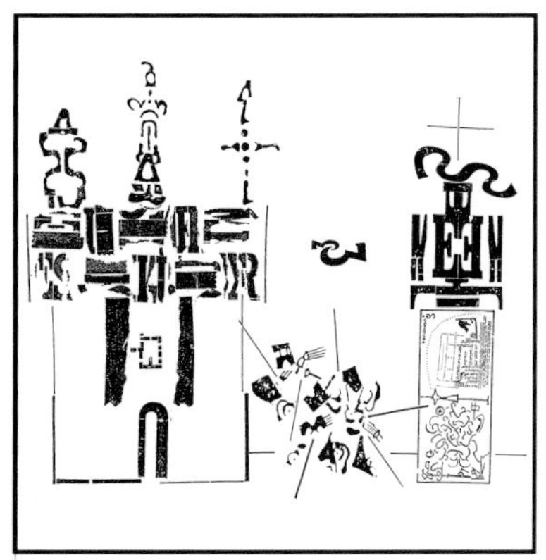

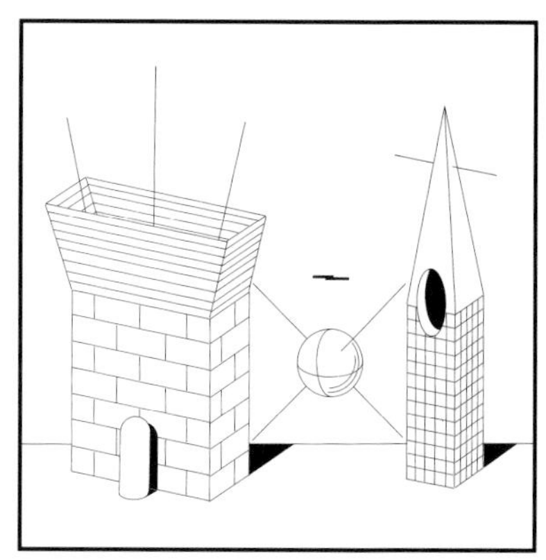

laundry detergent

tide

		regular size	net wt. 17oz. 1lb. 1oz.
		regular scent	037000036107
		tough cleaning	
1 always measure tide	adjust if necessary based on water hardness heavily soiled clothes or extra large loads		tear back to indicated line tear back to here recloseable top! lock tab in opening notch! to reclose push in tab close top to keep tide fresh
2 wash	sort your clothes select water temperature hot white,colorfast prints,pastels warm colorfast brights,light colors that bleed, nylons,woolens,polyester cold dark or bright colors that bleed stains like blood and chocolate	**ingredients**	perfume and agents to prevent deposition cleaning agents anionic surfactants and enzymes water softeners aluminosilicates,sodium carbonates processing aids sodium sulfate water protection agents fabric whitener tide contains less than 0.5% phosphorus less than 0.5 grams per cup use level the surfactants in tide are biodegradable
3 rinse	use cold water		
		caution caution:eye irritant	in case of eye contact flush with water call a physician keep out reach of children
			the world's leading washer makers approve tide for use in their top-loading machines
		under one or more patents	3,985,699 4,379,080 4,490,271
			made in the u.s.a. by proctor & gamble cincinatti,ohio 45202

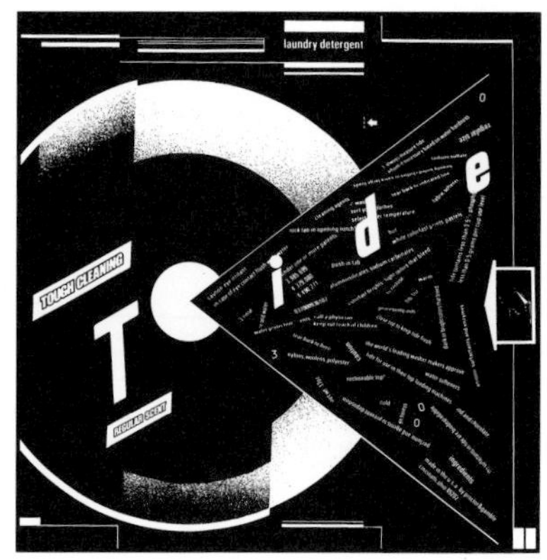
laundry detergent
TOUGH CLEANING
T
i
d
e

Three Musketeers Vernacular Message Sequence 1986
Edward Fella, designer; Cranbrook Studio assignment.
Four steps of a progressive sequence in which a candy wrapper's verbal message is reinterpreted to build a personal mythology. The series begins with an objective analysis of the message content and a strict grid organization of the text. Progressively more personal interpretations are expressed through the development of symbolic imagery. A page from the designer's daily sketchbook led to the medieval architectural imagery.

Tide Vernacular Message Sequence 1987
Andrew Blauvelt, designer; Cranbrook Studio assignment.
Four steps of a progressive sequence in which a detergent-box text is progressively reinterpreted to build a personal mythology. The gender-stereotyped routines of washing and housekeeping led the designer to ideas about female lunar cycles and television soap operas.

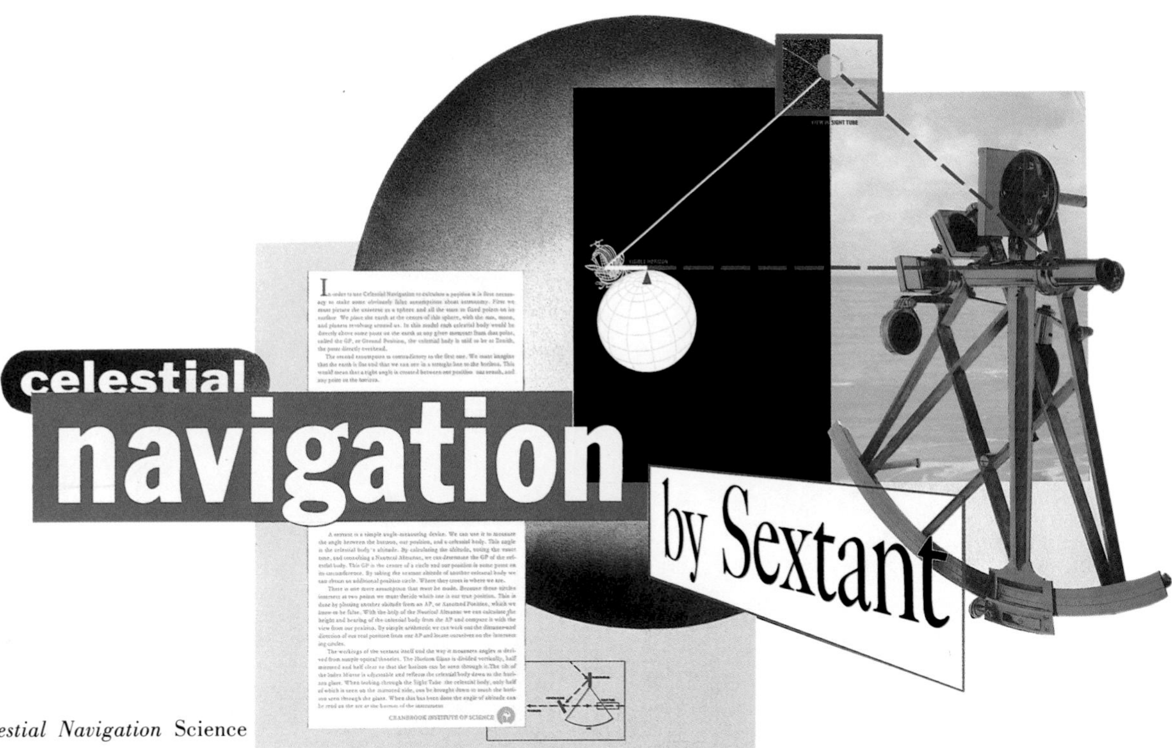
celestial
navigation
by Sextant

Celestial Navigation Science Concept Poster Prototype 1985
Edward McDonald, designer; Cranbrook Studio assignment.
A scientific concept is graphically visualized for potential sales in science museum shops. The poster conveys the profoundly three-dimensional quality of this navigational method in its two-dimensional format. The poster becomes an object in space through its irregular die-cut edges.

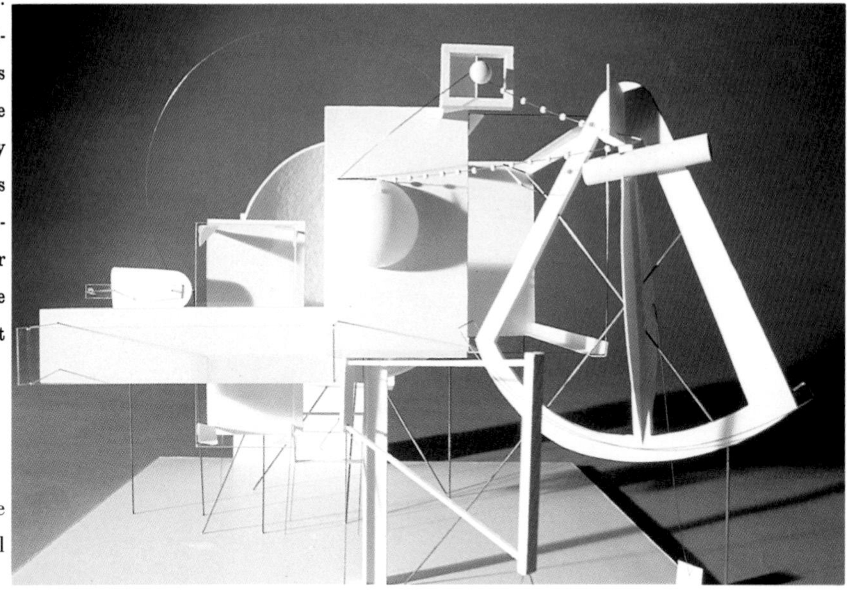

Celestial Navigation Science Concept Poster Study Model 1985
Edward McDonald, designer; Cranbrook Studio assignment.
This paper model aided the designer in visualizing navigation's three-dimensional relationships in space.

Foucault Pendulum Science Concept Poster Prototype 1985
Robert Nakata, designer; Cranbrook Studio assignment.
The concept of a Foucault Pendulum is graphically visualized for potential sales in science museum shops. Printed on flat board and die-cut, its perforated pieces would be punched out by the viewer and assembled as a three-dimensional poster.

FOUCAULT

The French physicist, L.J.B. Foucault (1819-1863), was best known for his light and motion experiments. Full of invention and measurement, his investigations included the velocity of light in various media, the gyroscope and a modern glass silvering technique. Foucault was recognized mostly for his 1851 Pendulum Experiment for which he received the Copely Medal. Using the principle that a pendulum tends to maintain its plane of oscillation unless acted upon by an external force, Foucault suspended an iron ball with an over 200 foot long wire from the Paris Pantheon dome. Once the device was set in motion, an eventual rotation was observed; because of the nature of the pendulum, Foucault deduced that the phenomena could only be accounted for by the rotation of the Earth about an axis beneath the freely suspended system.

Foucault's time projection for one rotation of the system in Paris, 31 hours, 47 minutes, was confirmed during the demonstration. Applying the formula to either Earth pole, the pendulum system would comlplete itself in 24 hrs.

right object
AND ITS
image
a=b
c=a
its pair
the object
the mirror image
DIRECTIONS MEAN SOMETHING ONLY TO AN OBSERVER.
PARITY

Parity Science Concept Poster 1989

Darice Koziel, designer; Cranbrook Studio assignment.

A self-published edition makes a visual/verbal pun, pairing pairs of pared pears to explain the physics law of parity in which an object, its pair, and its mirror image are identical.

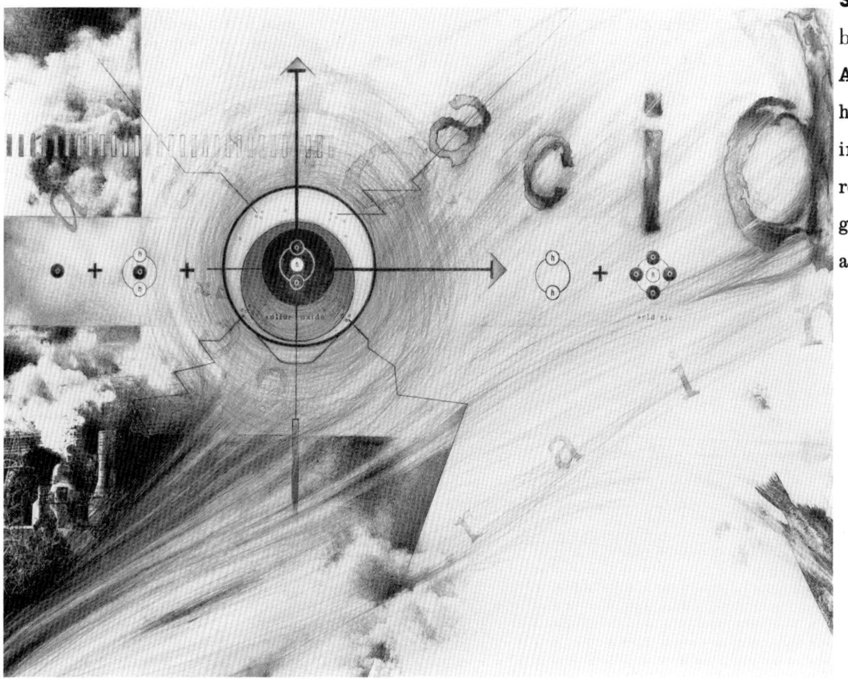
acid

Acid Rain Science Concept Poster Prototype 1989

Susan Lally, designer; Cranbrook Studio assignment.

A montage of photographic and hand-drawn typography and imagery charts the chemical reaction of acid rain and maps its geographic course eastward around the globe.

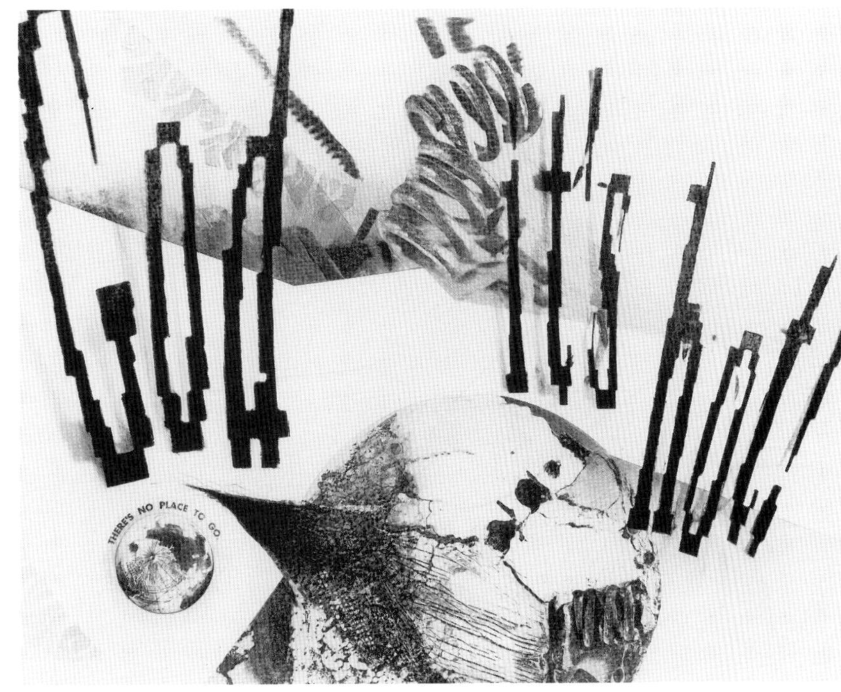
THERE'S NO PLACE TO GO

God It's Hot Concept Poster Prototype 1989

Susan Lally, designer; Cranbrook Studio project.

A montage of photographic and drawn typography and imagery deals with the phenomenon and environmental issue of global warming.

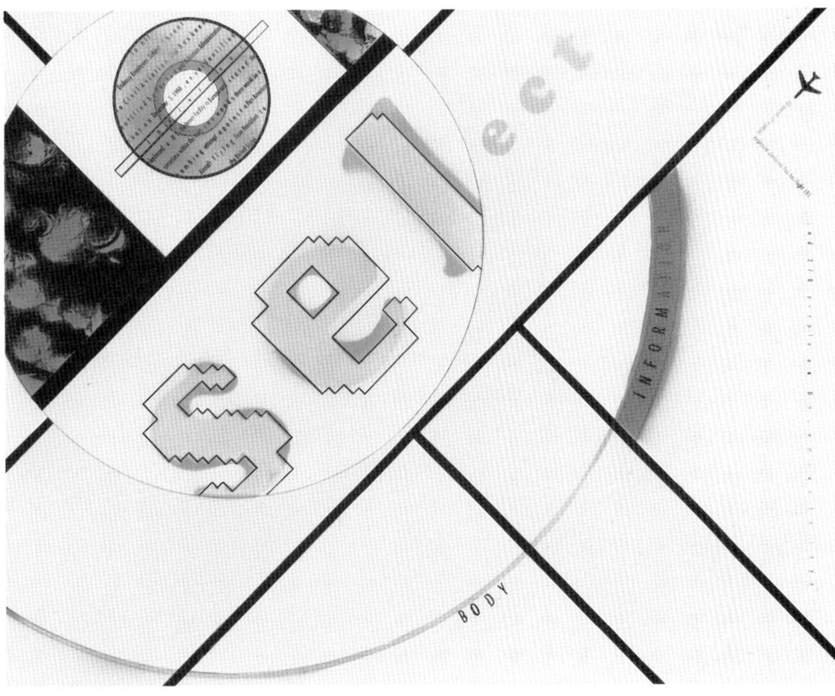
BODY

Select Concept Poster Prototype 1989

Susan Lally, designer; Cranbrook Studio project.

A montage of photographic and hand-drawn typography and imagery on how information is selectively disseminated.

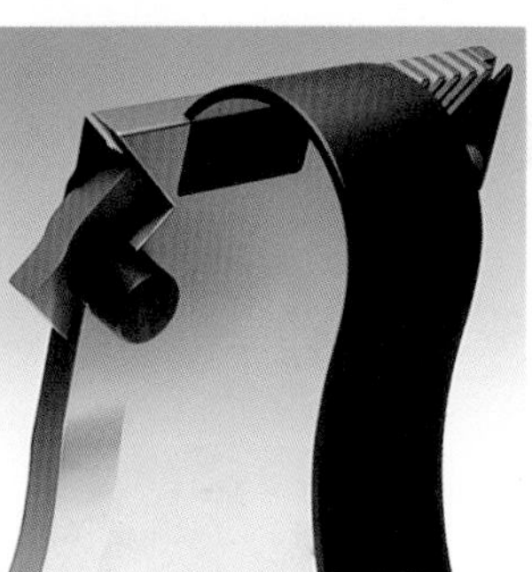

Picture Phone Video Telephone
Model 1986

Paul Montgomery, designer; Cranbrook Studio project.

The screen of this videophone is surrounded by an ornate structure (containing the camera and handset) which acts to domesticate the product through its resemblance to a picture frame.

MESG.1 IT'S MARTHA- HEY WHAT'S
WITH THE MESSAGE? I JUST CALLED
TO SAY THAT IF YOU GET ENOUGH
PHONE
RECORD
PRINT
PHONEBOOK

Phonebook Telephone Answering Machine Model 1987

Lisa Krohn with Tucker Viemiester, designers; Cranbrook Studio project.

This telephone-answering machine acts as its own instructional manual. By turning the electronic pages different modes are accessed. It is also contextual in its form, fitting in with the address books, papers, and other paraphenalia found on a desk top.

Power
On Line
Failure

Book Computer Model 1985
David Gresham, designer;
Cranbrook Studio project.
The modules added to this computer are offered in different shapes and sizes, making reference to the process of adding new books to a library.

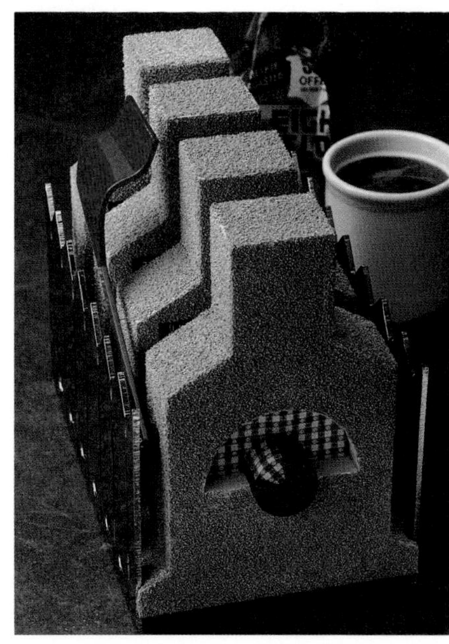

Suburban Toaster Model 1986
Paul Montgomery, designer;
Cranbrook Studio project.
The neighborhood context is satirized in this toaster surrounded by a picket fence. The mailbox flag pops up when the toast is done.

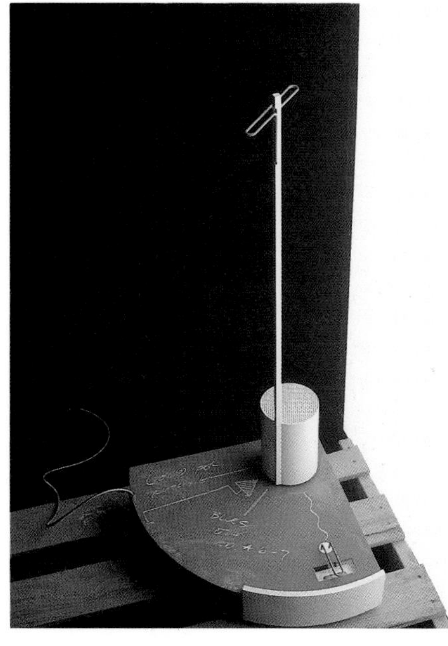

Radio Model 1987
Paul Montgomery, designer;
Cranbrook Studio project.
Favorite stations can be marked on the chalkboard dial at the base of this floor-standing radio.

POWER
1 Preset Tuner
Memory
Scan
1
2
3
4
5
6
7
8
2 Auto Tuner
Muting
High
Mid
Low
3 Manual Tuner
AM
52 61 70 79 88 97 106 133 142 151 160
FM
88 90 92 94 96 98 100 102 104 106 108
102.30
Stereo
4 Monitor
Tape 1
Tape 2
Copy 1-2
5 Phono
MM
MC
6 Auxiliary
On
V O L U M E
Phones
Remote
Main
Filter
Mono
Stereo
Right
Left
Loud
Bass
Treble
Balance

Stereo Receiver Model 1985

Robert Nakata, designer;

Cranbrook Studio project.

The images of musical notation and traditional instruments are used to organize the operation and convey the use of this receiver.

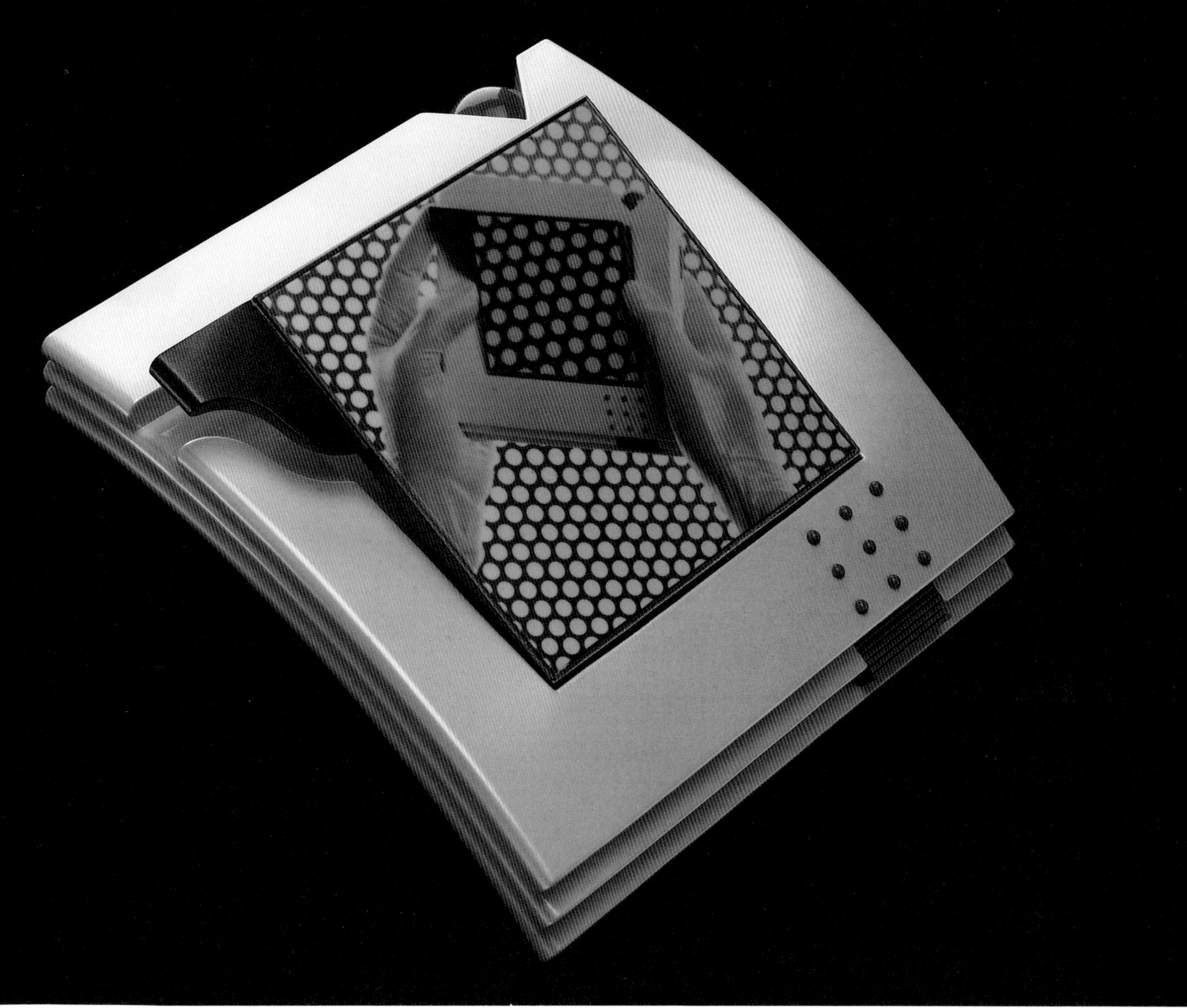

Electronic Still Camera Model
1987

Paul Montgomery, designer; Cranbrook Studio project sponsored by frogdesign.

The camera takes the form of a stack of photos and an eye. The camera is held in the hand and a picture is taken by pressing a button underneath. Once a photograph is taken it is stored in memory and can be displayed on the flip-up display screen.

MALEVICH

Kasimir Malevich Design History Poster 1980

Lori Barnett, designer; Cranbrook Studio assignment.

A self-published, limited-edition poster presents biographical information and pays homage to this distinguished historical design figure's vocabulary of forms.

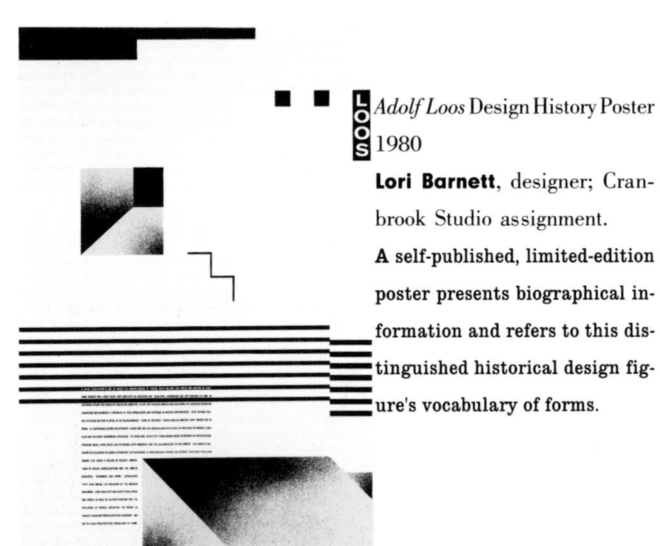
LOOS

Adolf Loos Design History Poster 1980

Lori Barnett, designer; Cranbrook Studio assignment.

A self-published, limited-edition poster presents biographical information and refers to this distinguished historical design figure's vocabulary of forms.

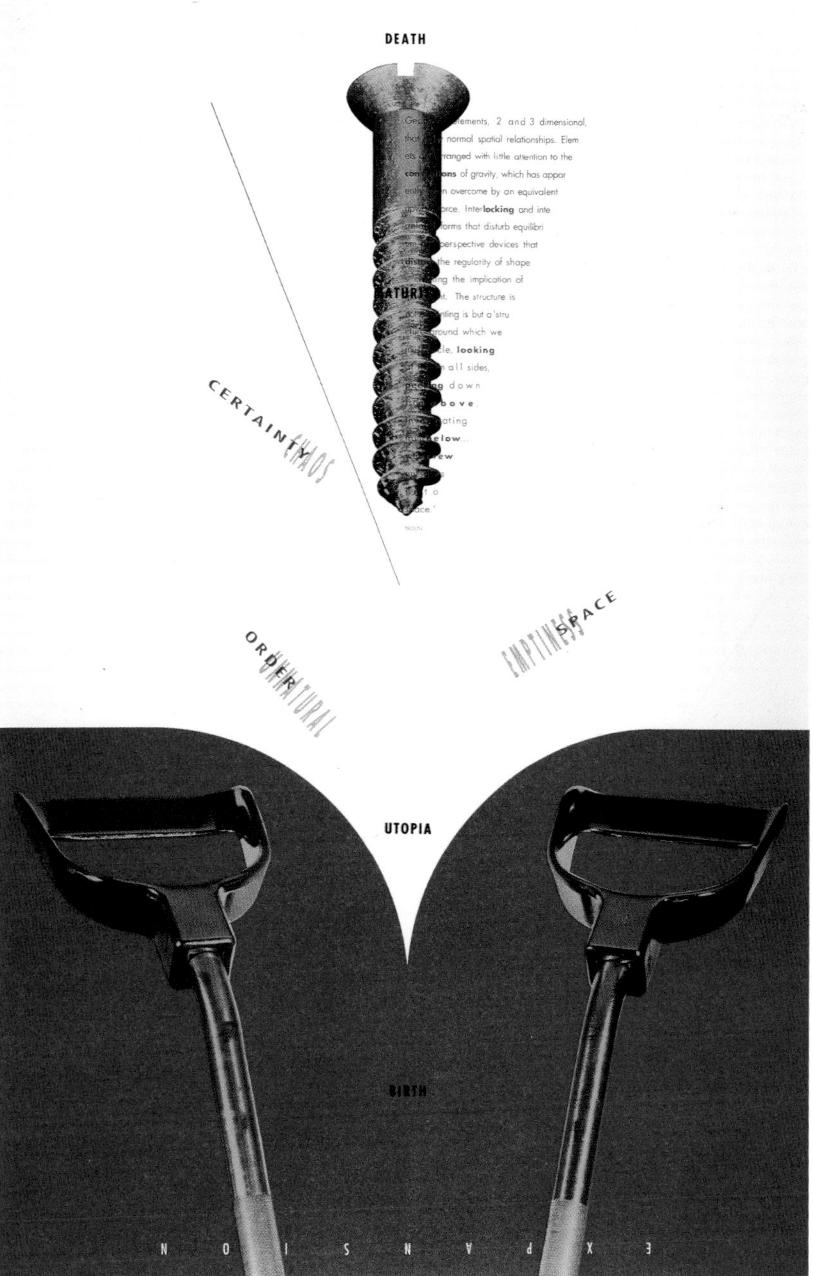
C O N T R A C T I O N
DEATH
CERTAINTY
CHAOS
ORDER
UNNATURAL
EMPTINESS
SPACE
UTOPIA
BIRTH
E X P A N S I O N

El Lissitzsky Design History Poster 1989
Darice Koziel, designer; Cranbrook Studio assignment.
A self-published, limited-edition poster relates quotations from this Russian Constructivist's philosophical writings on birth, life, and death to this student's personal forms and feminist concerns.

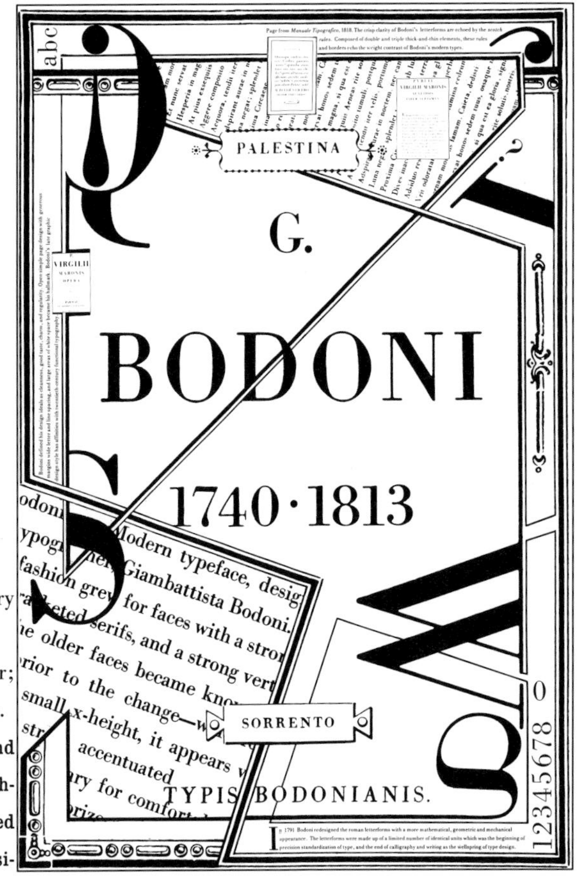
abc
PALESTINA
G.
BODONI
1740·1813
SORRENTO
TYPIS BODONIANIS.
0
12345678

Bodoni Typographic History Poster Prototype 1984
Jeffery Keedy, designer; Cranbrook Studio assignment.
This venerable Italian type and book designer's early-nineteenth-century forms are reconfigured in a freely irreverent composition that imbeds biographical information in its structure.

AGGRAVATE
Ample Notice Is Given As The Precious Becomes Girth
Robert Thorne, no doubt a portly gent, thin limbed and top hatted, cheeky & dark, born unknown, a foundling for sure, finds only a euphony of eye where a body of exuberance is needed. Stretching, he DOUBLED, then drew the very first fat face letterforms in the Great Britain of 1803. Turning to the bold of the Industrial Revolution (1760 1840), he fills out the demand for bloat.
As power SHIFTS in a great hundredfold INCREASE from sweat to steaming: throbbing, cranking, hurling quavering & in flux:
into this age for the expansive, that rise of the vast; DREAD along with the cheap and the quick. And NOW observe the newly corpulent in a role of substance pad the ephemera of PRINTED VERBOSITY from out of the tiny title page textfaces to the scale change of building side DISPLAY faces, posted in a great SHOW of mingled garrulity.

Robert Thorne Fat Face Typographic History Poster 1986
Edward Fella, designer; Cranbrook Studio assignment.
A self-published, limited-edition poster presents historical information on this vernacular typeface of the nineteenth century that was instrumental in the development of the handbill. A giant a becomes a "fat" face in a sly critique.

Dwiggins creates an illusion of machines.
But his machines are a masquerade. There are
no men inside them.
Strange case
of
W. A. not modernist
DWIGGINS
Modernist printing design? Modernism is not a
system of design—it is a state of mind. It is a
natural and wholesome reaction against an
overdose of traditionalism. W. A. D.
METRO 1929
W. A. DWIGGINS
1880-1956
In discussing Dwiggins' work, George Salter wrote: "Dwiggins' work has always impressed me as more truly American than the work of any other graphic artist in this country. It is without signs of visible influence. There is no traceable movement leading to him."
IN HIS BOOK Layout in Advertising, Dwiggins criticized sans serifs, writing 'The typefounders will do a service if they will provide a Gothic of good design.'
The Merganthaler Linotype Company challenged Dwiggins to design a better sans serif. Metro was accepted and cut in 1929. This challenge with Linotype led to a long and fruitful association which Dwiggins maintained throughout the rest of his life. His first book type, Electra, appeared in 1935 and in 1939 Dwiggins produced Caledonia, his best and most successful type which is a modified eighteenth century Scotch face
technology of Linotype in view while stil
background. Dwiggins designed several experimental types for Linotype including Stuyvesant, Winchester, Arcadia and Hingham, all interesting but idiosyncratic types, which are now fairly obscure. His last type, Eldorado, was released three years before his death in 1956.
Caledonia 1939

W. A . Dwiggins Design History
Poster 1988
Glenn Suokko, designer;
Cranbrook Studio assignment.

A self-published, limited-edition poster presents biographical information on this distinguished American book designer. Dwiggins' philosophy and eccentric individualism are reflected in selected quotations and the visual forms of the poster.

SUTNAR
visual design in action
Design is the synthesis of function, flow, and form. Design must satisfy all aspects of a given need. According to the design problem, this need may be analytically polarized into function and form, content and format, utility and beauty, the rational and irrational. The function of design may thus be defined as one of resolving the conflict of such polarities into a new entity.
design synthesis is the objective
good design cannot be obtained by prescription
Product Design File
1955
Sweet's Catalog Service
a design pointed to the future inspires improvement and progress
divergence from the conventional can make the common exciting
the designer must think first, work later
CUNO

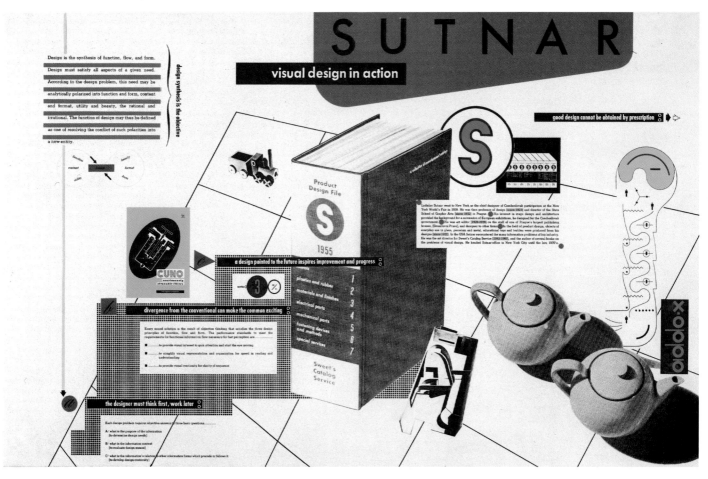

Ladislav Sutnar History Poster 1981

Christopher Ozubko, designer; Cranbrook Studio assignment.

This poster captures the spirit and forms of this influential designer of the 1940s and 1950s.

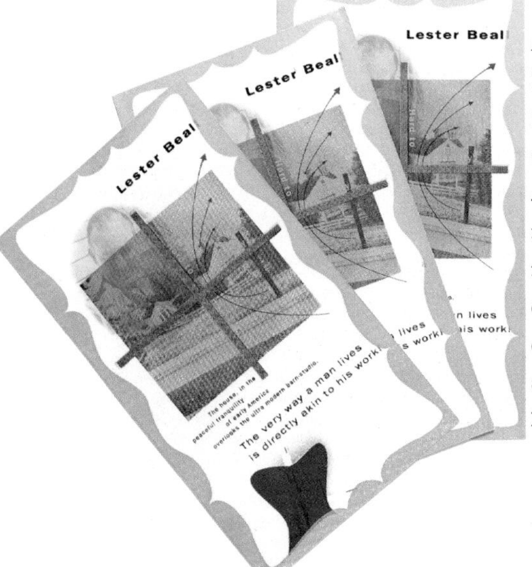
Lester Beal
The very way a man lives is directly akin to his work

Lester Beal Design History Poster 1989

Lisa Anderson, designer; Cranbrook Studio assignment.

A self-published, limited-edition miniature poster contains information on this mid-twentieth-century American Modernist's design in a "flash card" format as a humorous proposal for a design history series.

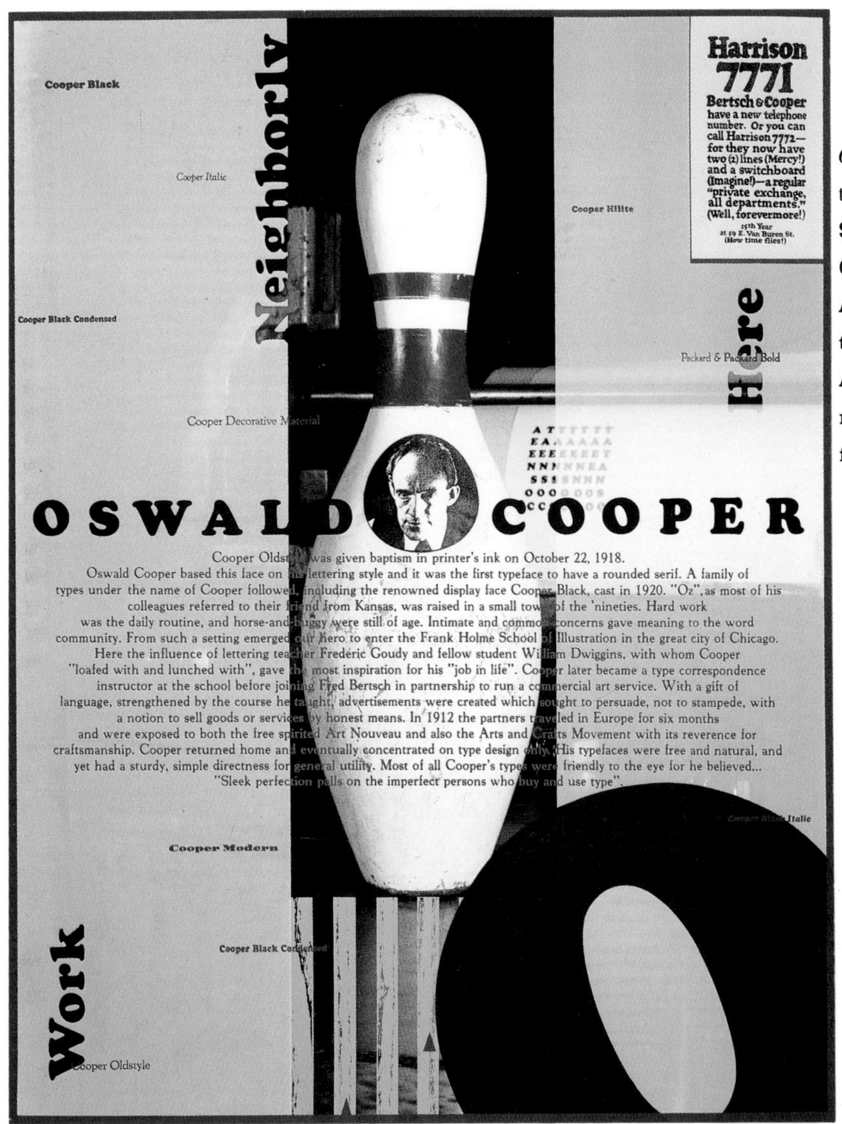
Harrison
7771
Bertsch & Cooper
have a new telephone number. Or you can call Harrison 7772—for they now have two (2) lines (Mercy!) and a switchboard (Imagine!)—a regular "private exchange, all departments." (Well, forevermore!)
25th Year
at 59 E. Van Buren St.
(How time flies!)
Cooper Black
Cooper Italic
Neighborly
Cooper Hilite
Cooper Black Condensed
Here
Packard & Packard Bold
Cooper Decorative Material
OSWALD COOPER
Cooper Oldst was given baptism in printer's ink on October 22, 1918.
Oswald Cooper based this face on lettering style and it was the first typeface to have a rounded serif. A family of types under the name of Cooper followed, including the renowned display face Cooper Black, cast in 1920. "Oz", as most of his colleagues referred to their friend from Kansas, was raised in a small tow of the 'nineties. Hard work was the daily routine, and horse-and-buggy were still of age. Intimate and commo concerns gave meaning to the word community. From such a setting emerged our hero to enter the Frank Holme School of Illustration in the great city of Chicago. Here the influence of lettering teacher Frederic Goudy and fellow student William Dwiggins, with whom Cooper "loafed with and lunched with", gave the most inspiration for his "job in life". Cooper later became a type correspondence instructor at the school before joining Fred Bertsch in partnership to run a commercial art service. With a gift of language, strengthened by the course he taught, advertisements were created which sought to persuade, not to stampede, with a notion to sell goods or services by honest means. In 1912 the partners traveled in Europe for six months and were exposed to both the free spirited Art Nouveau and also the Arts and Crafts Movement with its reverence for craftsmanship. Cooper returned home and eventually concentrated on type design only. His typefaces were free and natural, and yet had a sturdy, simple directness for general utility. Most of all Cooper's types were friendly to the eye for he believed... "Sleek perfection palls on the imperfect persons who buy and use type".
Italic
Cooper Modern
Cooper Black Condensed
Work
Cooper Oldstyle

Cooper Black Typographic History Poster Prototype 1988

Scott Santoro, designer; Cranbrook Studio assignment.

A rolling O and bowling pin refer to Oswald Cooper's Midwest American heritage and the vernacular popularity of this typeface.

max bill

Max Bill Design History Poster 1981

Craig Minor, designer; Cranbrook Studio assignment.

A self-published, limited-edition poster presents biographical information and pays homage to this distinguished historical design figure's vocabulary of forms.

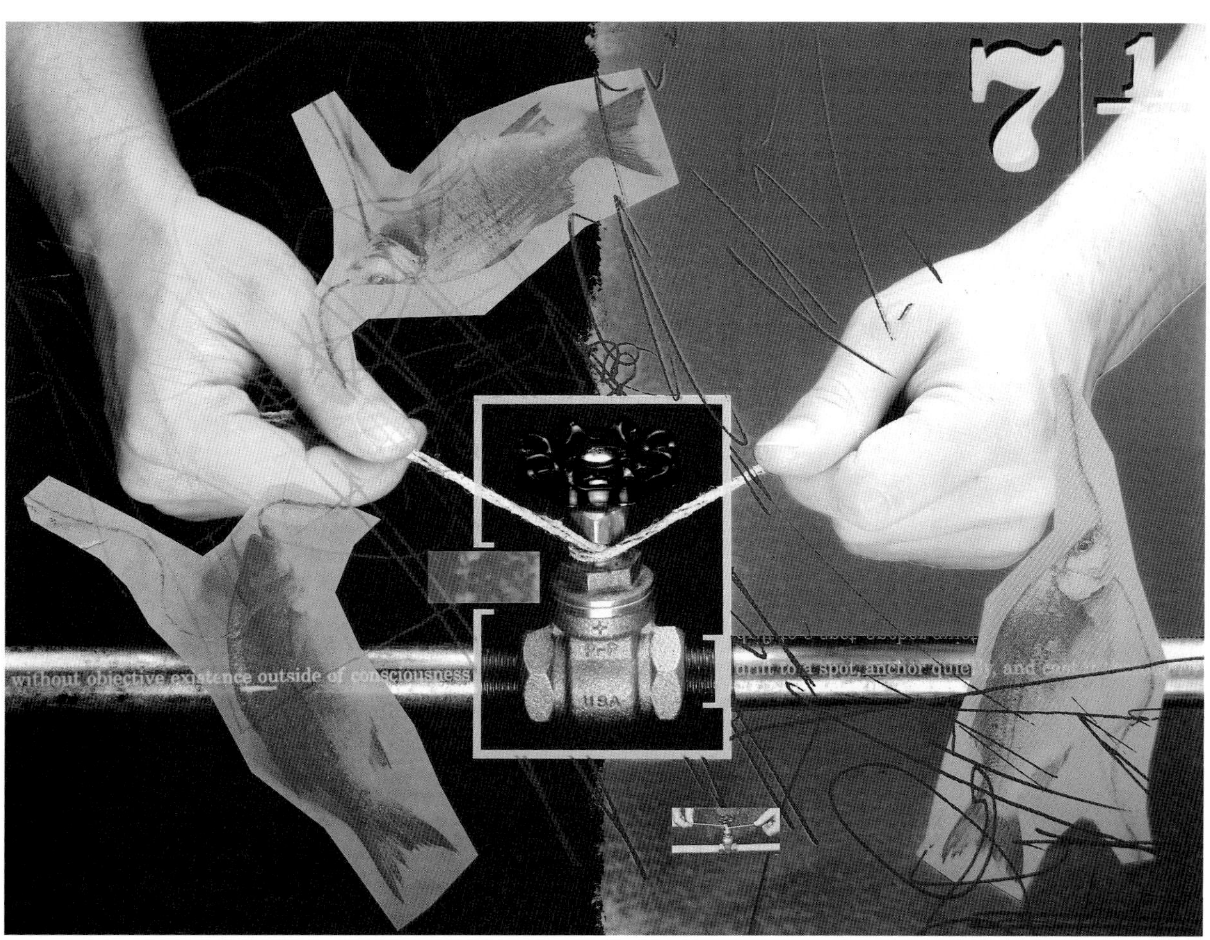
without objective existence outside of consciousness

Humor and the Subconscious
Degree Project 1988
Scott Santoro, designer;
Cranbrook Studio project.
Plumbing references become a metaphor for this student's design strategy in a large staged photograph montaged with silk-screened imagery.

JOKES
and
the

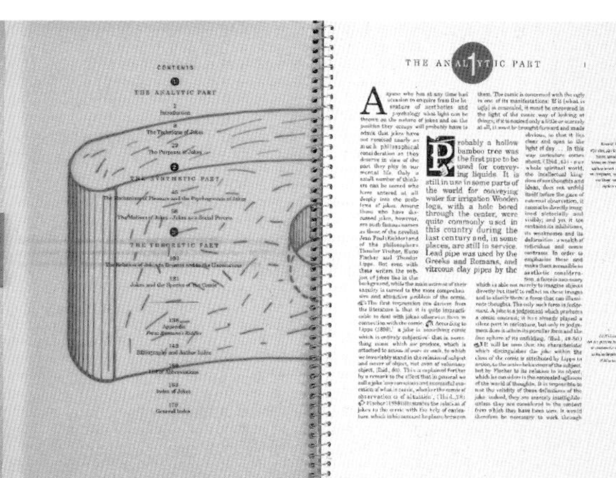

Humor and the Subconscious
Book Format 1988
Scott Santoro, designer;
Cranbrook Studio assignment.
Illustrations from a plumbing manual take on new symbolic content when juxtaposed with Sigmund Freud's classic text on humor. The format's structure and typography refer to the old plumbing manual's vernacular book design.

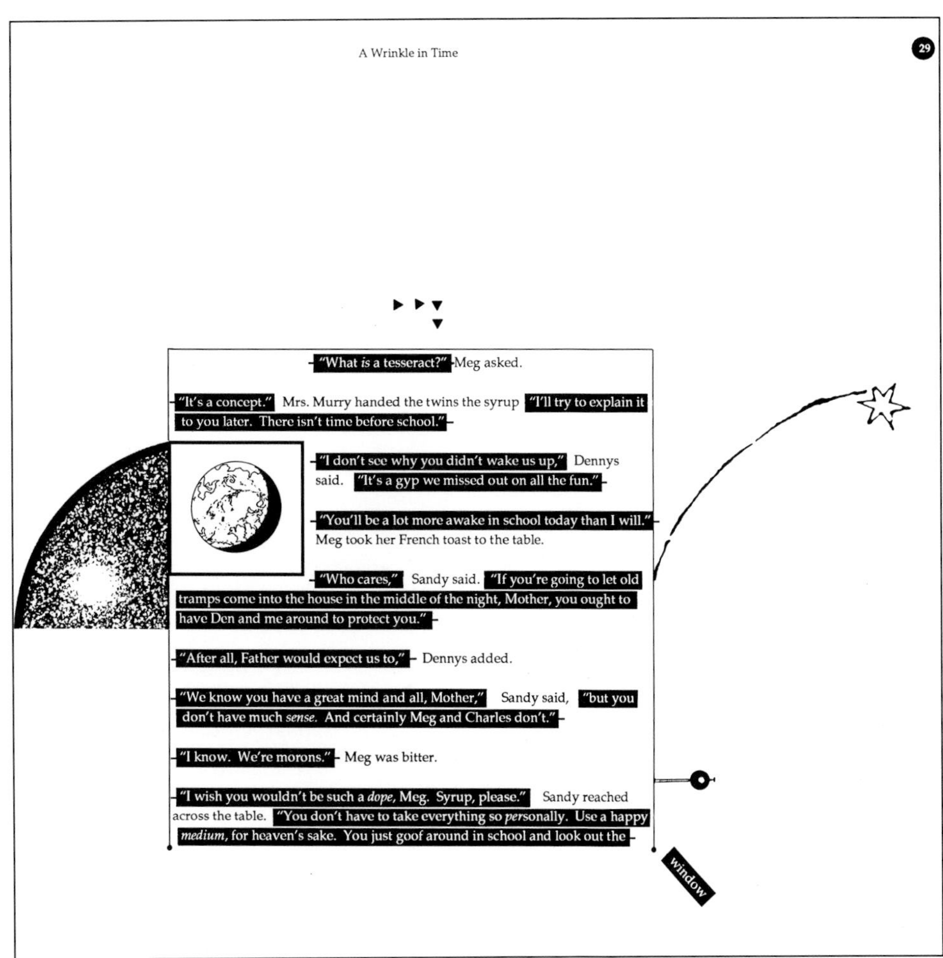
A Wrinkle in Time

29

"What *is* a tesseract?" Meg asked.

"It's a concept." Mrs. Murry handed the twins the syrup "I'll try to explain it to you later. There isn't time before school."

"I don't see why you didn't wake us up," Dennys said. "It's a gyp we missed out on all the fun."

"You'll be a lot more awake in school today than I will." Meg took her French toast to the table.

"Who cares," Sandy said. "If you're going to let old tramps come into the house in the middle of the night, Mother, you ought to have Den and me around to protect you."

"After all, Father would expect us to," Dennys added.

"We know you have a great mind and all, Mother," Sandy said, "but you don't have much *sense.* And certainly Meg and Charles don't."

"I know. We're morons." Meg was bitter.

"I wish you wouldn't be such a *dope,* Meg. Syrup, please." Sandy reached across the table. "You don't have to take everything so *per*sonally. Use a happy *medium,* for heaven's sake. You just goof around in school and look out the

window

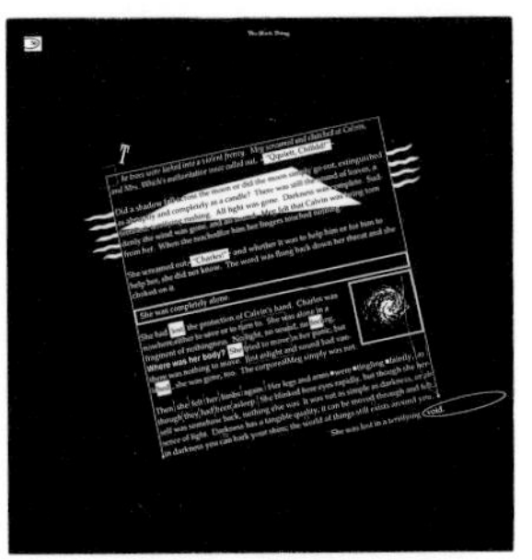

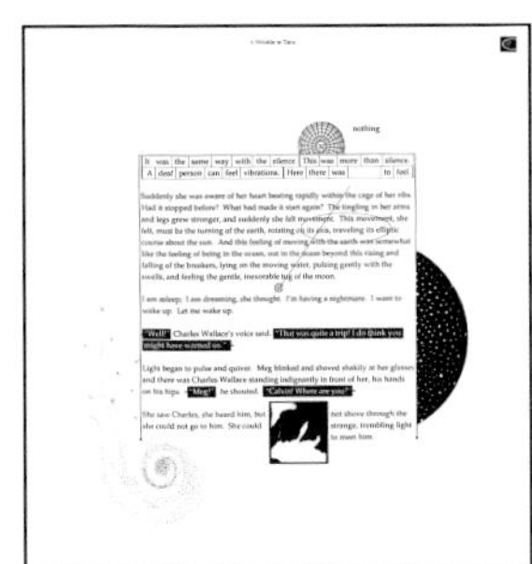

A Wrinkle in Time Book Format

1988

Tamar Rosenthal, designer; Cranbrook Studio assignment. The page format for this children's classic develops in size progressively through the chapters. First-person quotations are highlighted and imagery is integrated into the text in this syntactical experiment.

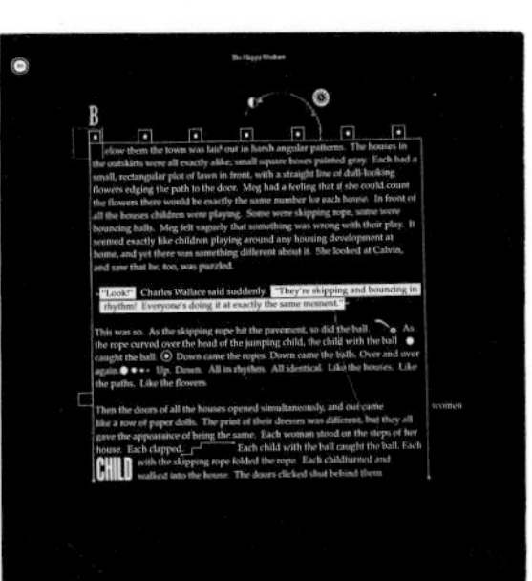

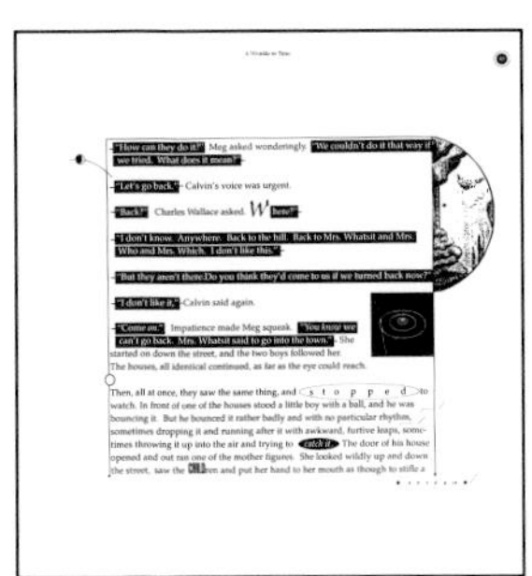

Palms
TEL

Palms Motel Street Signs Project 1981
Lori Barnett, designer; Cranbrook Studio assignment.
One block of a commercial main street is recorded photographically and combined in collage form in an interpretive graphic essay.

ACANCY

barry
PACKAGE DEALER
CIGARETTES
4 89
HOMO MILK
179
plastic gallon
LIQUOR
WINE BEER
SANDERS
candy
at its best
P R E S C R I P T I O N S
FREE
BLOOD PRESSURE
CHECK
NO APPOINTMENT NECESSARY
DRUGS
BOOKS
HARDCOVERS
TECHNICAL
CHILDRENS
PAPERBACKS MAGAZINES RACING FORMS EDUCATIONAL
The Bookworm Bookstore
Tropical Fish Pond
PET SUPPLIES REPTILES
OPEN 6 DAYS
out of town newspapers
fixtures
lamps
The Horseman Inc.
apparel.tack
gifts.supplies
Lampcraft
DOG FOOD
50 lbs $10.95 25 lbs $5.60
P.D.Q. INSTANT PRINTING
WHILE-U-WAIT
STOCKED & CUSTOM SHADES
CUSTOM LAMP MOUNTING
Gandalf
Leather clothing & accessories
ALL CITY TV
color TV
RCA
kitchen aid
handcrafted
zenith TV
CB RADIO
5PM
last pick up 5pm
US Mail

barry
PACKAGE DEALER
CIGARETTES
4 89
HOMO MILK
179
plastic gallon
LIQUOR
WINE BEER
SANDERS
candy
at its best
P R E S C R I P T I O N S
FREE
BLOOD PRESSURE
CHECK
NO APPOINTMENT NECESSARY
DRUGS

Barry Drugs Street Signs Project 1981

Lucille Tenazas, designer; Cranbrook Studio assignment.

One block of a commercial main street is recorded photographically and combined in collage form in an interpretive graphic essay.

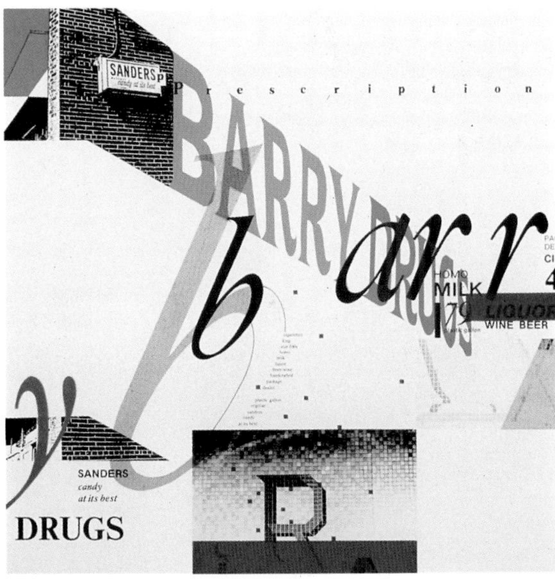
SANDERS
P r e s c r i p t i o n
BARRY DRUGS
barr
HOMO MILK
LIQUOR
WINE BEER
SANDERS
candy
at its best
DRUGS

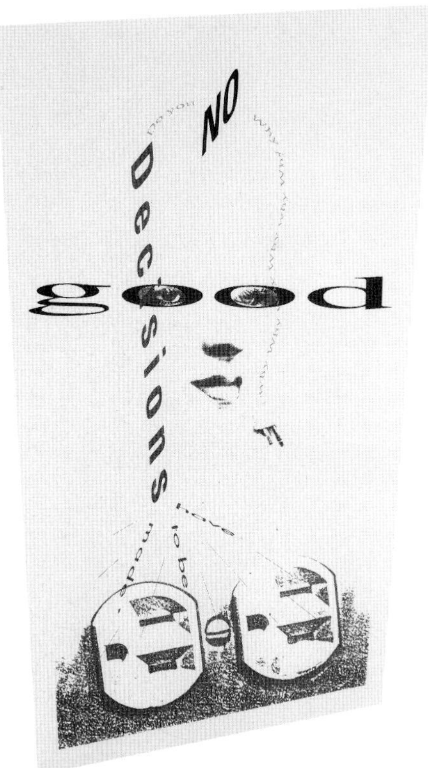
NO
good
Decisions

No Good Power Poster Prototype
1988

James Mason, designer; Cranbrook Studio assignment.

Text presenting opposing viewpoints about housing for the homeless and government power intermix, allowing the viewer to make his/her own interpretation. The text forms a woman's face, and the electrical outlets represent her breasts, a source of sustenance.

Sex Goddess Poster Prototype
1989

Paul Scott Makela / Laurie Haycock, designers; Cranbrook Studio project.

A digital photographic montage of two versions of the same woman's draped torso against a Hollywood landscape raises questions about gender and androgyny, glamor and sexual values. The text can be read in several ways, leading to questions about excess and godlessness.

SEX
LESS
GOD
EXC
ESS

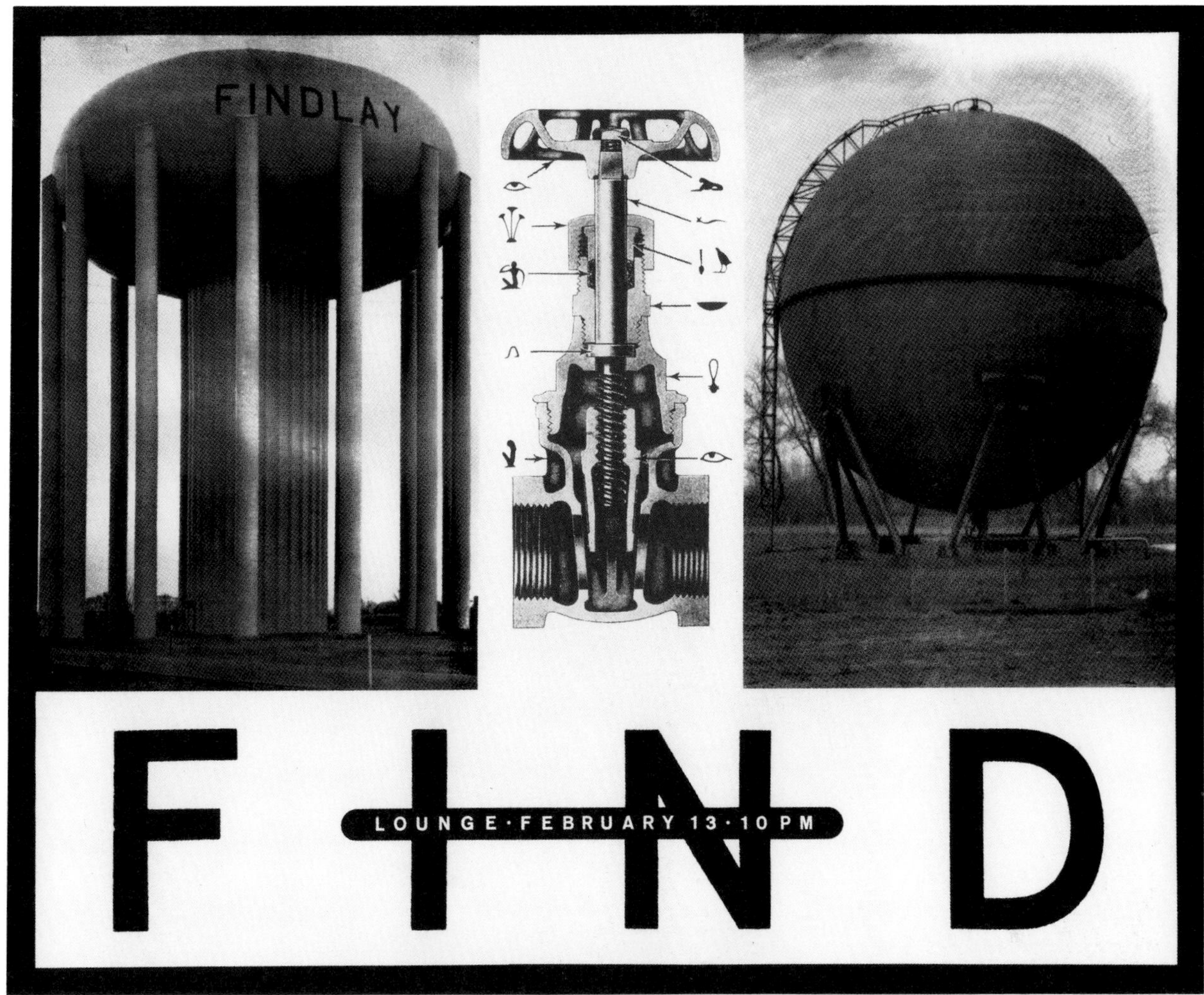
FINDLAY
F I N D
LOUNGE · FEBRUARY 13 · 10 PM

Findlay Valentine's Day Party Poster 1988

Scott Santoro, designer; Cranbrook Studio project.

A self-published, limited-edition poster that makes verbal and visual puns on the syllables of the water tank's name. Plumbing imagery and Freudian symbolism interact with the words to make a sly comment on the purpose of attending such a party.

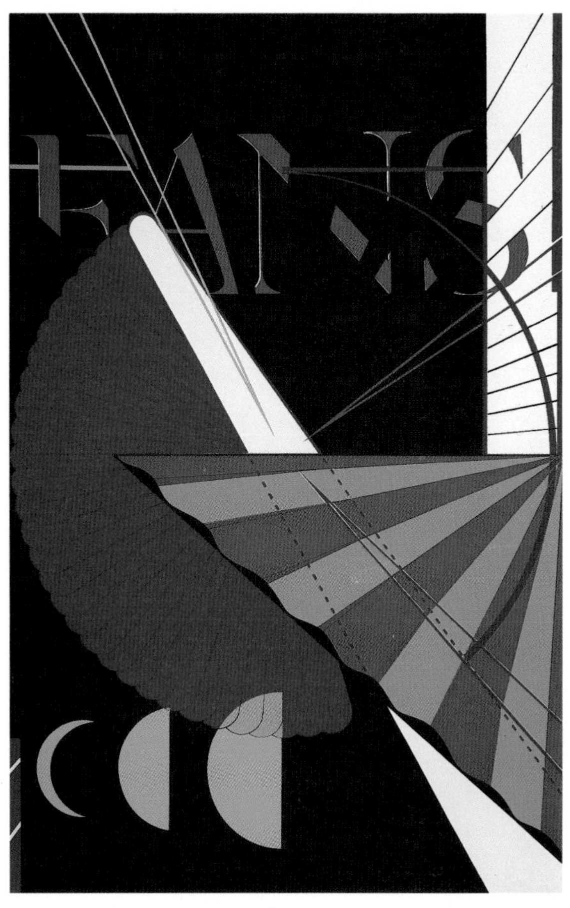

FANS

Fans Degree Project Posters
1983

Constance Birdsall, designer;
Cranbrook Studio project.

This self-published, limited-edition poster draws on Japanese symbolism and mythology about fans.

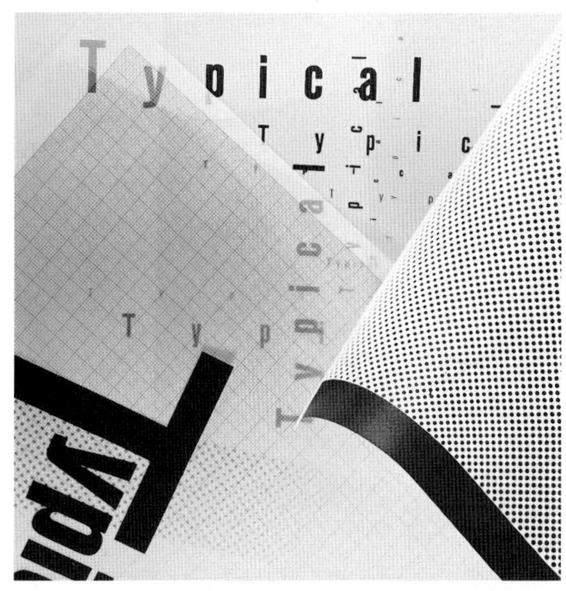
Typical

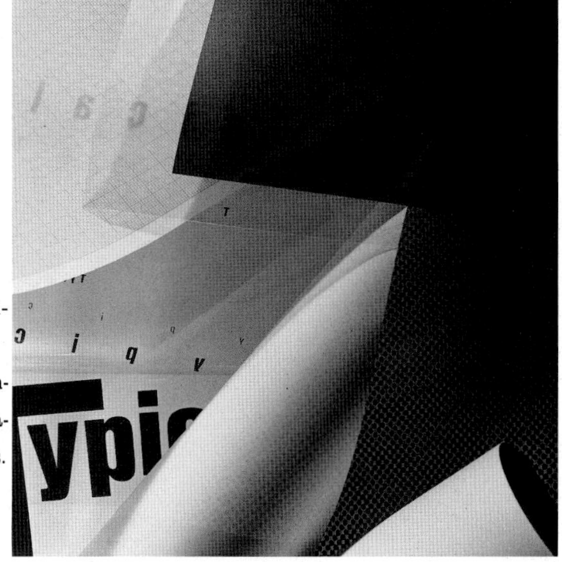

Typical Degree Project 1982
Craig Minor, designer; Cranbrook Studio project.
These staged photographs montage layers of "typical" typography and graphic-arts materials.

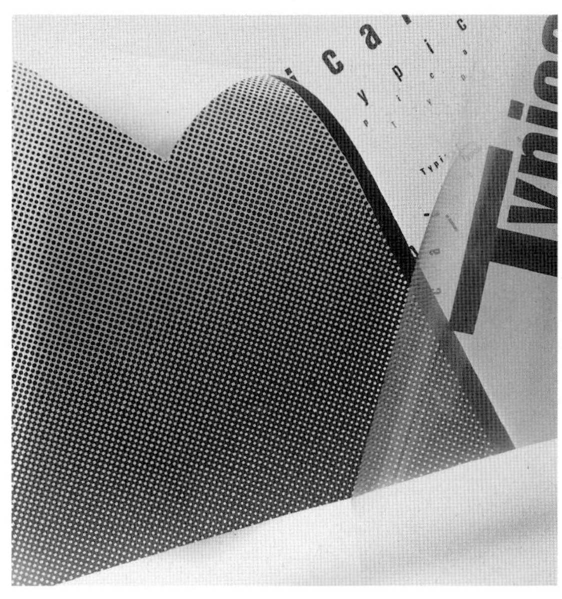

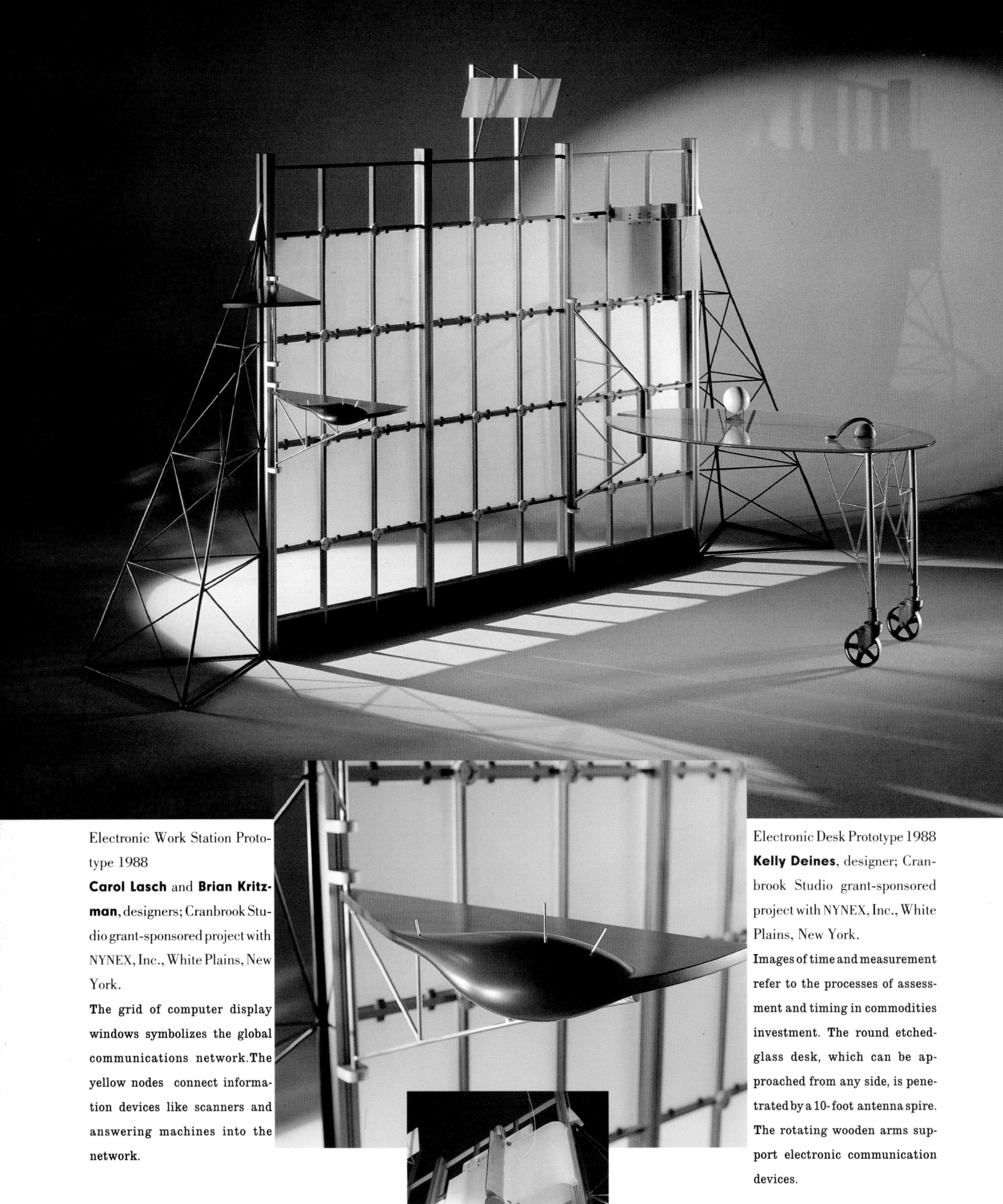

Electronic Work Station Prototype 1988
Carol Lasch and **Brian Kritzman**, designers; Cranbrook Studio grant-sponsored project with NYNEX, Inc., White Plains, New York.
The grid of computer display windows symbolizes the global communications network. The yellow nodes connect information devices like scanners and answering machines into the network.

Electronic Desk Prototype 1988
Kelly Deines, designer; Cranbrook Studio grant-sponsored project with NYNEX, Inc., White Plains, New York.
Images of time and measurement refer to the processes of assessment and timing in commodities investment. The round etched-glass desk, which can be approached from any side, is penetrated by a 10-foot antenna spire. The rotating wooden arms support electronic communication devices.

Electronic Desk Prototype 1988
Mike Scott, designer; Cranbrook Studio grant-sponsored project with NYNEX, Inc., White Plains, New York.
Dynamic skeletal support structures covered with translucent rubber skin give movement and gesture to the computer display and desk elements in this medical-research work station.

Electronic Chair Prototype 1988
Tod Lawrence, designer; Cranbrook Studio grant-sponsored project with NYNEX, Inc., White Plains, New York.
This electronic armchair unfurls its keyboard and computer display, like a transformer toy, for working and then folds them back into itself for relaxing.

Intellectual Sandbox Study Device Prototype 1989
Tod Lawrence, designer; Cranbrook Studio project.
The sliding glass planes hold areas of translucent glass beads for viewing images projected from below. Objects and books can be positioned on other planes for studying relationships and connections between images, objects, and text.

Electronic Desk Prototype 1988
Ken Krayer, designer; Cranbrook Studio grant-sponsored project with NYNEX, Inc., White Plains, New York.
Cast-aluminum connectors position leg supports and work surfaces of different materials in reference to the commodities being traded on this work station.

Electronic Desk Prototype 1988
Peter Stathis, designer; Cranbrook Studio grant-sponsored project with NYNEX, Inc., White Plains, New York.
A serene, undulating work surface is supported by a geologic mass housing the computer and printer. The electronic writing tablet can be "docked" on the surface of the desk to access the computer.

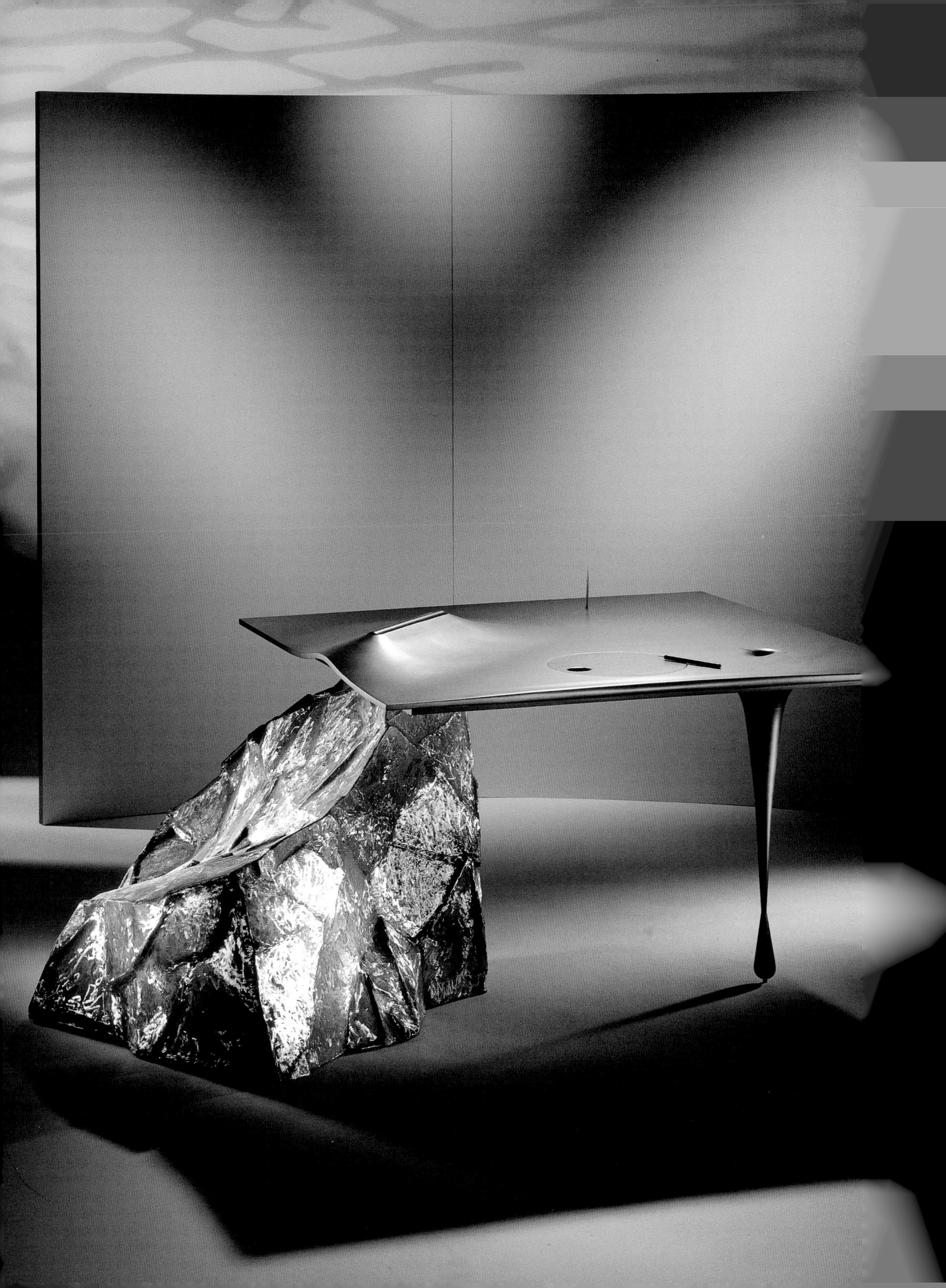

Remembrance Has a Rear and a Front House Architectural Model
1986
Ron Chung, designer; Cranbrook Studio project.
A psychological portrait of a house.

Interiors Initiative Project Interior Design Studio Concept Installation, New York 1985
Brian Carney and **Alan Cooper**, designers; Cranbrook Studio project designed for *Interiors* magazine, New York.
This prototypical interior design studio, symbolizing the computerized studio, was sponsored by Intergraph, Formica, and Atelier International and was built full scale at the International Design Center, New York (IDCNY).

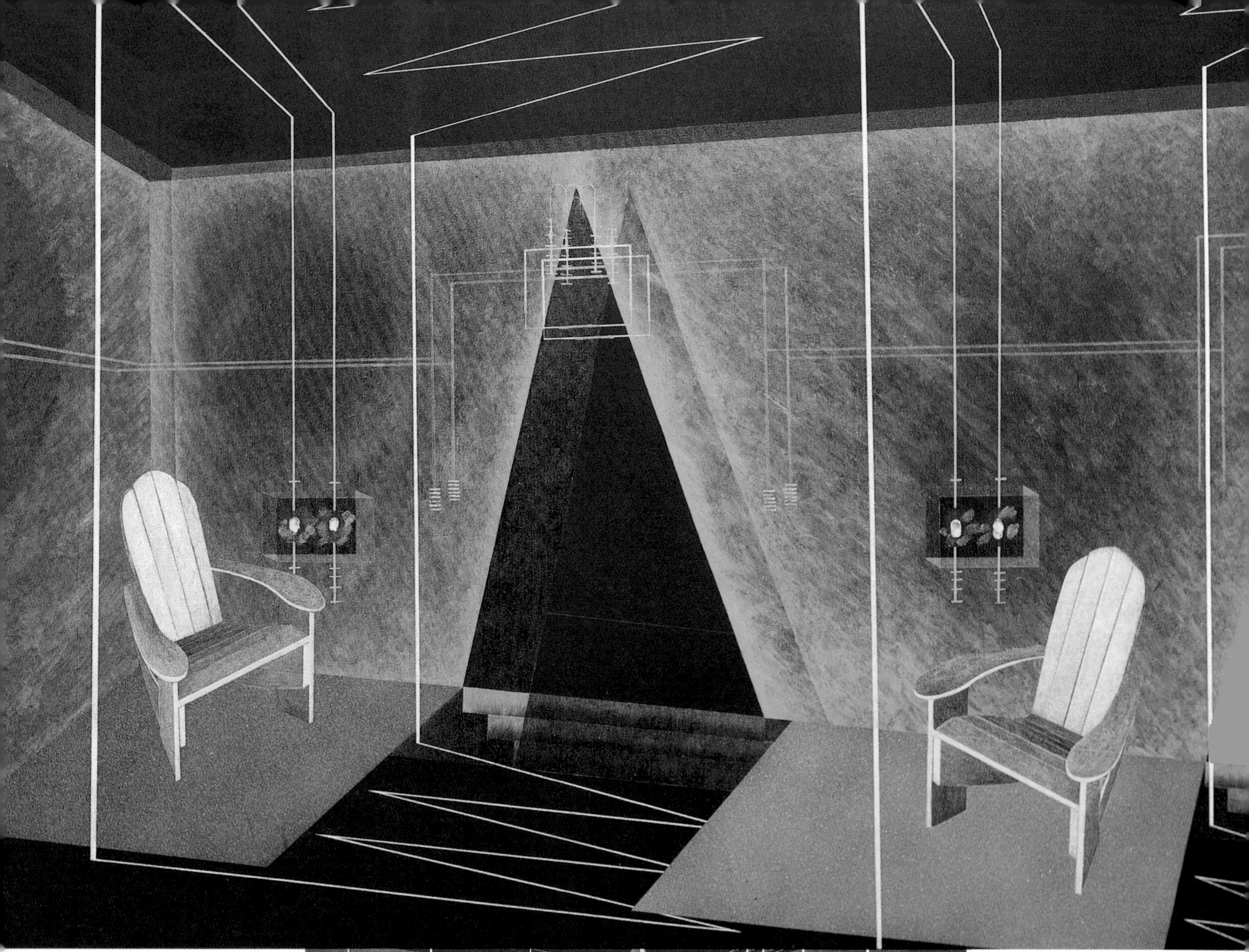

Techno Café Interior Model and Drawings 1987

Pam Carpenter, designer; Cranbrook Studio project.

A café, in the tradition of the early Modernist cabarets, for the contemporary Minimalist movement. Double walls of glass both conceal and reveal the technological metabolism of the space.

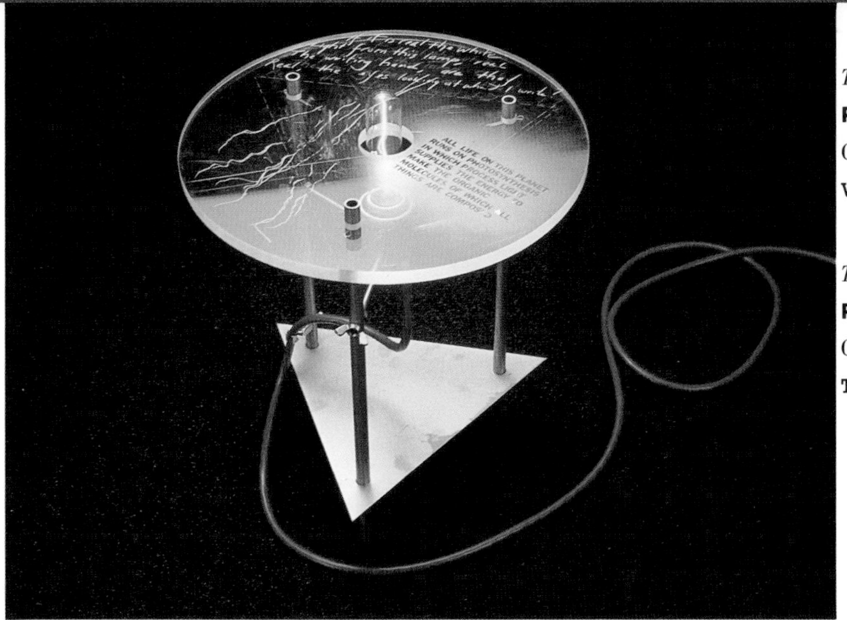
ALL LIFE ON THIS PLANET
RUNS ON PHOTOSYNTHESIS
IN WHICH PROCESS LIGHT
SUPPLIES THE ENERGY TO
MAKE THE ORGANIC
MOLECULES OF WHICH ALL

Techno Café Models 1987
Pam Carpenter, designer;
Cranbrook Studio project.
Wall details for the café.

Techno Café Prototypes 1987
Pam Carpenter, designer;
Cranbrook Studio project.
Table lamps for the café.

see,

THEY TOLD YOU

everything.

See Everything Concept Poster 1986

David Frej, designer; Cranbrook Studio project.

A self-published, limited-edition poster on the process of seeing and knowing. The audience is provoked to explore multiple interpretations by linking the phrases together in a variety of reading orders.

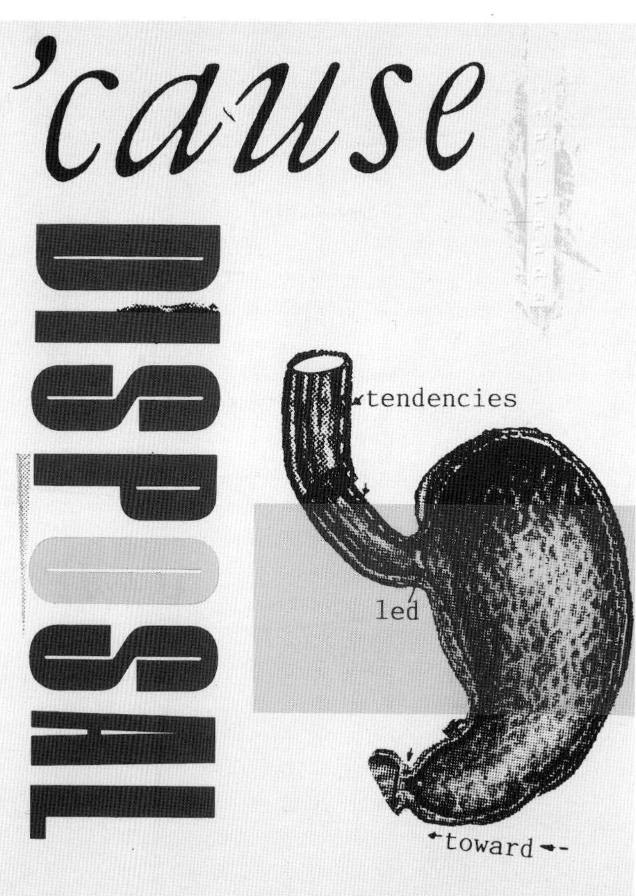
'cause
DISPOSAL
tendencies
led
toward

'Cause Tendencies Led to Disposal Concept Poster 1986

David Frej, designer; Cranbrook Studio project.

A self-published, limited-edition poster on the instant consumption of images and ideas in art and design, trends that are discarded before they are digested thoroughly.

LOAF
HE IS AN IDLE MAN.

Loaf Concept Poster 1986
Scott Zukowski, designer; Cranbrook Studio project.
This self-published, limited-edition poster provokes its audience to consider multiple interpretations about a working man's life of work and leisure as a "breadwinner." The texts, *Loaf* and *He is an idle man*, interact with symbolic images of vernacular objects. Each element carries a variety of possible meanings.

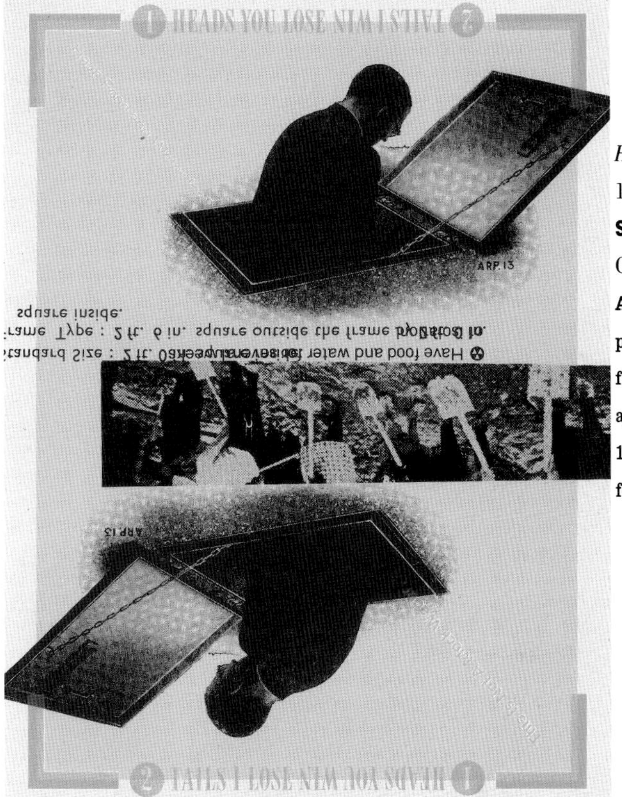
HEADS YOU LOSE

Heads You Lose Concept Poster 1986
Scott Santoro, designer; Cranbrook Studio project.
A self-published, limited-edition poster that comments on the fruitless outcome of nuclear war, appropriating an image from a 1950s fall-out shelter civil-defense manual.

In Flux Concept Poster 1 1988
David Frej, designer; Cranbrook Studio project.
This self-published, limited-edition poster initiates a discussion of personal polemics on design and designing. The first of the series proclaims *In Flux Forever* as the constant condition of design sensibilities and solutions. This visual/verbal dialogue was continued by three studio colleagues who each contributed a statement to the image area of the poster format designed by David Frej.

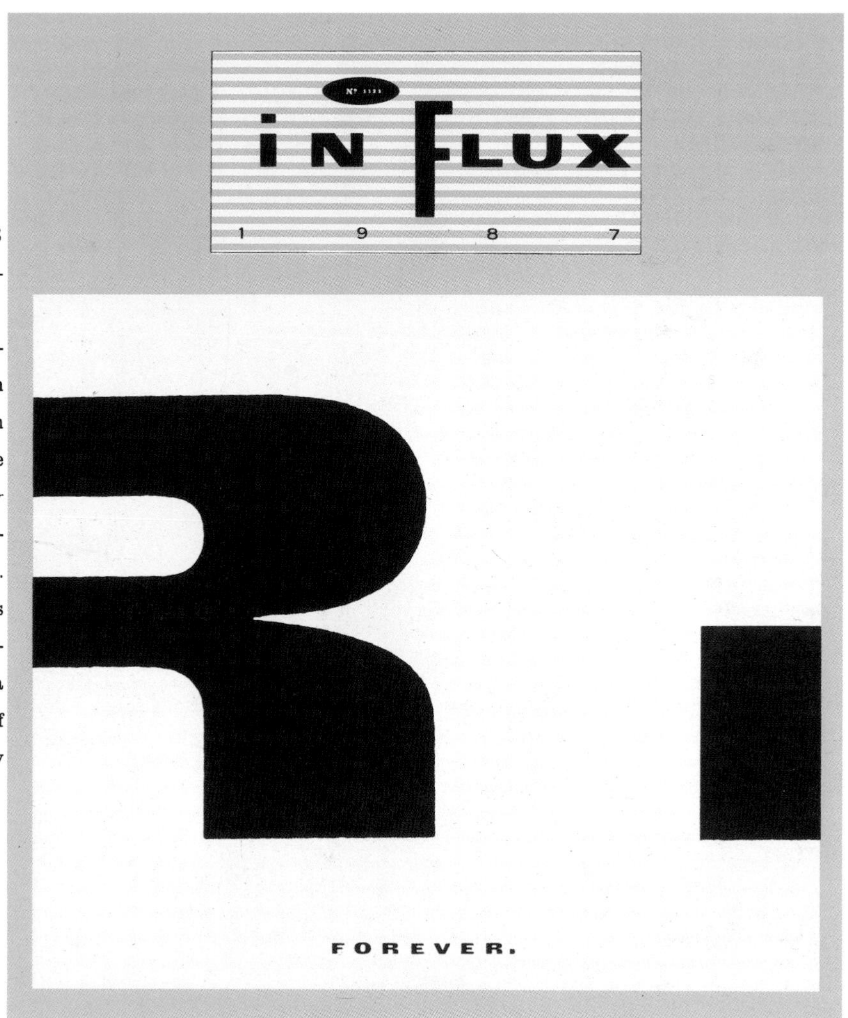
IN FLUX
1 9 8 7
FOREVER.

IN FLUX
1 9 8 7

In Flux Concept Poster 2 1988
Edward Fella, designer; Cranbrook Studio project.
In an emphatic rhymed answer to the first poster's statement of *Forever*, this poster's message itself is "in flux." An ambiguous figure-ground relationship allows the alternate reading of *ever* and *never* when the negative space is read as an *N*.

In Flux Concept Poster 3 1988
David Frej, designer; Cranbrook Studio project.
Fear of gear titles this poster on the need for hand-generated images and letterforms in a very technological age of design. The hand-drawn elements contrast with the technological gear image in the background.

IN FLUX
1 9 8 7
OF
fear
GEAR

In Flux Concept Poster 4 1988
Scott Santoro, designer; Cranbrook Studio project.
This poster's hero enters a world of mechanical plumbing gear "in flux." The hand-generated elements continue the theme of mechanics versus the hand.

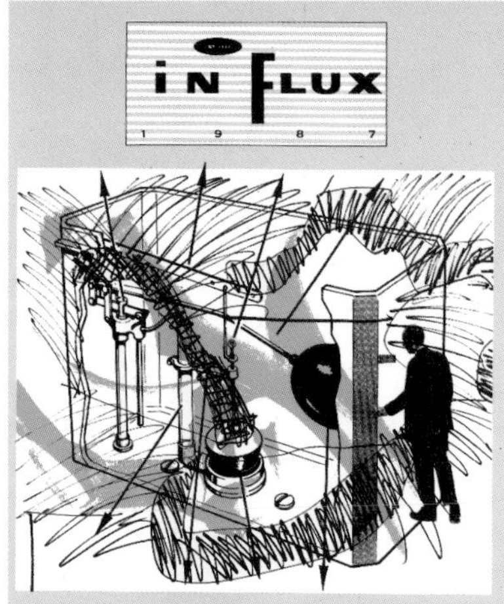
IN FLUX
1 9 8 7

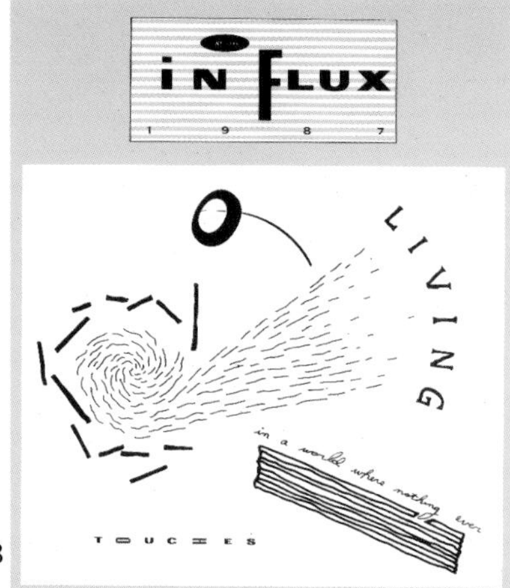
IN FLUX
1 9 8 7
O
LIVING
in a world where nothing ever
TOUCHES

In Flux Concept Poster 5 1988
David Frej, designer; Cranbrook Studio project.
Living in a world where nothing ever touches titles an assemblage of separated gestures held together by positive tension, referring to the designer's appreciation of two-dimensional graphic elements in flat space.

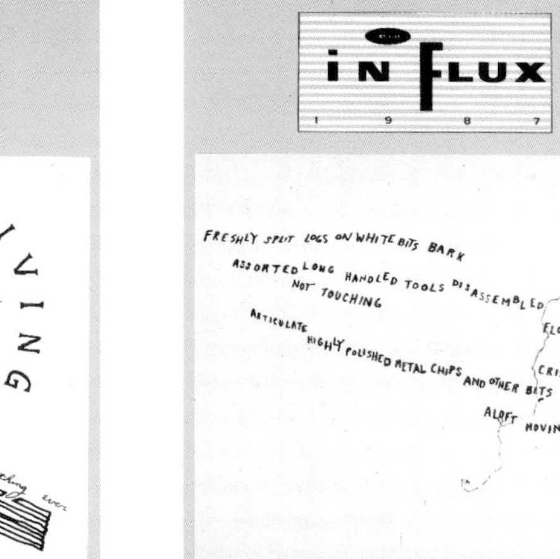
IN FLUX
1 9 8 7
FRESHLY SPLIT LOGS ON WHITE BITS BARK
ASSORTED LONG HANDLED TOOLS DISASSEMBLED
NOT TOUCHING
ARTICULATE
HIGHLY POLISHED METAL CHIPS AND OTHER BITS
FLOATING
CRISP
ALOFT
MOVING
CLEAN

In Flux Concept Poster 6 1988
Scott Zukowski, designer; Cranbrook Studio project.
Picture This titles calligraphic hand-rendered typographic forms that relate a poetic image of natural forms and simple tools. The "automatic" writing of the lyrical text decays like wood in a forest.

Personal Process Concept Poster 1986
Scott Santoro, designer; Cranbrook Studio project.
This self-published, limited-edition poster appropriates clichés from the commercial art of past decades to summarize this designer's sources of influence.

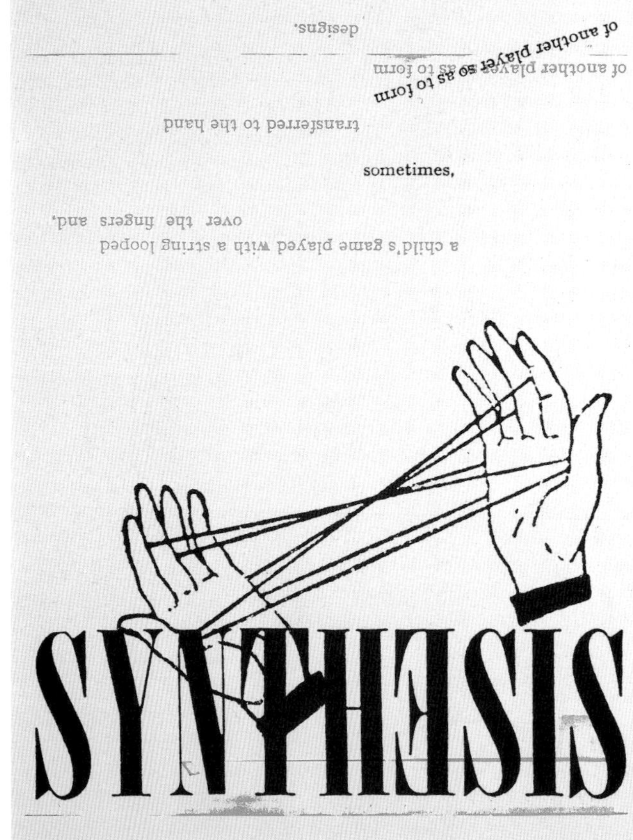

designs.
of another player so as to form
transferred to the hand
sometimes,
a child's game played with a string looped over the fingers and,
SYNTHESIS

Synthesis Concept Poster 1986
Glenn Suokko, designer; Cranbrook Studio project.
A self-published, limited-edition poster that uses an image of the child's game of cat's cradle as an analogy to this designer's personal creative process.

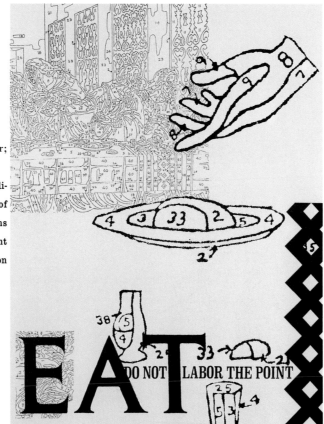

Eat Concept Poster 1986
Glenn Suokko, designer;
Cranbrook Studio project.
This self-published, limited-edition poster uses elements of "paint-by-number" instructions for *The Last Supper* as a comment on modern culture's consumption of art and religion.

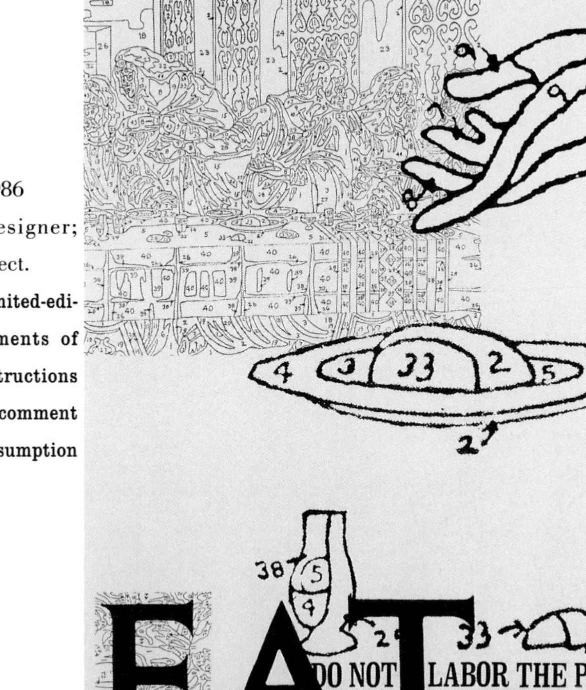
EAT
DO NOT LABOR THE POINT

Yoke Concept Poster 1986
Glenn Suokko, designer;
Cranbrook Studio project.
A self-published, limited-edition poster that makes a feminist statement. Each image poses an alternate meaning of the word *Yoke*.

(on pair of oxen)
(on dress)
1. 2. 3. 4. 5.
YOKE
or
(yOke)

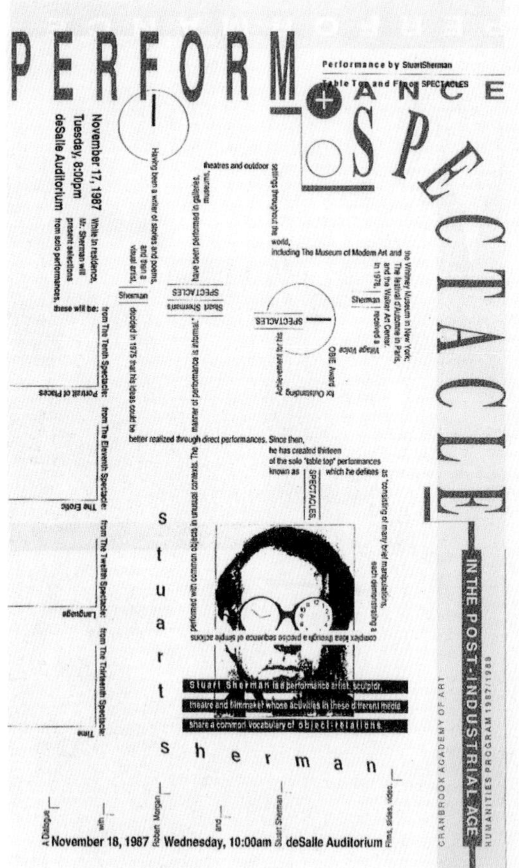
PERFORM
ANCE
SPECTACLE
Performance by Stuart Sherman
Stuart Sherman is a performance artist, sculptor,
theatre and filmmaker whose activities in these different media
share a common vocabulary of object-relations.
s t u a r t
s h e r m a n
November 18, 1987 Wednesday, 10:00am deSalle Auditorium
IN THE POST-INDUSTRIAL AGE
CRANBROOK ACADEMY OF ART
HUMANITIES PROGRAM 1987/1988

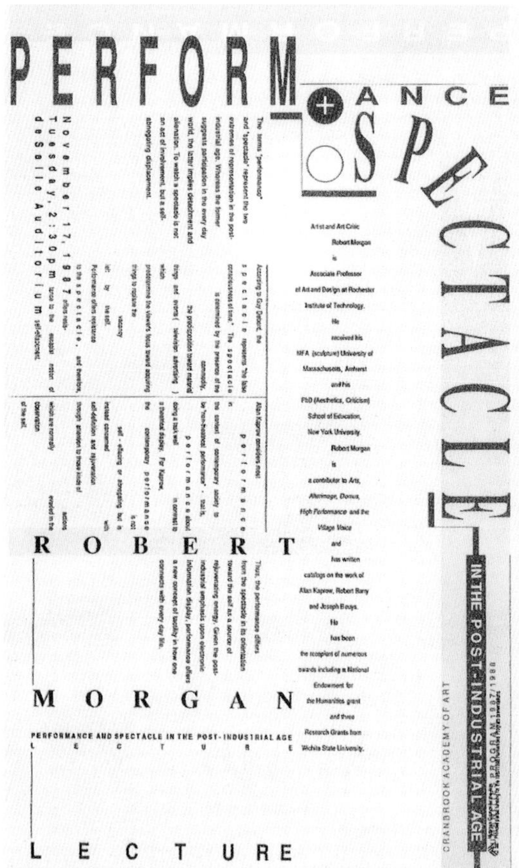
PERFORM
ANCE
SPECTACLE
ROBERT
MORGAN
PERFORMANCE AND SPECTACLE IN THE POST-INDUSTRIAL AGE
LECTURE
L E C T U R E
IN THE POST-INDUSTRIAL AGE
CRANBROOK ACADEMY OF ART

Performance and Spectacle
Poster Series 1987
Allen Hori, designer; Cranbrook Studio project; Cranbrook Academy of Art, client and publisher.
Publicity for a Cranbrook Humanities Program explores and challenges the syntactic conventions of word, phrase, sentence, and paragraph.

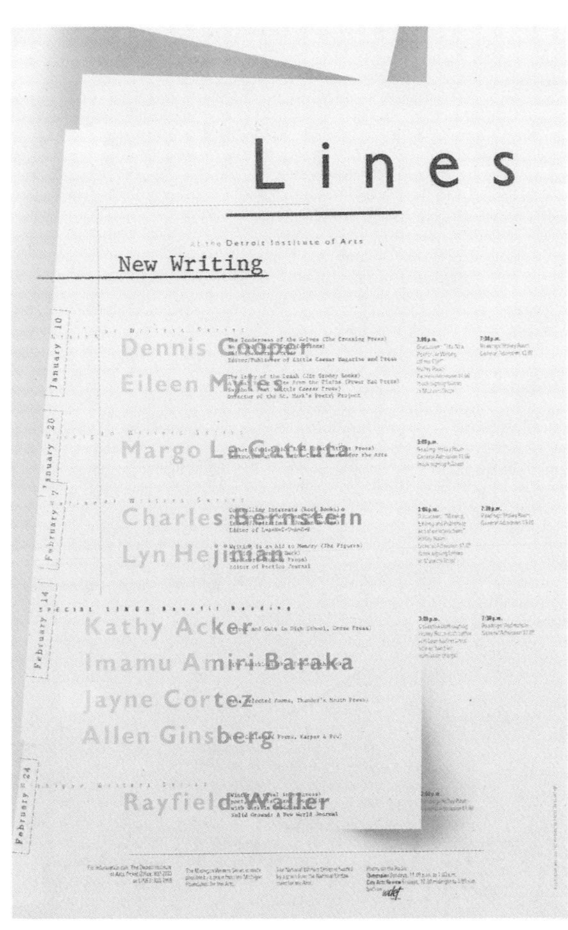
Lines
New Writing
January 10
Dennis Cooper
Eileen Myles
January 20
Margo La Gattuta
February 7
Charles Bernstein
Lyn Hejinian
February 14
Kathy Acker
Imamu Amiri Baraka
Jayne Cortez
Allen Ginsberg
February 24
Rayfield Waller

Lines Poster 1985

Jan Marcus Jancourt, designer; Cranbrook Studio project; The Detroit Institute of Arts, Detroit, Michigan, client and publisher.

A poster announcing an experimental poetry series.

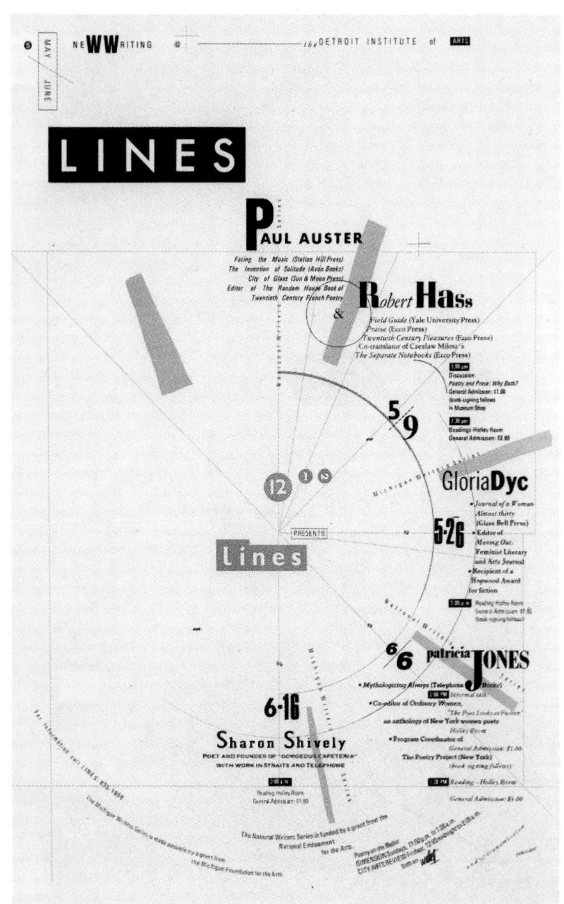
MAY
JUNE
NEWWRITING
DETROIT INSTITUTE of ARTS
LINES
PAUL AUSTER
Robert Hass
5/9
GloriaDyc
5·26
Lines
6/6 patricia JONES
6·16
Sharon Shively

Lines Poster 1985

Jan Marcus Jancourt, designer; Cranbrook Studio project; The Detroit Institute of Arts, Detroit, Michigan, client and publisher.

A diagrammatic typographic structure organizes the schedule of an experimental poetry series.

ARTIST LECTURE:
Saturday, MAY 16, 2pm, at the gallery
RECEPTION immediately FOLLOWING
DETROIT FOCUS GALLERY
MORRIS BROSE:
A SUSTAINED VISION
APRIL 25
May 23
1987
(313) 962-9025

Morris Brose: A Sustained Vision Poster 1987

Edward Fella, designer; Cranbrook Studio project; Detroit Focus Gallery, Detroit, Michigan, client and publisher.

Graphic-arts darkroom processes warp typography and construct the artist's name out of "stat garbage," the refuse of graphic design.

LINES:
NEW
WRITING
DETROIT
INSTITUTE
OF ARTS
MARCH
APRIL
1986
OPEN FIELD SERIES
Faruq Z. Bey
SUNDAY APRIL 27
THE SECOND ANNUAL
LINES BENEFIT READING TUESDAY APRIL 17
JESSICA HAGEDORN
RICHARD HELL
PEDRO PIETRI
NTOZAKE SHANGE
SUNDAY
CARL TOTH
MARCH 16
"Literary Models And Photography"
TUESDAY 13 MARCH
SONIA SANCHEZ
NATIONAL WRITERS SERIES

MARK TUCKER
R. TIM MILLER
LINDA KENNEDY
SUSAN CARMAN
1987
APRIL 17
MARCH 20
NU-BODIES
Review Committee Selects
DETROIT FOCUS GALLERY
Opening Reception: Friday
March 20
6:00-8:30 p.m.
(313) 962-9025

Nu-Bodies Poster 1987

Edward Fella, designer; Cranbrook Studio project; Detroit Focus Gallery, Detroit, Michigan, client and publisher.

Graphic-arts darkroom processes warp, distort, and abuse typography to create new typefaces out of the familiar classics.

Typography Explorations 1985 -1987

Edward Fella, designer; Cranbrook Studio project; Detroit Focus Gallery and Detroit Artists Market, Detroit, Michigan, clients and publishers.

"Normal" expectations of typography are investigated and challenged by this series of typographic details from larger posters that range from low parody to high seriousness.

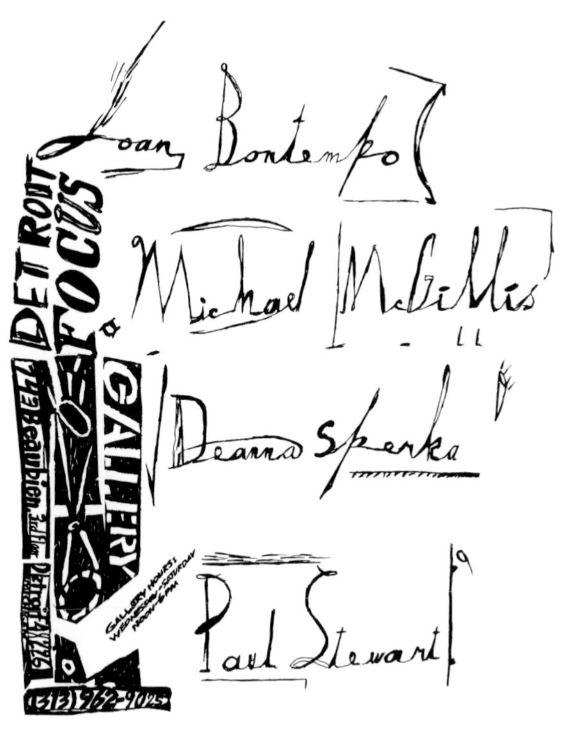
DETROIT FOCUS GALLERY
Joan Bontempo
Michael McGillis
Deanna Sperka
Paul Stewart
GALLERY HOURS: WEDNESDAY-SATURDAY NOON-6 PM
(313) 962-9025

THE DETROIT ARTISTS MARKET PRESENTS
JANUARY 9 1987 FEBRUARY 6
PHILLIP FIKE
& BILL RAUHAUSER
OPENING RECEPTION: FRIDAY JANUARY 9 5-7:30 PM

Brian Fekete
David Griffith
Robin Luebs
Wendy MacGaw
Anat Shiftan
Paul Wittenbraker

"
'-:;!?"
A MATTER OF PAINTING/
AREA
MFA
CANDIDATES

MICHIGAN STATE
JAMES SNYDER
GORDON BOARDMAN
CHING-KAN-TSENG

EASTERN MICHIGAN UNIVERSITY
BENITA GOLDMAN

UNIVERSITY OF MICHIGAN
RICHARD CULLING
SARAH INNES BLOS
JOEL LONGENECKER

WAYNE STATE UNIVERSITY
GREGG TARRANT
LAVERNE FLAKE

CRANBROOK ACADEMY OF ART
CHRIS DIMMICK
KURT COLEMAN
BYRON SHEN

MICHIGAN

DETROIT FOCUS GALLERY
ARTISTS SPACES
COLLABORATE
ARTEMISIA GALLERY
CHICAGO
OCTOBER 16
NOVEMBER 15, 1987

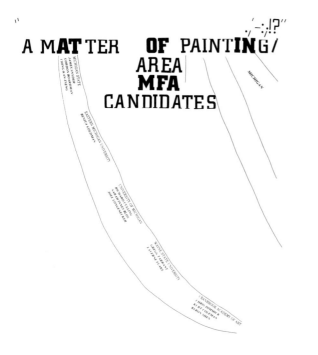

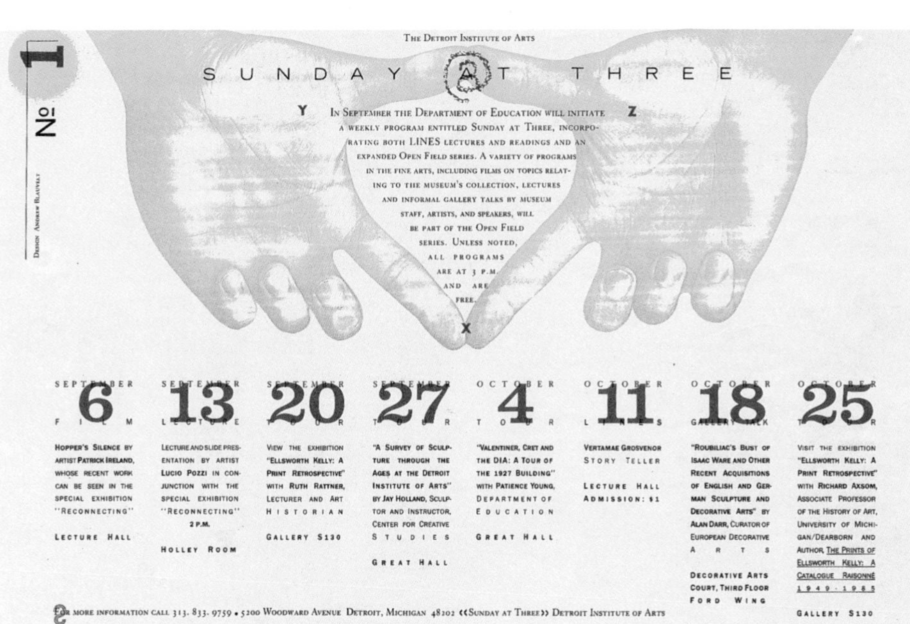

The Detroit Institute of Arts
SUNDAY AT THREE
No 1
Design Andrew Blauvelt
In September the Department of Education will initiate a weekly program entitled Sunday at Three, incorporating both LINES lectures and readings and an expanded Open Field series. A variety of programs in the fine arts, including films on topics relating to the museum's collection, lectures and informal gallery talks by museum staff, artists, and speakers, will be part of the Open Field series. Unless noted, all programs are at 3 p.m. and are free.
September 6 Film
Hopper's Silence by artist Patrick Ireland, whose recent work can be seen in the special exhibition "Reconnecting"
Lecture Hall
September 13 Lecture
Lecture and slide presentation by artist Lucio Pozzi in conjunction with the special exhibition "Reconnecting" 2 P.M.
Holley Room
September 20 Tour
View the exhibition "Ellsworth Kelly: A Print Retrospective" with Ruth Rattner, lecturer and art historian
Gallery S130
September 27 Tour
"A Survey of Sculpture through the Ages at the Detroit Institute of Arts" by Jay Holland, sculptor and instructor, Center for Creative Studies
Great Hall
October 4 Tour
"Valentiner, Cret and the DIA: A Tour of the 1927 Building" with Patience Young, Department of Education
Great Hall
October 11 Lines
Vertamae Grosvenor Story Teller
Lecture Hall Admission: $1
October 18 Gallery Talk
"Roubiliac's Bust of Isaac Ware and Other Recent Acquisitions of English and German Sculpture and Decorative Arts" by Alan Darr, Curator of European Decorative Arts
Decorative Arts Court, Third Floor Ford Wing
October 25 Tour
Visit the exhibition "Ellsworth Kelly: A Print Retrospective" with Richard Axsom, Associate Professor of the History of Art, University of Michigan/Dearborn and author, The Prints of Ellsworth Kelly: A Catalogue Raisonné 1949-1985
Gallery S130
For more information call 313.833.9759 • 5200 Woodward Avenue Detroit, Michigan 48202 «Sunday at Three» Detroit Institute of Arts

The Department of Education of the Detroit Institute of Arts Presents

SUNDAY AT THREE

January · February

Sunday at Three January 3 Tour
Dorothy Kostuch, Assistant Professor, Center for Creative Studies, will discuss selected works from "The Art That is Life: The Arts and Crafts Movement in America, 1875-1920." Exhibition admission required.

LINES: New Writing January 10 Films on Artists
Two film documents of contemporary artists:
1. Spiral Jetty by Robert Smithson on the creation of a work of environmental art;
2. North Star - Mark di Suvero by Francois de Menil (with music by Philip Glass) on the sculptor at work.
Lecture-Recital Hall, $1 general admission.

Sunday at Three January 17 Tour
Thomas W. Brunk, Architectural Historian, will discuss Charles Lang Freer and his residence as an embodiment of American art in architecture.
Freer House, 71 East Ferry Street
(space is limited: call 833-7888 to reserve).

LINES: New Writing January 24 Reading
Lydia Lunch, a rare Detroit appearance by the outrageous New York poet and performance artist, author of *Incriminating Evidence* (Illiterati Press) and *Hysterie* (Widowspeak LP).
Lecture-Recital Hall, $3 general admission.

Sunday at Three January 31 Tour
William Rauhauser, Professor of Photography, Center for Creative Studies, will discuss selected works from the exhibition "Henri Cartier-Bresson: The Early Years."
Albert and Peggy de Salle Gallery of Photography

Sunday at Three February 7 Lecture
William Porter, Designer and Historian, will speak on "Integrity for All: American Arts and Crafts Furniture."
Lecture-Recital Hall

LINES: New Writing February 14 Lecture
Houston A. Baker, Jr., Greenfield Professor of Human Relations, University of Pennsylvania, will speak on "Literary Theory and the Poetics of Afro-American Women's Writing."
Holley Room, $1 general admission.

Sunday at Three February 21 Tour
James Tottis, Department of American Art, will discuss selected works from "The Art That is Life: The Arts and Crafts Movement in America, 1875-1920."
Exhibition admission required.

LINES: New Writing February 28 Reading
Charles Johnson, novelist and critic, author of *The Sorcerer's Apprentice* (Atheneum) and *The Oxherding Tale* (Grove Press), will read from his work.
Holley Room, $3 general admission.

Unless otherwise indicated, all events are at 3 pm on Sundays and are free of charge.

For more information call LINES at 313.833.1858 or the Department of Education at 313.833.9759

Made possible in part by a general operating support grant from American Natural Resources Pipeline Company.

The Detroit Institute of Arts 5200 Woodward Avenue Detroit Michigan 48202

Design Andrew Blauvelt

The Detroit Institute of Arts Presents
SUNDAY•AT•THREE

The Detroit Institute of Arts Presents
SUNDAY AT THREE

Sunday at Three Poster Series
1987-1988

Andrew Blauvelt, designer; Cranbrook Studio project; The Detroit Institute of Arts, Detroit, Michigan, client and publisher.

Each of the four posters is based on one of the alchemic elements of fire, earth, water, and wind to announce a diverse series of poetry and fine-arts events. The typography is organized into a symbolic structuring system based on historic alchemic diagrams.

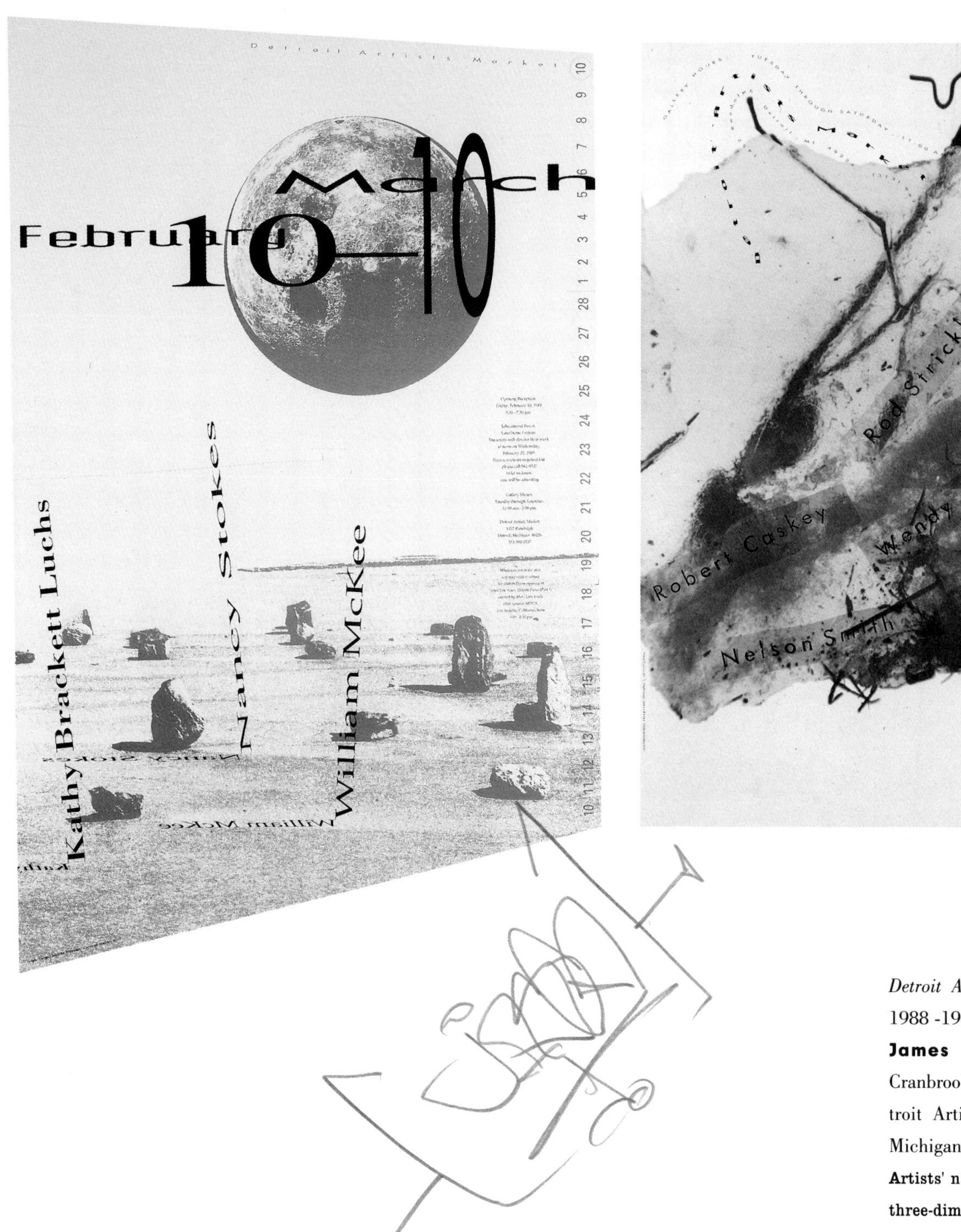
Detroit Artists Market
February 10 — 10 March
Kathy Brackett Luchs
Nancy Stokes
William McKee
MARCH 17 APRIL 14
Robert Caskey
Rod Strickland
Wendy MacGaw
Nelson Smith

Detroit Artists Market Posters 1988 -1989

James Mason, designer; Cranbrook Studio project; Detroit Artists Market, Detroit, Michigan, client and publisher.

Artists' names are presented in three-dimensional environments and participate in the imagery.

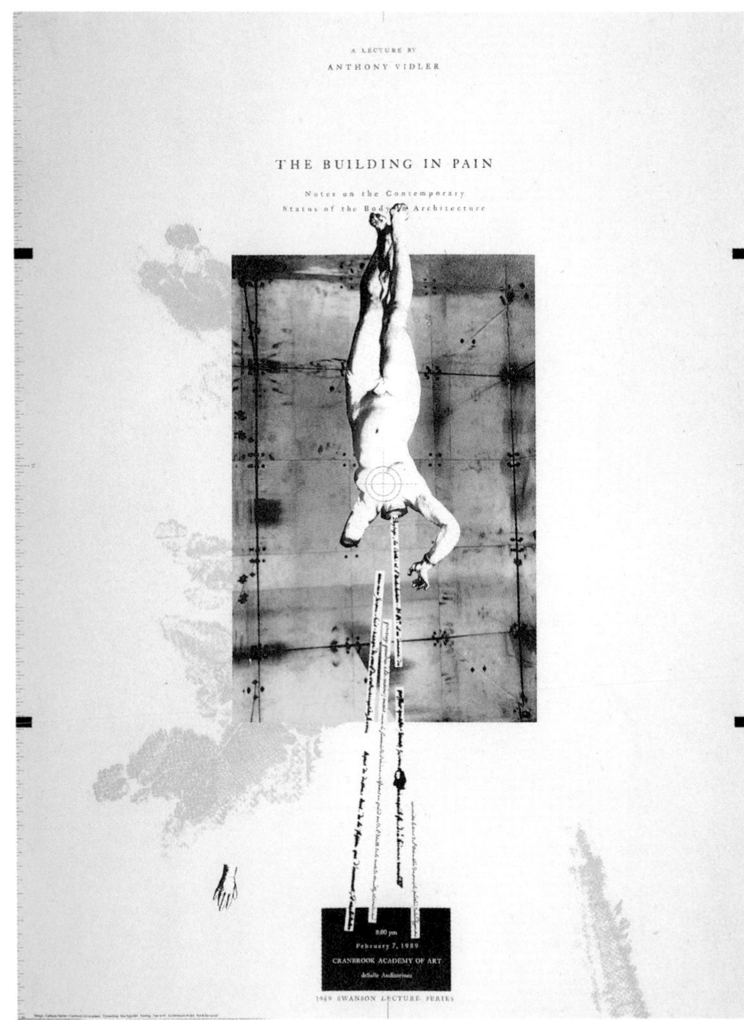
A LECTURE BY
ANTHONY VIDLER
THE BUILDING IN PAIN
Notes on the Contemporary
8:00 pm
February 7, 1989
CRANBROOK ACADEMY OF ART
1989 SWANSON LECTURE SERIES

The Building in Pain Poster 1989
Kathleen Palmer, designer; Cranbrook Studio project; Cranbrook Academy of Art, client and publisher.
Architecture and body analogies are the subjects of a lecture by distinguished architectural critic Anthony Vidler. A classical text spills from the beheaded body.

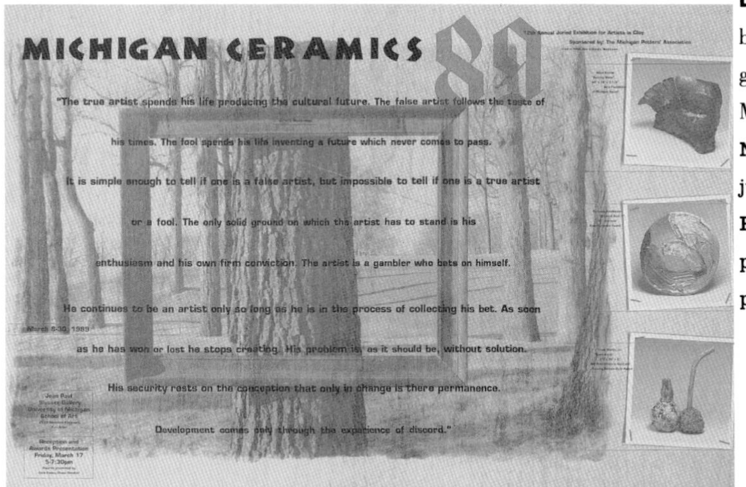
MICHIGAN CERAMICS 89
"The true artist spends his life producing the cultural future. The false artist follows the taste of
his times. The fool spends his life inventing a future which never comes to pass.
It is simple enough to tell if one is a false artist, but impossible to tell if one is a true artist
or a fool. The only solid ground on which the artist has to stand is his
enthusiasm and his own firm conviction. The artist is a gambler who bets on himself.
He continues to be an artist only so long as he is in the process of collecting his bet. As soon
as he has won or lost he stops creating. His problem is, as it should be, without solution.
His security rests on the conception that only in change is there permanence.
Development comes only through the experience of discord."

Michigan Ceramics Poster 1989
Daniel Olsen, designer; Cranbrook Studio project; The Michigan Potters Association, Detroit, Michigan, client and publisher.
Nature is framed to announce a juried exhibition of ceramics. Plywood is reproduced as the poster's background in this exploration of natural materials.

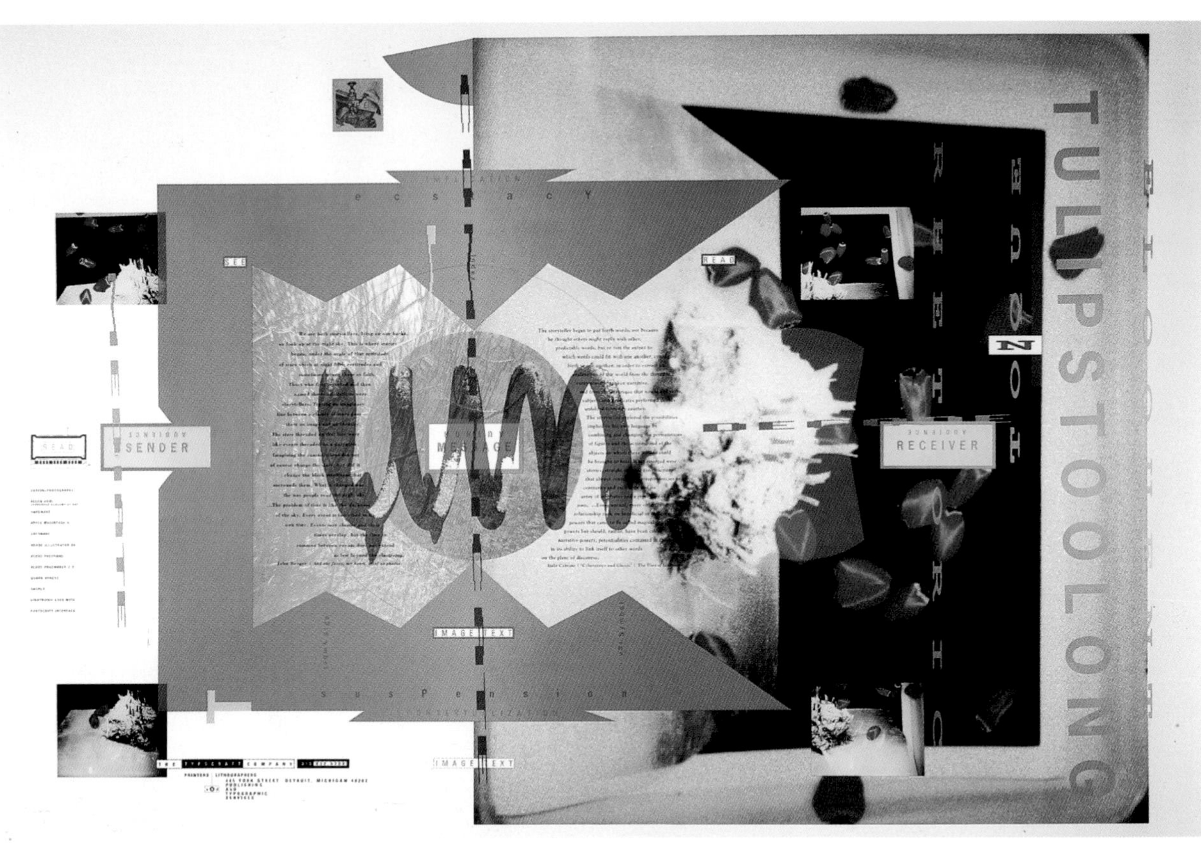
TULIPSTOOLONG
SENDER
MESSAGE
RECEIVER
IMAGE TEXT

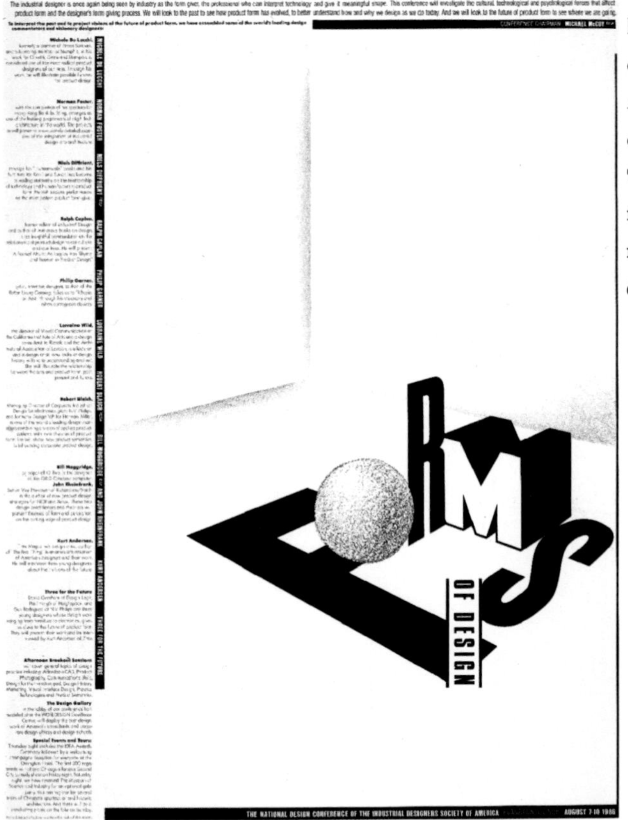
RMS
OF DESIGN
THE NATIONAL DESIGN CONFERENCE OF THE INDUSTRIAL DESIGNERS SOCIETY OF AMERICA

Forms of Design Poster 1986

Edward Fella, designer; Cranbrook Studio project; The Industrial Designers Society of America, Great Falls, Virginia, client and publisher.

Three-dimensional typographic forms announce the subject of a national conference on industrial design.

Too Lips Poster 1989

Allen Hori, designer; Cranbrook Studio project; The Typocraft Company, Detroit, Michigan, client.

Oral communication and storytelling are the subjects of a promotional poster for Typocraft, a commercial printer. Quotations from John Berger and Italo Calvino and communications theory terminology are montaged with photographic imagery. A verbal/visual pun connects tulip-petal imagery with the title.

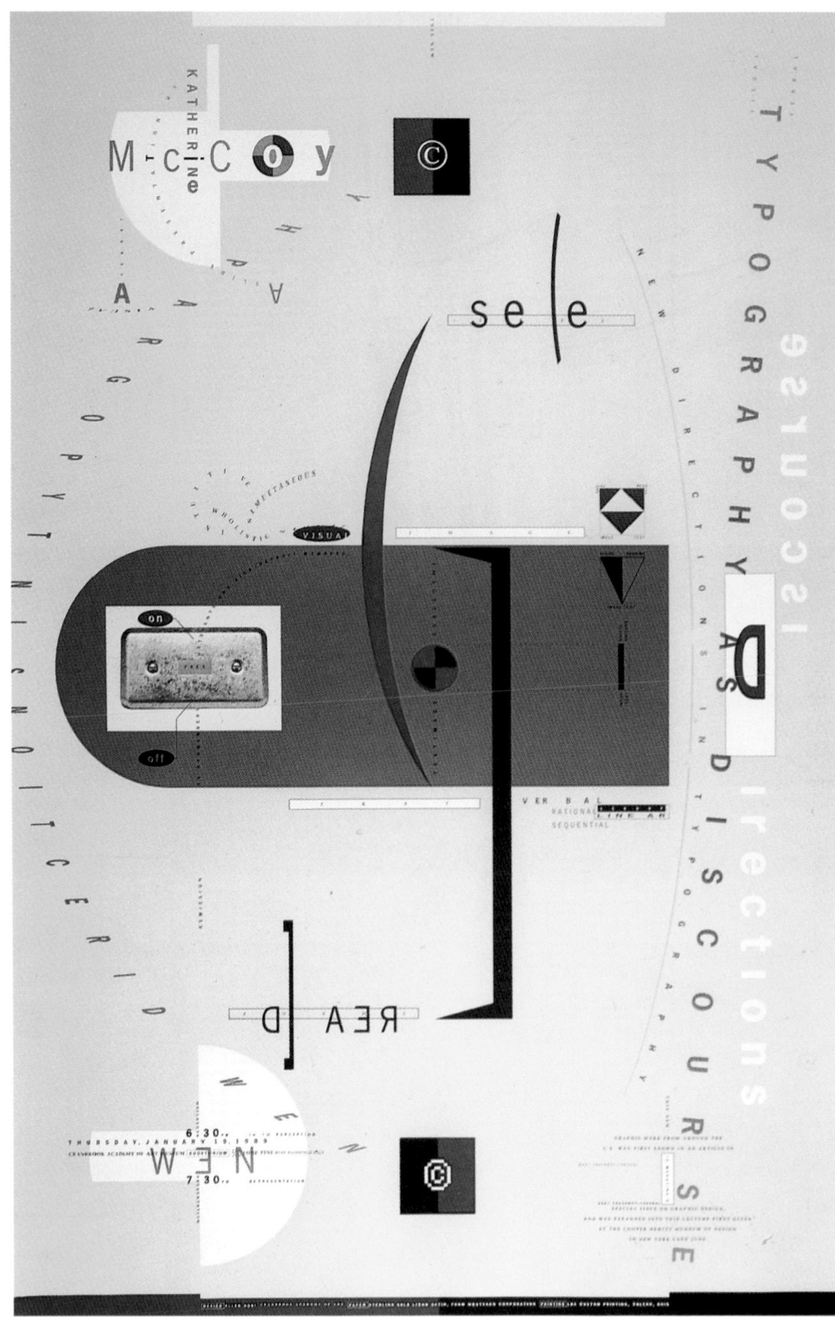
KATHERINE
McCoy
TYPOGRAPHY AS DISCOURSE
New Directions
VISUAL
on
off
VERBAL
RATIONAL
SEQUENTIAL
6:30
7:30

Typography as Discourse Poster 1989

Allen Hori, designer; Cranbrook Studio project; American Institute of Graphic Arts, Detroit, client and publisher.

New directions in American typography are the subject of the lecture announced by this poster. The poster bases its composition on a communications theory diagram discussed in the lecture. Information clusters become smaller diagrams that question the conventions of written language.

Three Dimensional Study Model 1981

Ting Hsieh, designer: Cranbrook Studio Project.

The imagery of traditional musical instruments is decomposed and recombined as formal elements in this composition. The designer drew on this study for subsequent audio component projects.

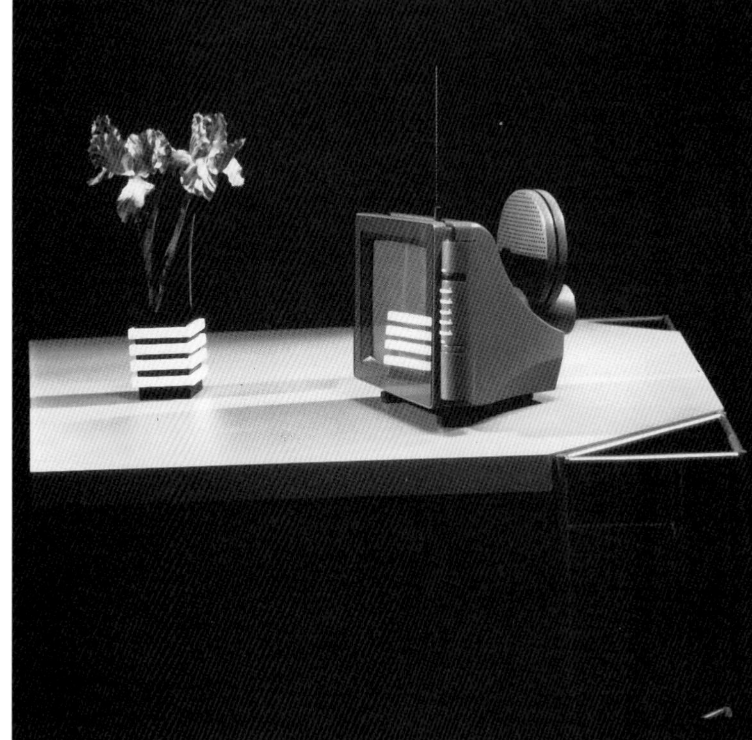

Portable Television Model 1982

Ting Hsieh, designer; Cranbrook Studio project.

The speaker, picture tube, and remote control are brought out of the box and articulated in this small television set.

Table Prototype 1982

Bruce Albinson, designer; Cranbrook Studio project.

The open structure of the table legs establishes scale without heavy mass.

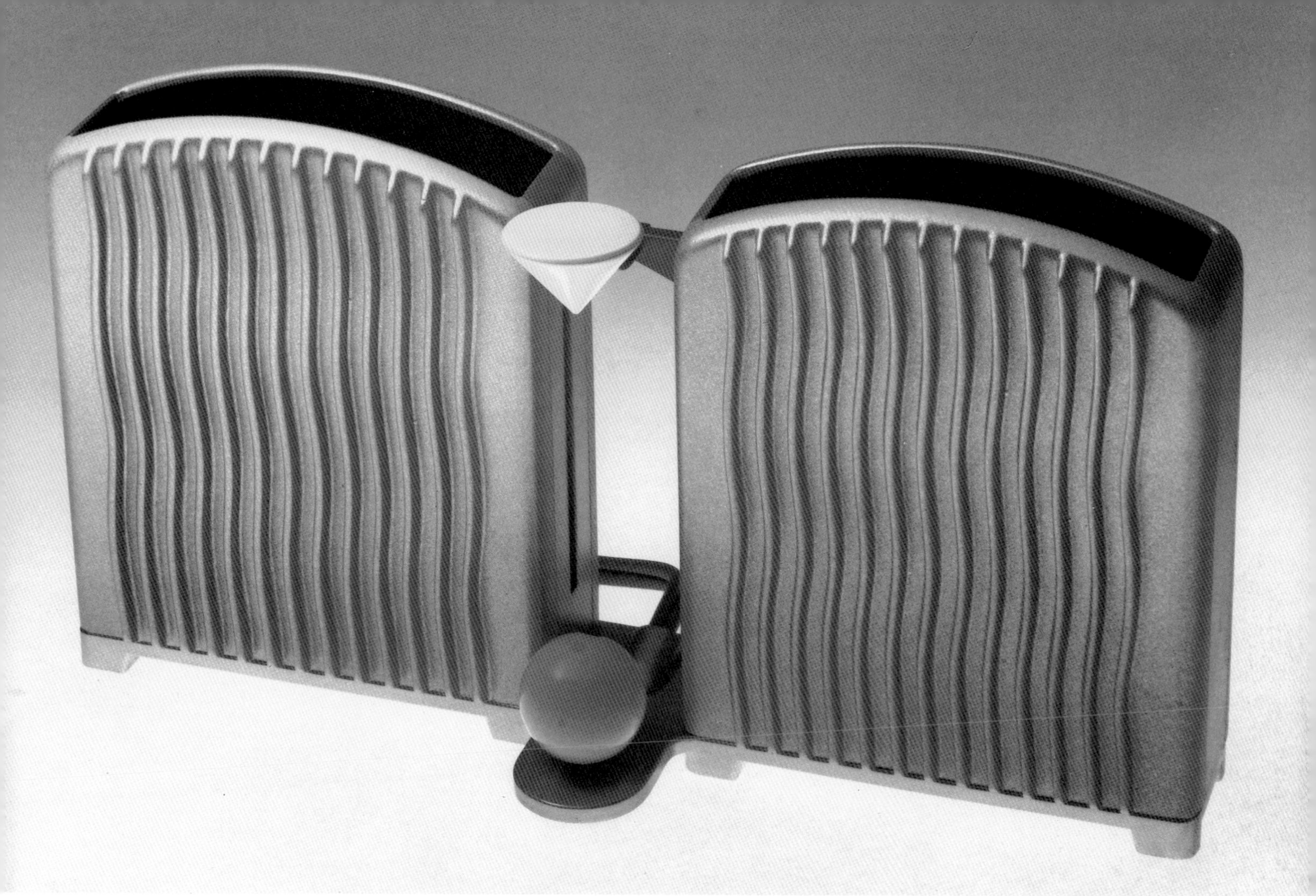

Toaster Model 1986
Van Hong Tsai, designer; Cranbrook Studio project.
The morning ritual of making toast is celebrated in this toaster with "friendly waves of heat" molded into the cast-aluminum housing.

Domestic Space Heater Model 1984
Don Harel, designer; Cranbrook Studio project.
The process of turning liquid fuel into radiant heat is diagrammed in this kerosene heater.

Room Dehumidifier Model 1987

Paul Montgomery, designer; Cranbrook Studio project.

The process of wringing moisture out of the air and draining it into the clear reservoir is symbolized by the vertical planes squeezed together in the center of this household appliance.

Electronic Forum Model 1986

Michael McCoy, **David Gresham**, and **Dan Ferguson**, designers.

An interactive information center, which can be checked out from the local library, to be used for group meetings on any subject. Information from the network-connected internal computer is displayed on a large screen for the group to see. Video conferences with distant groups are displayed on the smaller screen. The internal printer can make copies for everyone at the meeting to take home.

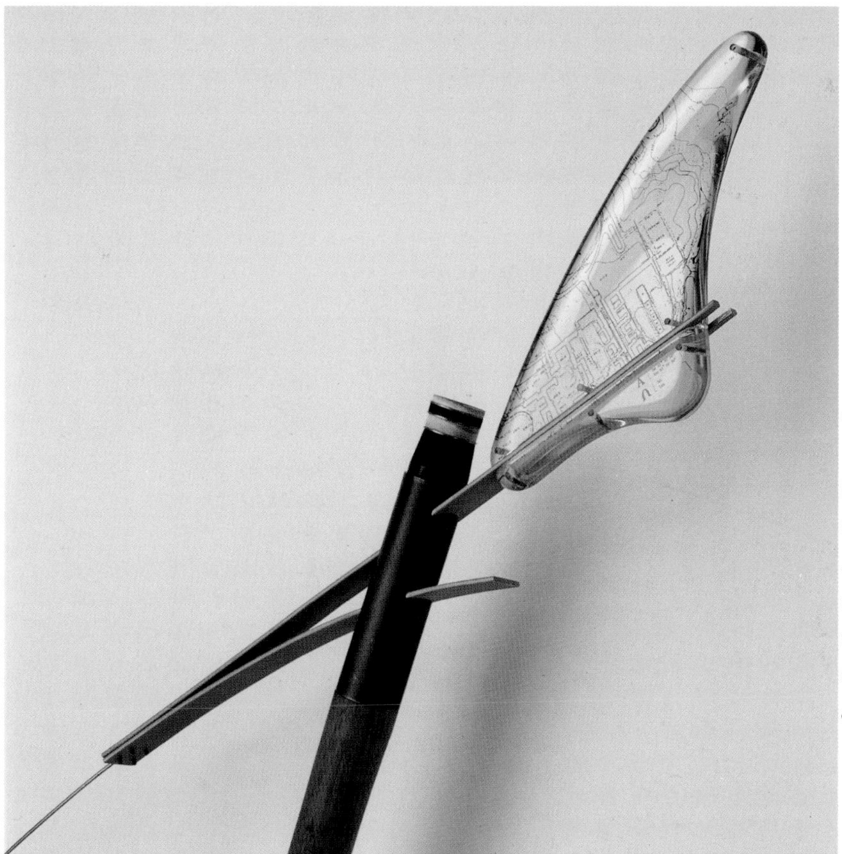

Celestial Navigator Model 1989

Brian Kritzman, designer; Cranbrook Studio project.

A walking staff that communicates with the satellite navigational system, displaying information in its liquid crystal head.

detail

Compact Disc Player Model
1987

Jin Dean Cheng, designer;
Cranbrook Studio project.

The axial symmetry of this CD player celebrates the music by conjuring up images of traditional "cathedral" radios and jukeboxes.

Videocassette Player Model
1987

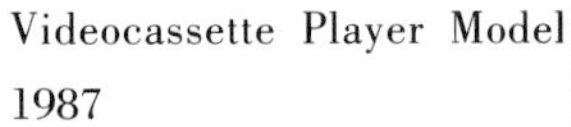

Jin Dean Cheng, designer;
Cranbrook Studio project.

The videocassette is placed center stage in this theatrical television.

Room Dehumidifier Model 1987
Paul Montgomery, designer;
Cranbrook Studio project.
The process of wringing moisture out of the air and draining it into the clear reservoir is symbolized by the vertical planes squeezed together in the center of this household appliance.

Electronic Forum Model 1986
Michael McCoy, **David Gresham**, and **Dan Ferguson**, designers.
An interactive information center, which can be checked out from the local library, to be used for group meetings on any subject. Information from the network-connected internal computer is displayed on a large screen for the group to see. Video conferences with distant groups are displayed on the smaller screen. The internal printer can make copies for everyone at the meeting to take home.

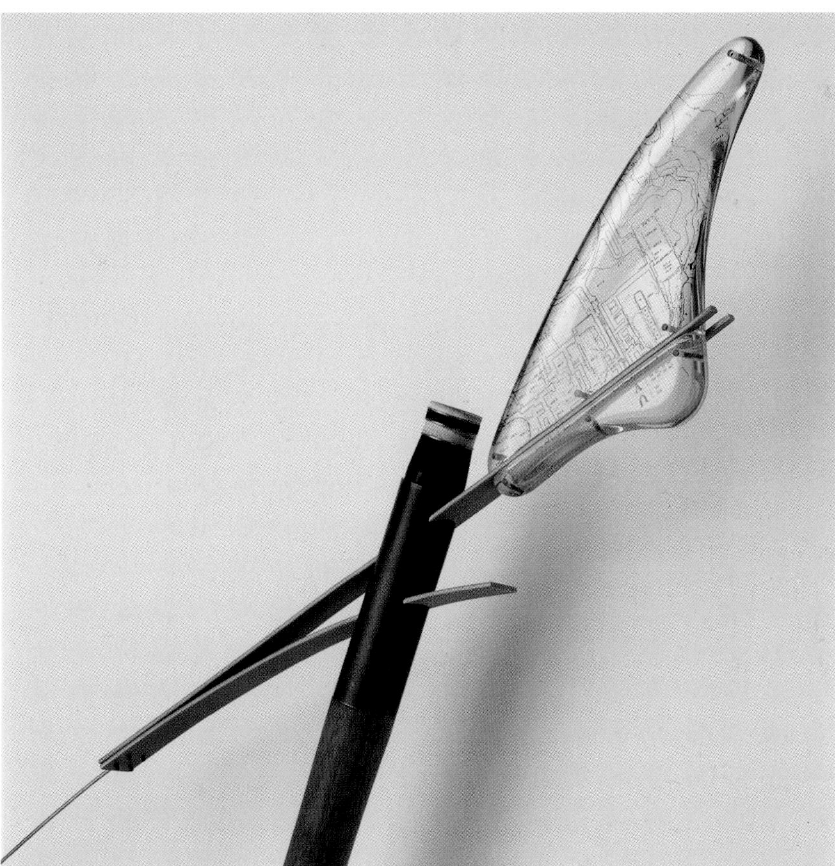

Celestial Navigator Model 1989
Brian Kritzman, designer;
Cranbrook Studio project.
A walking staff that communicates with the satellite navigational system, displaying information in its liquid crystal head.
detail

Compact Disc Player Model 1987

Jin Dean Cheng, designer; Cranbrook Studio project.

The axial symmetry of this CD player celebrates the music by conjuring up images of traditional "cathedral" radios and jukeboxes.

Videocassette Player Model 1987

Jin Dean Cheng, designer; Cranbrook Studio project.

The videocassette is placed center stage in this theatrical television.

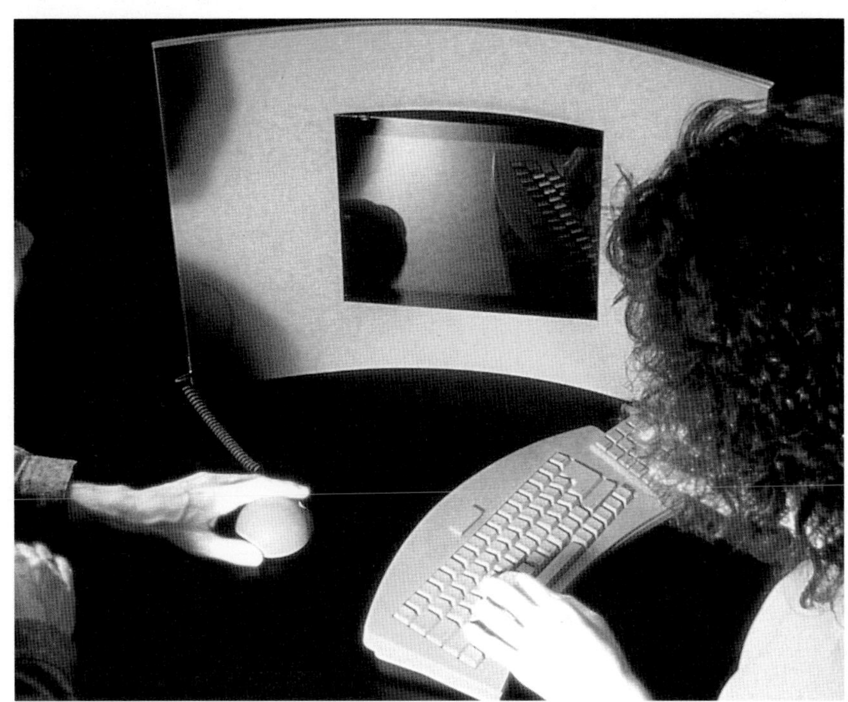

Curved Computer Model
1988
Ching-Liang Wang, designer; Cranbrook Studio project.
The gently curved form of this computer creates an inviting space for two people to share and interact with the information on the screen.

Coffee Maker for Two Model
1988
Ching-Liang Wang, designer; Cranbrook Studio project.
Water heated in the two glass columns joins together in the center filter to make coffee for two.

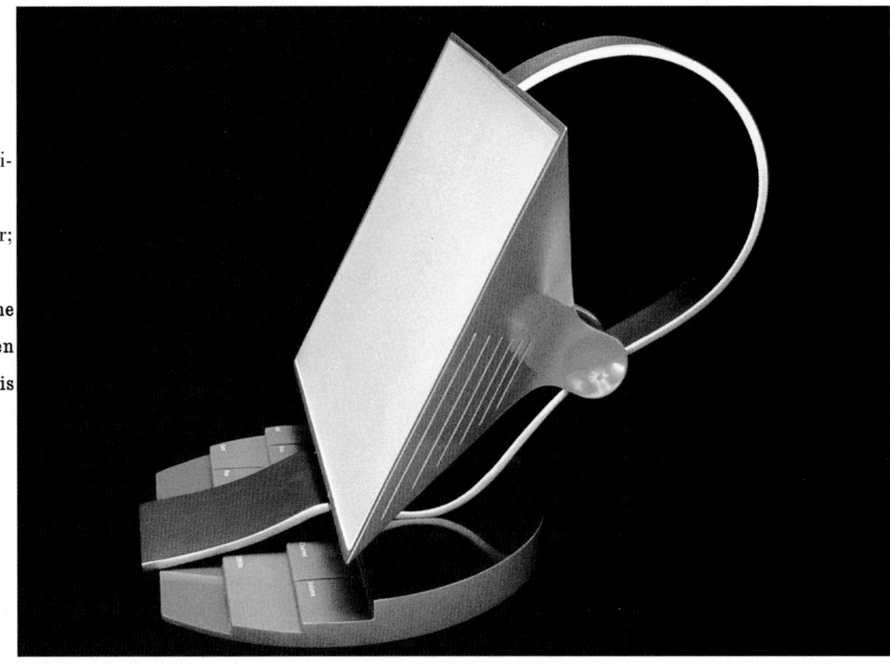

Portable Video Player / Television Model 1987
William Goralski, designer; Cranbrook Studio project.
The flow of the film out of the machine and into the screen forms the basic image for this 8mm videotape player.

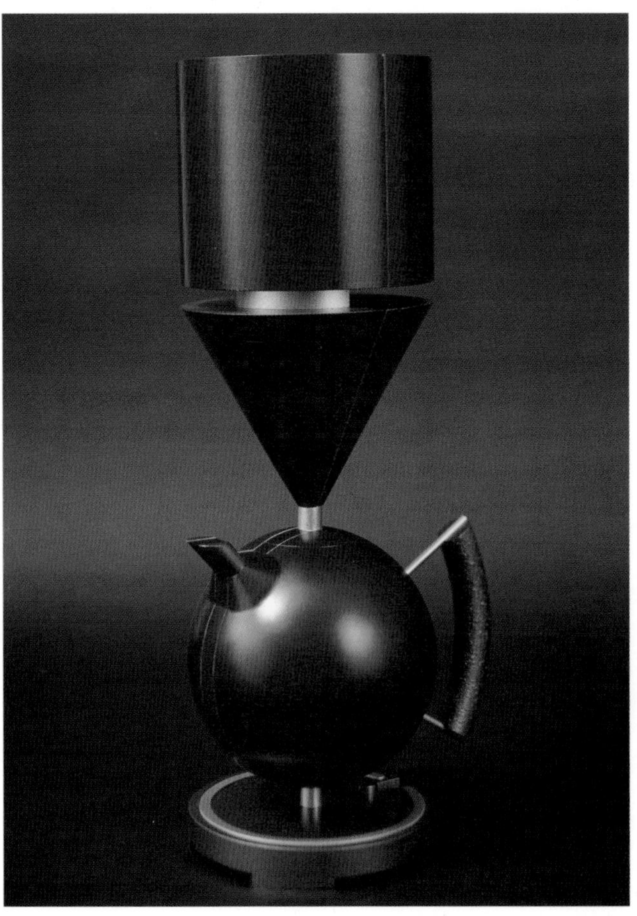

Coffeemaker Model 1988
Ken Krayer, designer; Cranbrook Studio project.
The coffeemaker celebrates the process and the warmth of coffeemaking in its form and color.

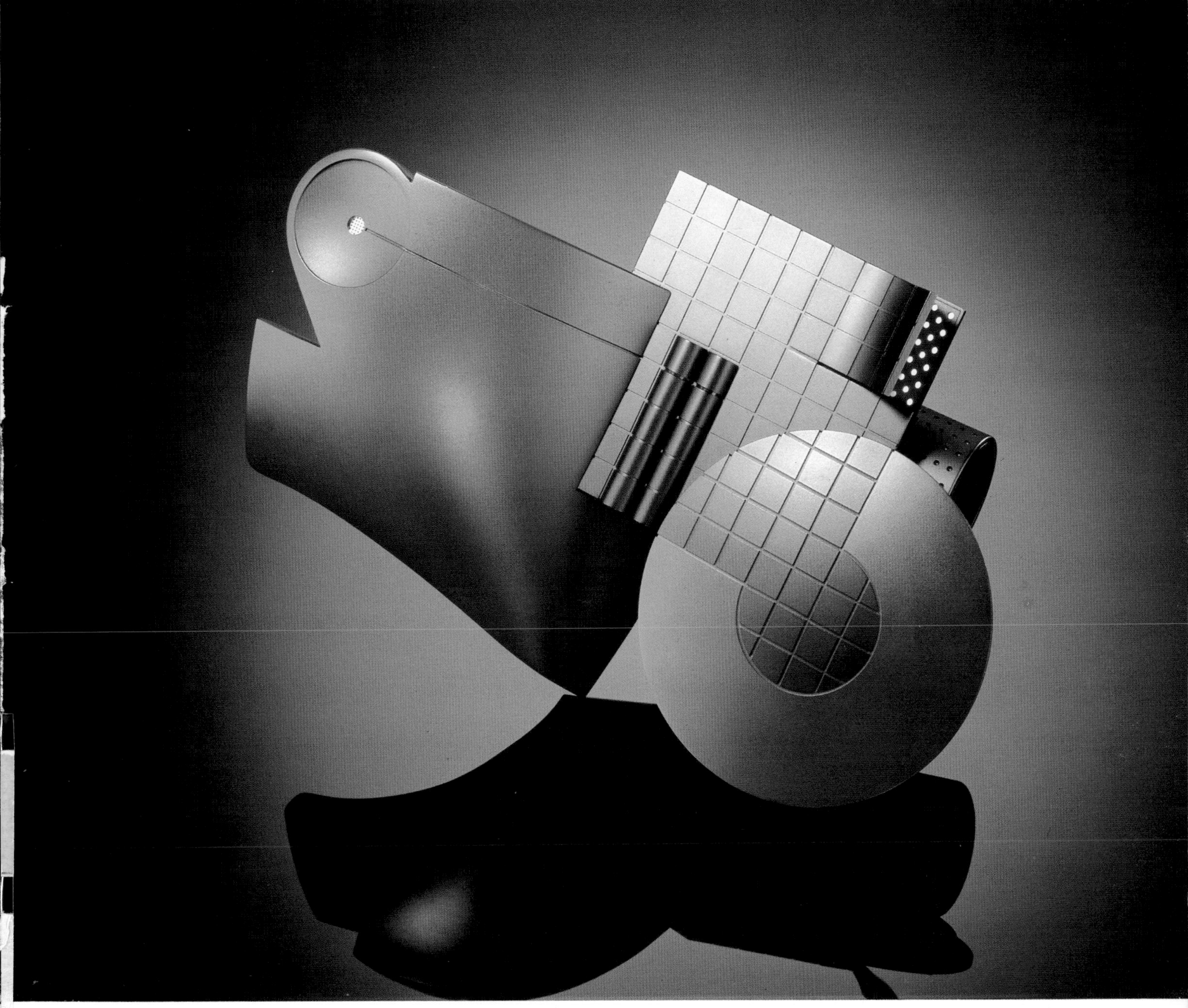

Videodisc Camera Model 1985
David Gresham with Martin Thaler, designers; Cranbrook Studio project.
The mask form of the camera symbolizes its role as an extension of the senses of sight, sound, and memory.

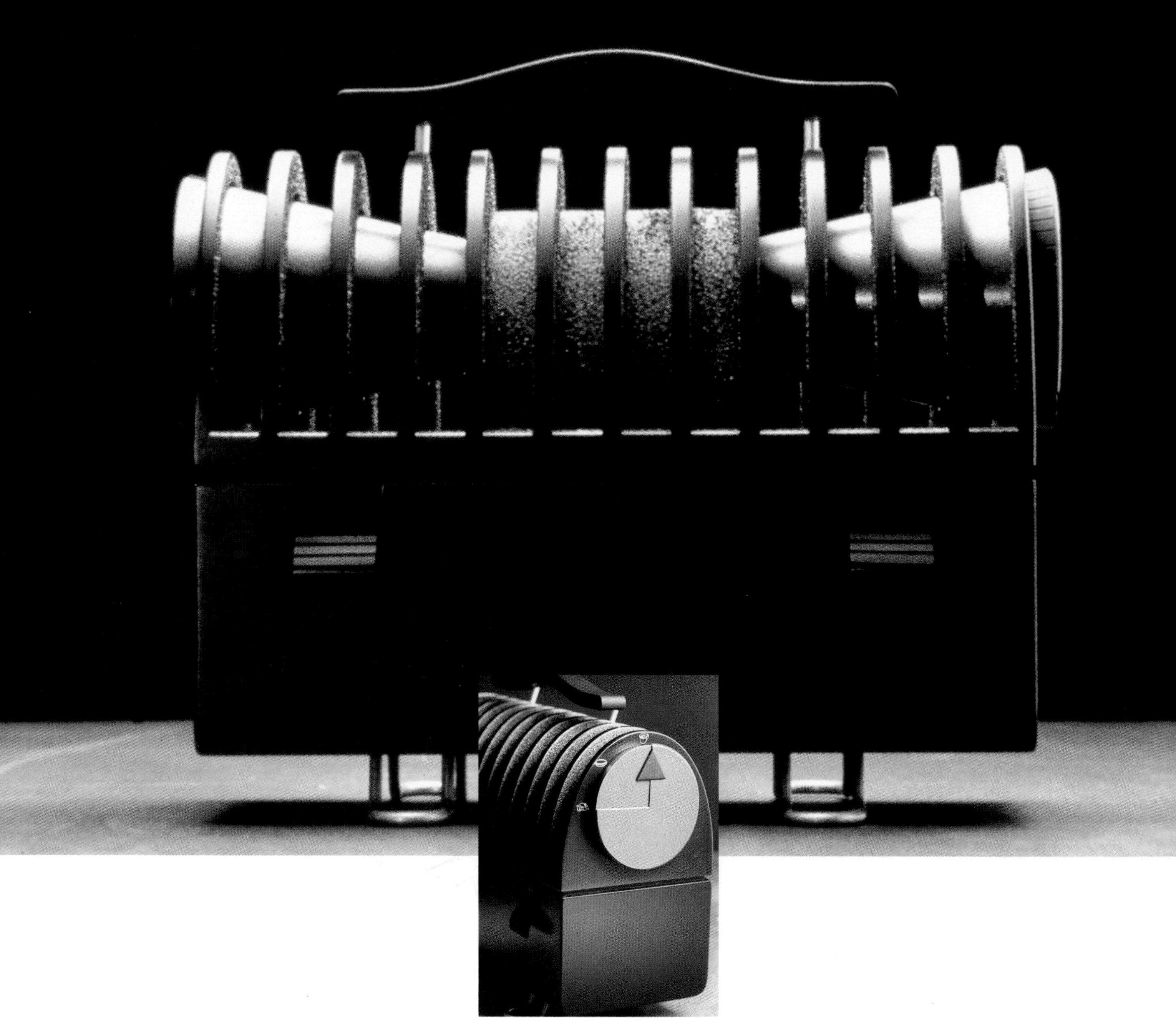

Portable Microwave Model 1986
Paul Montgomery, designer;
Cranbrook Studio project.
The form of this portable microwave oven refers to the traditional workman's lunchpail, the artifact which it has displaced.

Telephone Model 1988
William Goralski, designer; Cranbrook Studio project.
The upright stance of this telephone with its separate earpiece recalls the character of early telephones.

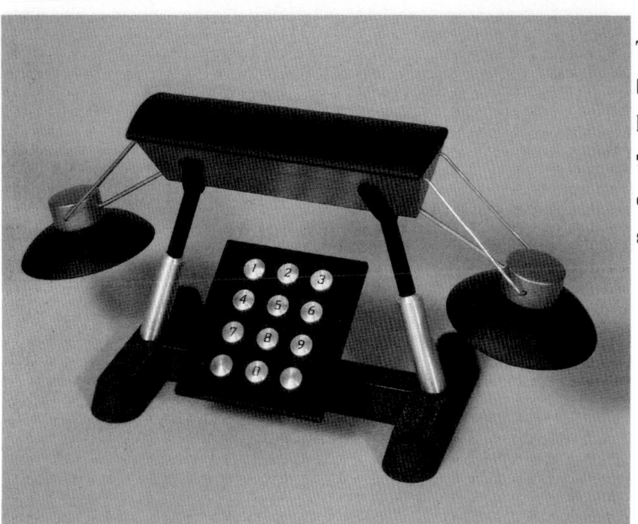

Telephone Model 1988
Ken Krayer, designer; Cranbrook Studio project.
The telephone reflects the imagery of the microwave communications systems to which it is attached.

Ultrasonic Humidifier Model 1987
Julie Sook Ah, designer; Cranbrook Studio project sponsored by frogdesign.
The humidifier takes its form from the ultrasonic waves transforming water into mist. It delivers the humid air high in the room where it is needed.

Computer Model 1989
William Wurz, designer; Cranbrook Studio project.
A computer that is like a "pool" of information. One may gather information together by passing a hand over the hemispherical, touch-sensitive display, and "tickle" the grasslike memory nodes to access certain memory banks.

Information Projector Model 1989

Masamichi Udagawa, designer; Cranbrook Studio project.

Computer images and information are projected up and reflected by the servo-controlled mirror onto a desk or table top, eliminating the need for a display screen.

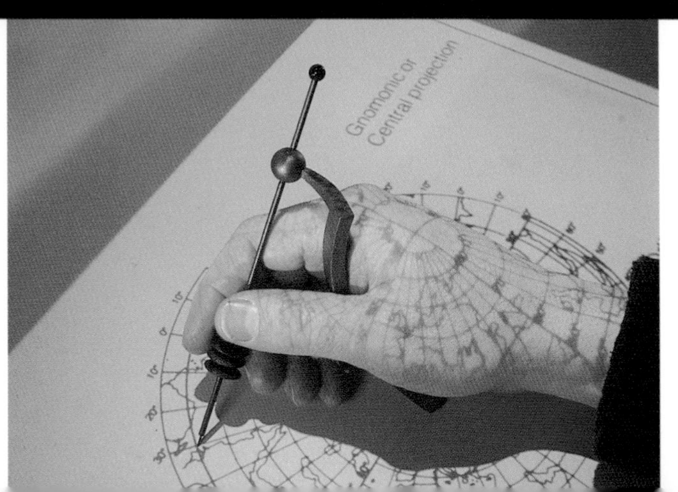
Gnomonic or
Central projection

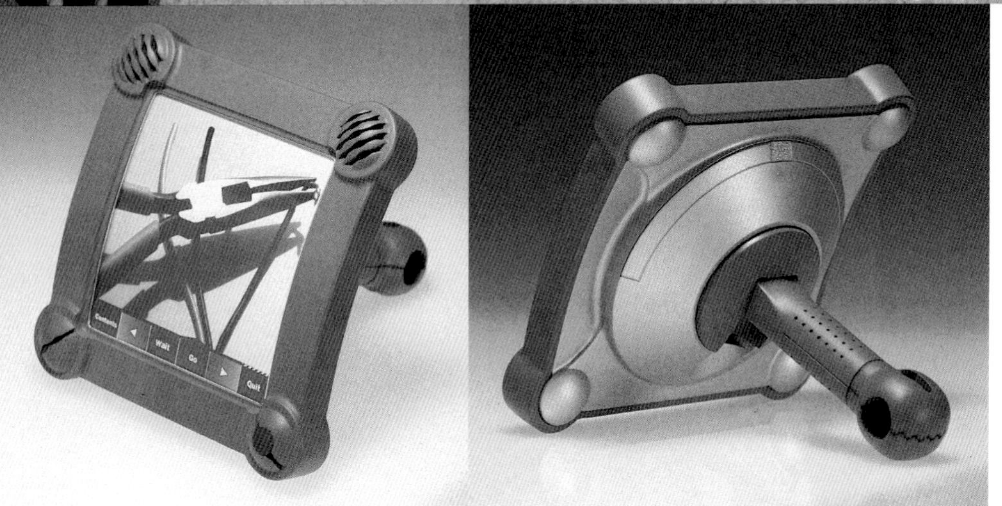

Home Office Prototype 1989
Rick Lewis, designer; Cranbrook Studio project.
The computer, scanner, and printer components are composed in the manner of a still-life. The computer is imbedded in a glowing block of translucent plastic.

Electronic Repair Manual Model 1989
Rick Lewis, designer; Cranbrook Studio project.
A voice-activated, interactive video display demonstrates household repairs with actual video instruction. The form of the manual recalls the shapes and textures of the hand tools used in the repair process.

Satori Television Model 1988
Peter Stathis, designer; Cranbrook Studio project.
A small personal television that "wakes up" when touched, turning its screen up to look at the user. The design presents the idea of technology as a companion or pet.

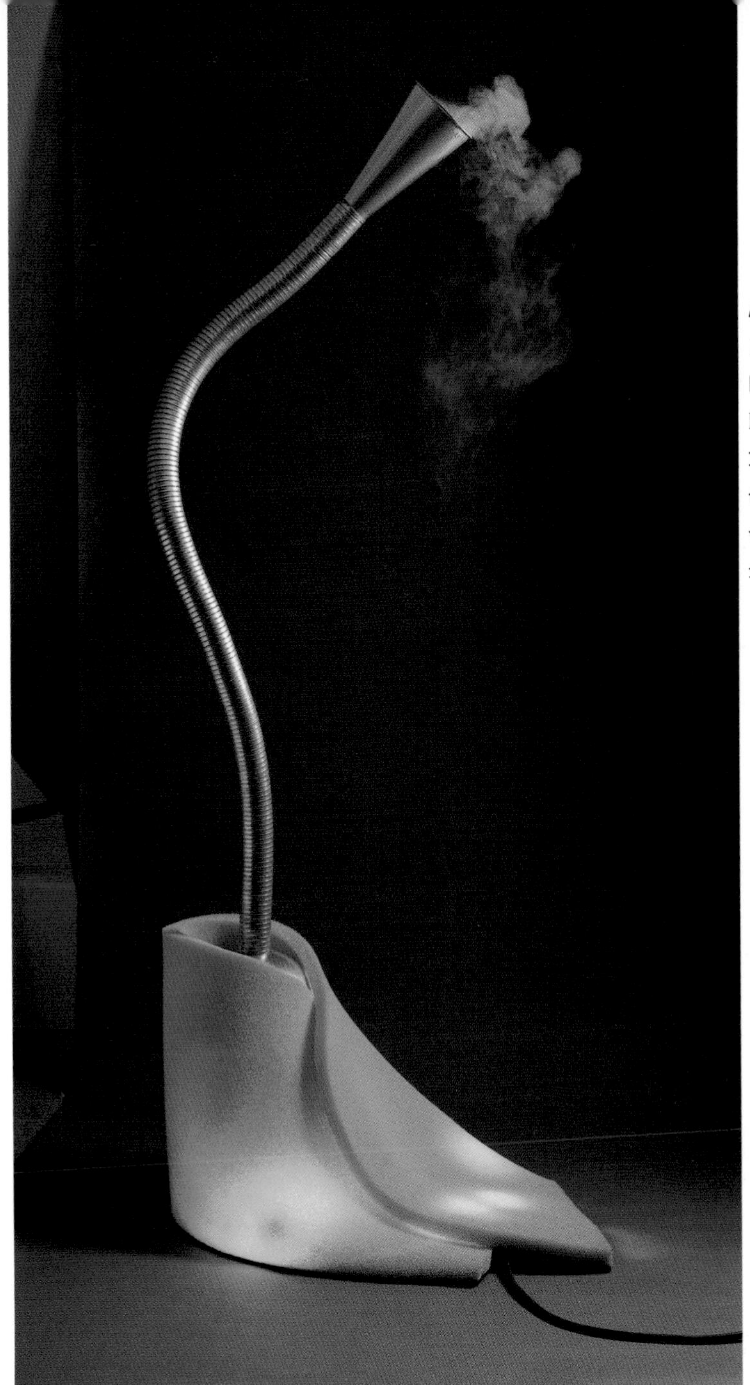

Hyper-natural Scenery series 2
1989
Peter Stathis, designer; Cranbrook Studio project.
Low mysterious light emits from the base while illuminated mist wafts from the spout of this environmental conditioner.

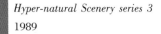

Hyper-natural Scenery series 3
1989
Peter Stathis, designer; Cranbrook Studio project.
The comforting glow of dancing flames illuminates the wall behind the sleek black form.

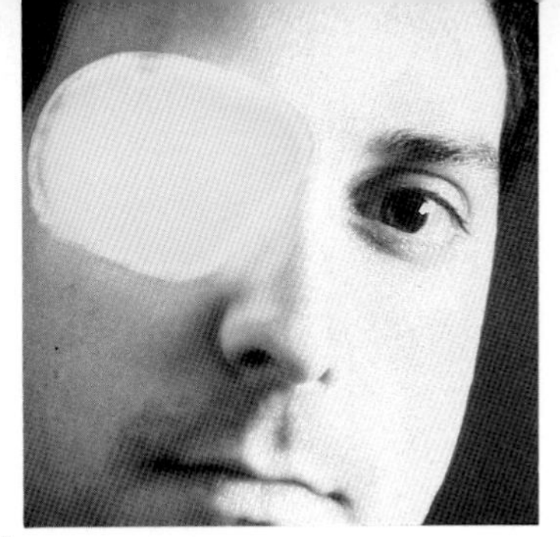

Informational Eyepatch 1989
Peter Stathis, designer; Cranbrook Studio project.
Information is transmitted directly into the eye in this luminous eyepatch computer display.

Manual Fax Model 1988
Lisa Krohn, designer; Cranbrook Studio project.
A portable fax that rolls up for transport. To send a fax the scanning wand is passed across the document, a more natural and personal physical gesture than feeding the document into a slot. An acoustical modem allows the fax to be used in a public phone booth.

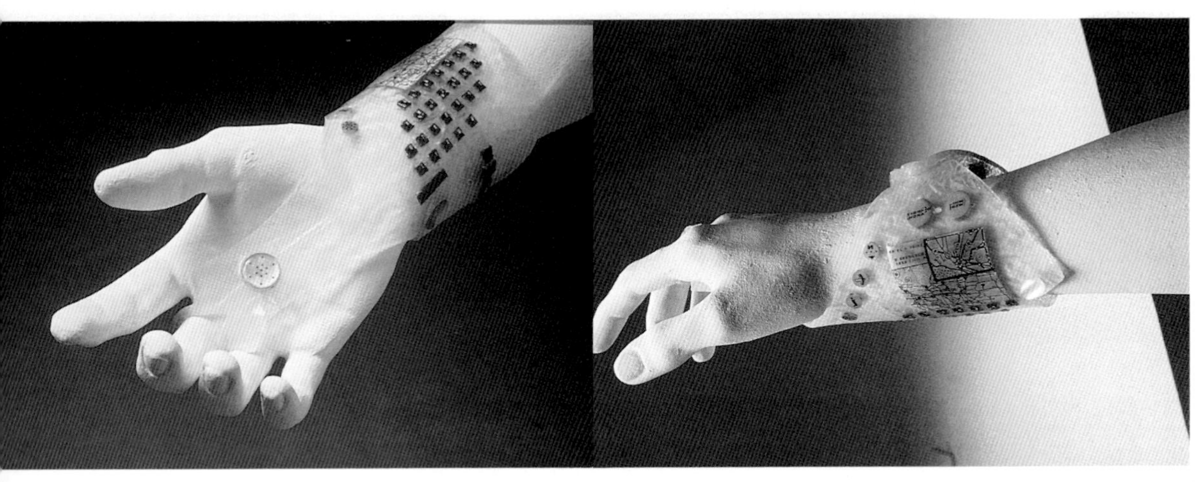

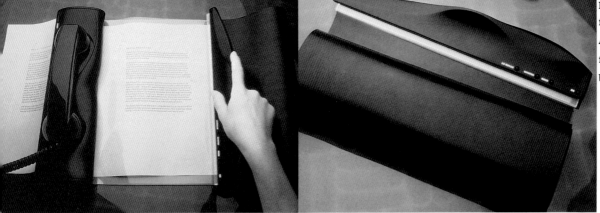

Wrist Computer Model 1988
Lisa Krohn, designer; Cranbrook Studio project.
A wearable information and navigation system that is in the form of a second "informational" skin.

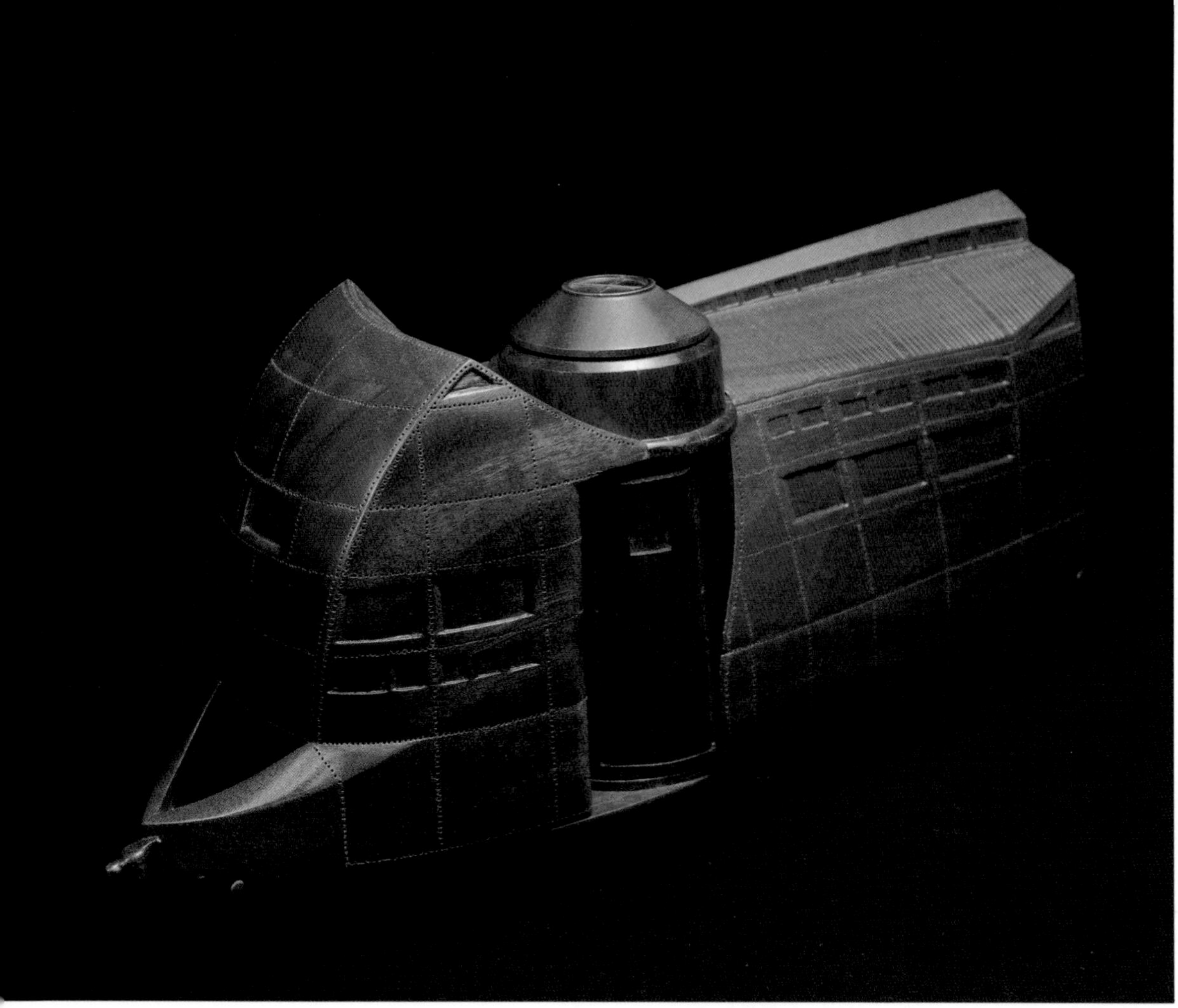

Housetrailer Model 1989

Kendall McAdams, designer; Cranbrook Studio project.

A house-trailer for an itinerant toymaker evokes the mythology of craft and the open road.

Viewphone Model 1989

Philip White, designer; Cranbrook Studio project.

This portable videophone is held in the hand like a mirror, allowing users to view their own images before transmission.

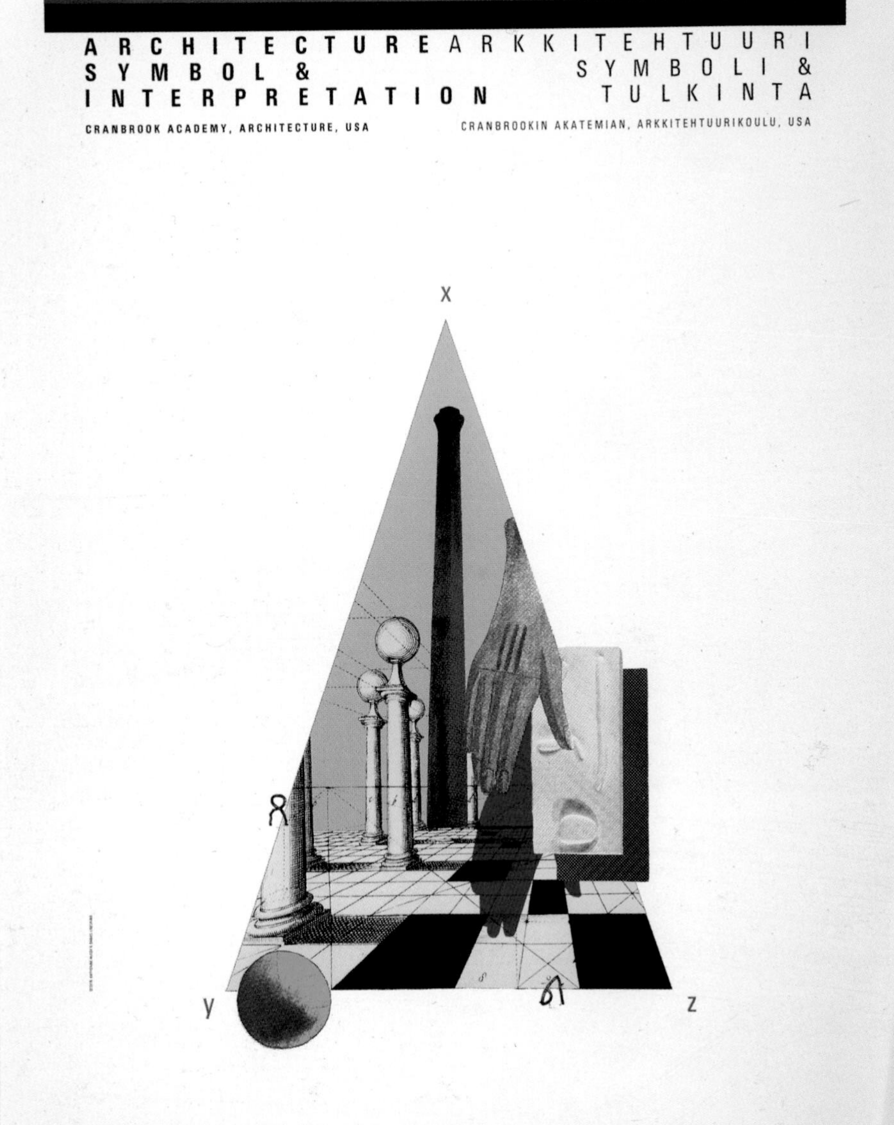
ARCHITECTURE ARKKITEHTUURI
SYMBOL & SYMBOLI &
INTERPRETATION TULKINTA
CRANBROOK ACADEMY, ARCHITECTURE, USA
CRANBROOKIN AKATEMIAN, ARKKITEHTUURIKOULU, USA
x
y
z
MUSEUM OF FINNISH ARCHITECTURE 6. 2.–19. 3. 1980 SUOMEN RAKENNUSTAITEEN MUSEO

Architecture Symbol and Interpretation Exhibition Poster 1981 **Katherine McCoy**, designer, in collaboration with Daniel Libeskind; Cranbrook Faculty project; Finnish Museum of Architecture, Helsinki, Finland, client and publisher.

An announcement for an exhibition refers to the rational and irrational in architecture. A reconstruction of a De Chirico painting includes an early Renaissance perspective drawing and diagrammatic notations from an Edgar Allan Poe short story.

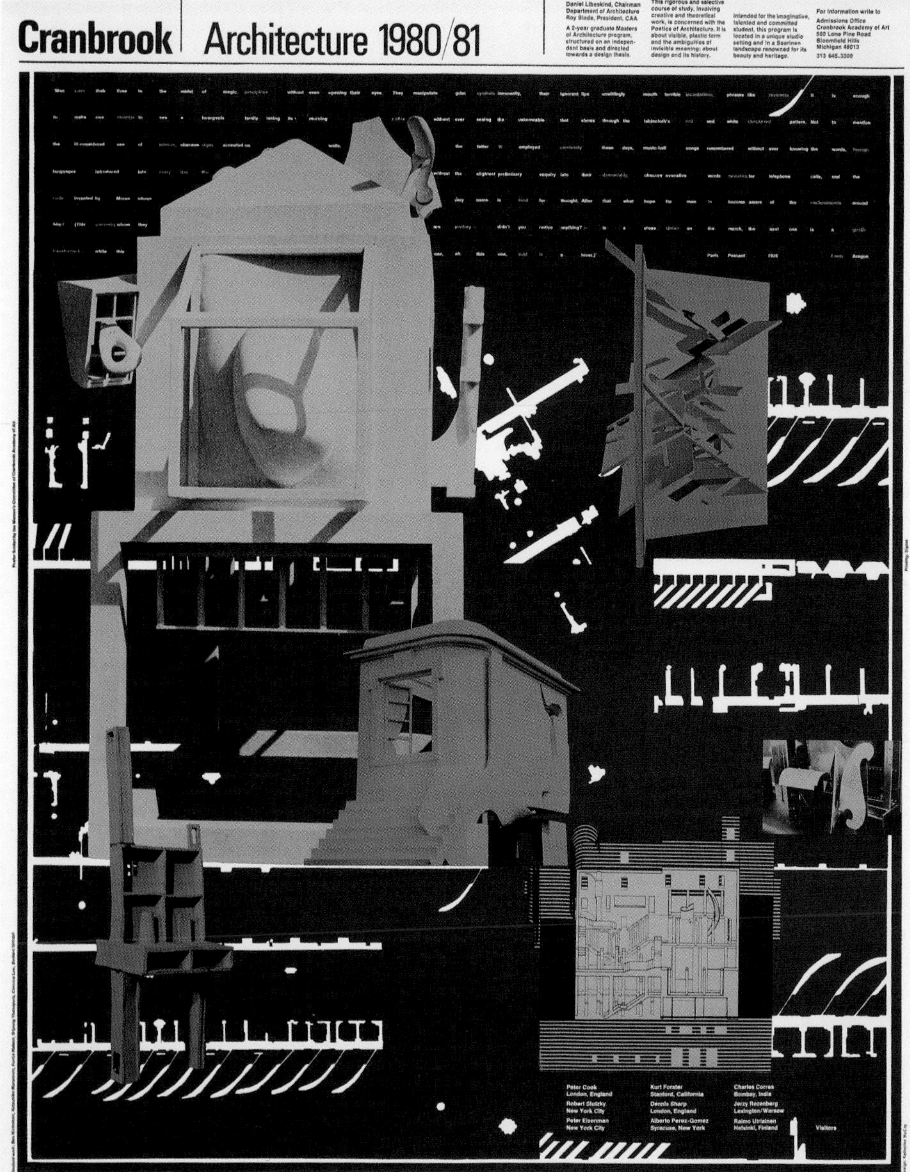
Cranbrook
Architecture 1980/81
Daniel Libeskind, Chairman
Department of Architecture
Roy Slade, President, CAA
A 2-year graduate Masters of Architecture program, structured on an independent basis and directed towards a design thesis.
This rigorous and selective course of study, involving creative and theoretical work, is concerned with the Poetics of Architecture. It is about visible, plastic form and the ambiguities of invisible meaning; about design and its history.
Intended for the imaginative, talented and committed student, this program is located in a unique studio setting and in a Saarinen landscape renowned for its beauty and heritage.
For information write to
Admissions Office
Cranbrook Academy of Art
500 Lone Pine Road
Bloomfield Hills
Michigan 48013
313 645.3300
Peter Cook
London, England
Robert Slutzky
New York City
Peter Eisenman
New York City
Kurt Forster
Stanford, California
Dennis Sharp
London, England
Alberto Perez-Gomez
Syracuse, New York
Charles Correa
Bombay, India
Jerzy Rozenberg
Lexington/Warsaw
Raimo Utriainen
Helsinki, Finland
Visitors

Cranbrook Architecture Poster
1980

Katherine McCoy, designer; Cranbrook Faculty project; Cranbrook Academy of Art, client and publisher.

A montage of student projects includes architectural models constructed of plaster, copper, and aluminum superimposed on a field of drawings based on Arabic calligraphy and Middle Eastern mosque plans. A Louis of Aragon quotation floats above the horizon.

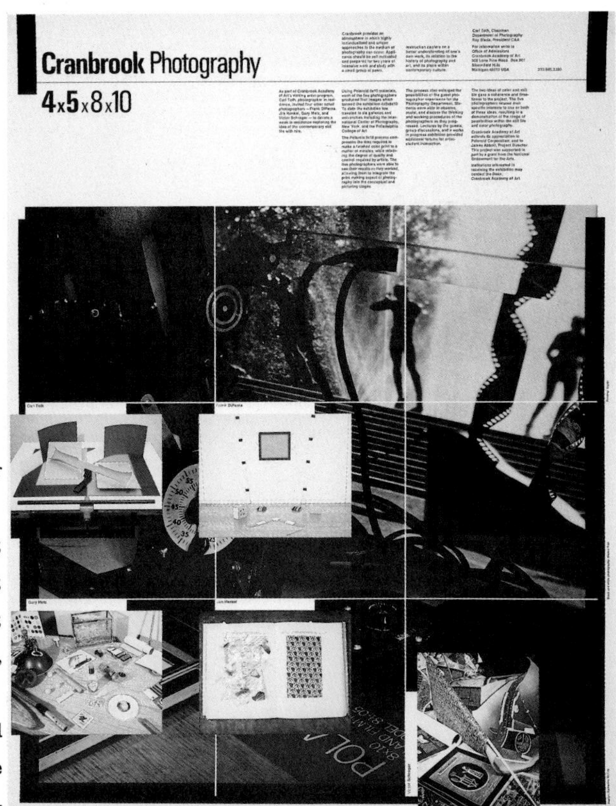
Cranbrook Photography
4x5x8x10

Cranbrook Photography Poster
1980
Katherine McCoy, designer; Steven Rost, photographer; Cranbrook Faculty project; Cranbrook Academy of Art, client.
A staged photograph of projected slides of a Cranbrook landscape over a student darkroom is overlaid with five color photographs documenting a photography workshop at Cranbrook.

Cranbrook Metalsmithing

Cranbrook Metalsmithing Poster
1985
Katherine McCoy, designer; Steven Rost, photographer; Cranbrook Faculty project; Cranbrook Academy of Art, client.
A staged photograph montages projected slides over art pieces by the department's chairman. The ladder form refers to a recurring symbol in this artist's work.

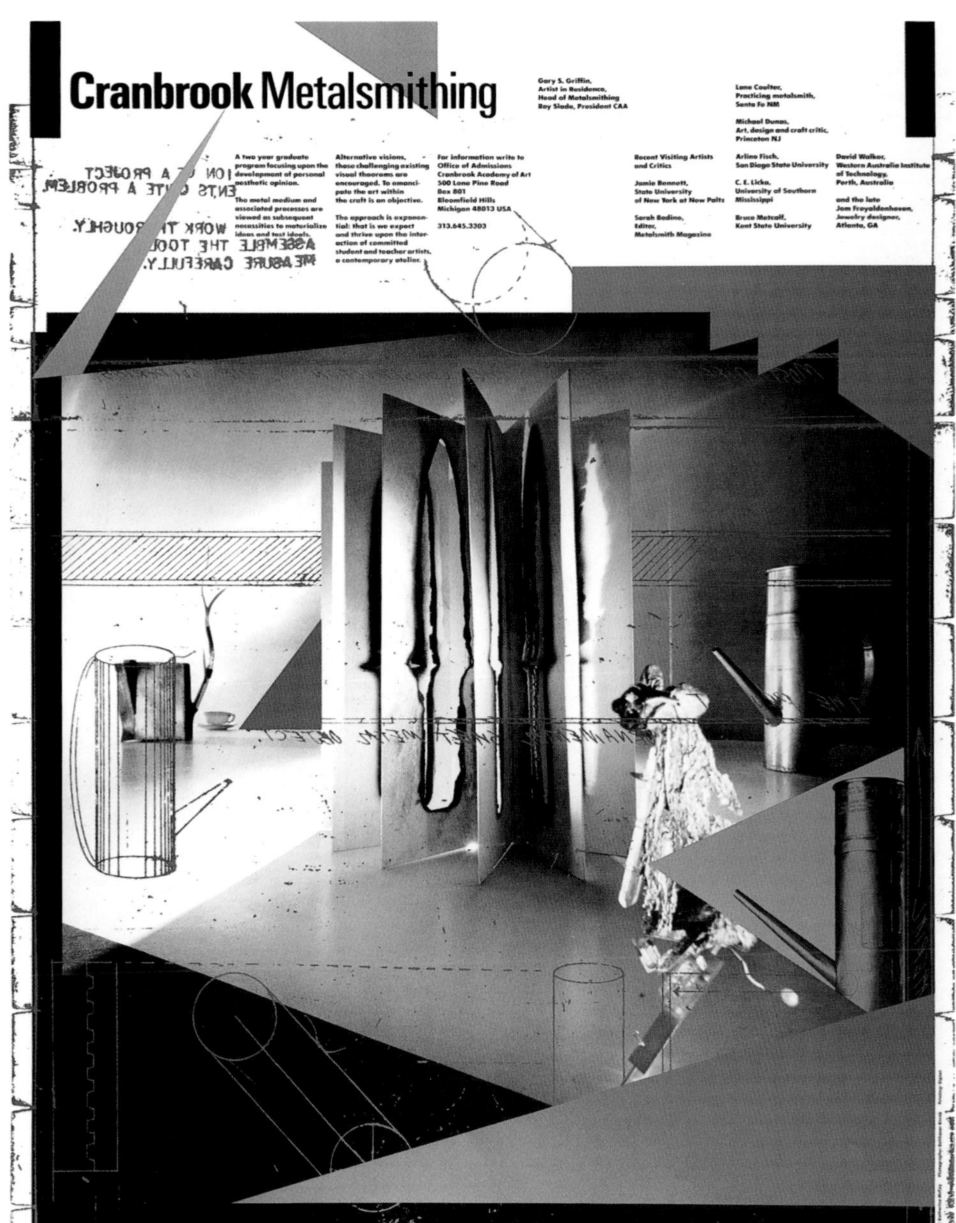
Cranbrook Metalsmithing
Gary S. Griffin, Artist in Residence, Head of Metalsmithing
Roy Slade, President CAA
Lane Coulter, Practicing metalsmith, Santa Fe NM
Michael Dunas, Art, design and craft critic, Princeton NJ
A two year graduate program focusing upon the development of personal aesthetic opinion.
The metal medium and associated processes are viewed as subsequent necessities to materialize ideas and test ideals.
Alternative visions, those challenging existing visual theorems are encouraged. To emancipate the art within the craft is an objective.
The approach is exponential: that is we expect and thrive upon the interaction of committed student and teacher artists, a contemporary atelier.
For information write to Office of Admissions Cranbrook Academy of Art 500 Lone Pine Road Box 801 Bloomfield Hills Michigan 48013 USA
313.645.3303
Recent Visiting Artists and Critics
Jamie Bennett, State University of New York at New Paltz
Sarah Bodine, Editor, Metalsmith Magazine
Arline Fisch, San Diego State University
C. E. Licka, University of Southern Mississippi
Bruce Metcalf, Kent State University
David Walker, Western Australia Institute of Technology, Perth, Australia
and the late Jem Freyaldenhoven, Jewelry designer, Atlanta, GA

Cranbrook Metalsmithing Poster
1986
Katherine McCoy, designer; Balthazar Korab, photographer; Cranbrook Faculty project; Cranbrook Academy of Art, client.

A staged photograph makes a landscape of recent student work. A schematic plan for the pitcher is superimposed and metallic forms of silver and copper cut into the photograph.

Cranbrook
Ceramics

Cranbrook Ceramics Poster 1987
Katherine McCoy, designer; Steven Rost, photographer; Cranbrook Faculty project; Cranbrook Academy of Art, client.
A staged photograph montages projected slides over an art piece by the department's chairman. The spiral-and-coil theme is reiterated by an engraving of a butterfly tongue, a prehistoric Japanese pot, and a photograph of the artist building a coiled piece.

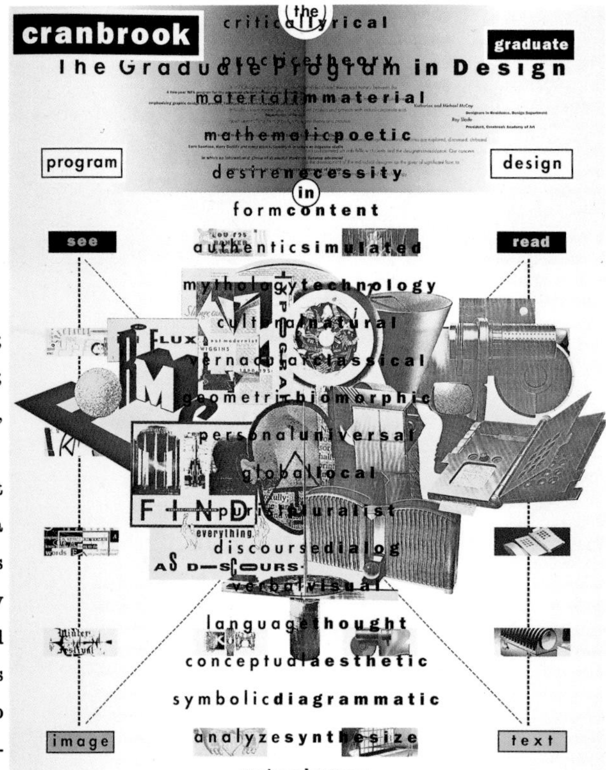
cranbrook
graduate
The Graduate Program in Design
materialimmaterial
mathematicpoetic
program
design
desirenecessity
in
formcontent
see
read
mythologytechnology
geometricbiomorphic
personaluniversal
globallocal
F+ND
discoursedialog
languagethought
conceptualaesthetic
symbolicdiagrammatic
image
analyzesynthesize
text
artscience

Cranbrook Design Poster 1989
Katherine McCoy, designer; Cranbrook Faculty project; Cranbrook Academy of Art, client.
A photographic collage of recent student work is overlayed by a list of possibly opposing values and a communications-theory diagram. The poster is bisected vertically by red and blue and is perforated, allowing recipients to remove sections as reply postcards.

Cranbrook Ceramics *graduate studies*

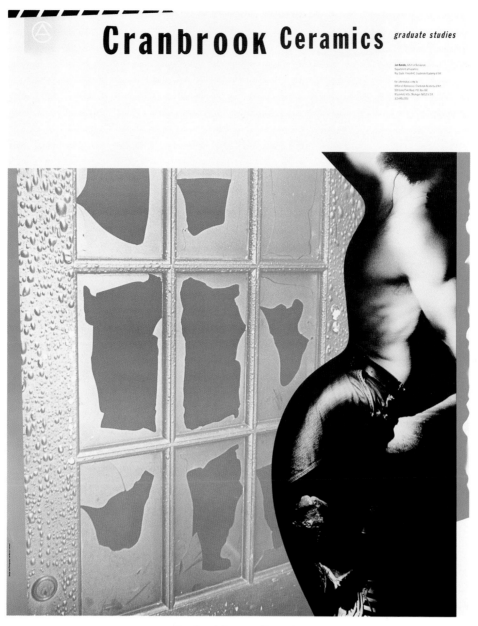

Cranbrook Ceramics Poster 1985
Jan Marcus Jancourt, designer; Cranbrook Studio project; Cranbrook Academy of Art, client.

Fire, water, and the human form are symbolized by a photomontage of a water- and soot-covered door blown out by a kitchen fire, overlayed by a partial human form.

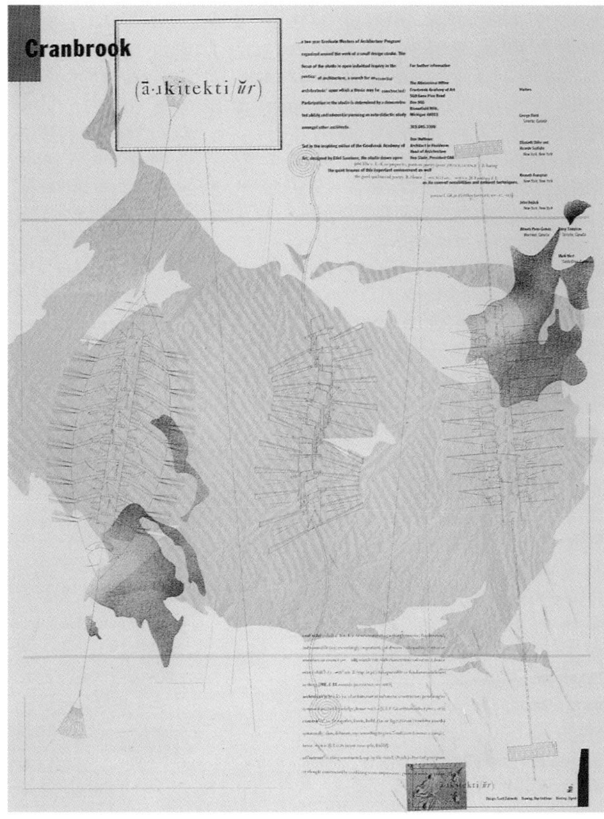
Cranbrook

Cranbrook Architecture Poster
1987
Scott Zukowski, designer; Cranbrook Studio project; Cranbrook Academy of Art, client.
A drawing by the department's chairman is ambiguously scaled, suggesting forms from the size of a continent to those of fossils or cellular material.

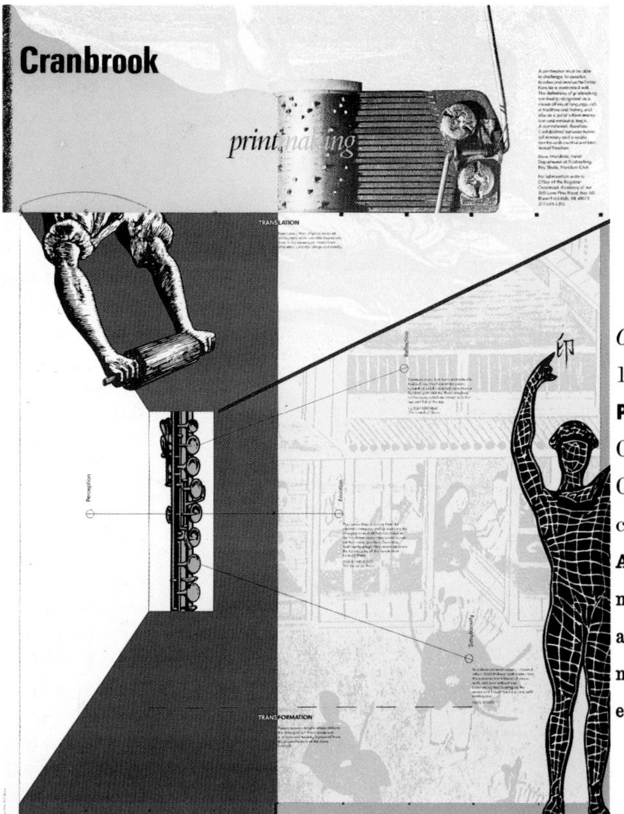
Cranbrook

Cranbrook Printmaking Poster
1985
Peter Wong, designer; Cranbrook Studio project; Cranbrook Academy of Art, client and publisher.
A music-box mechanism and musical instruments draw an analogy between the making of music and the printmaking process.

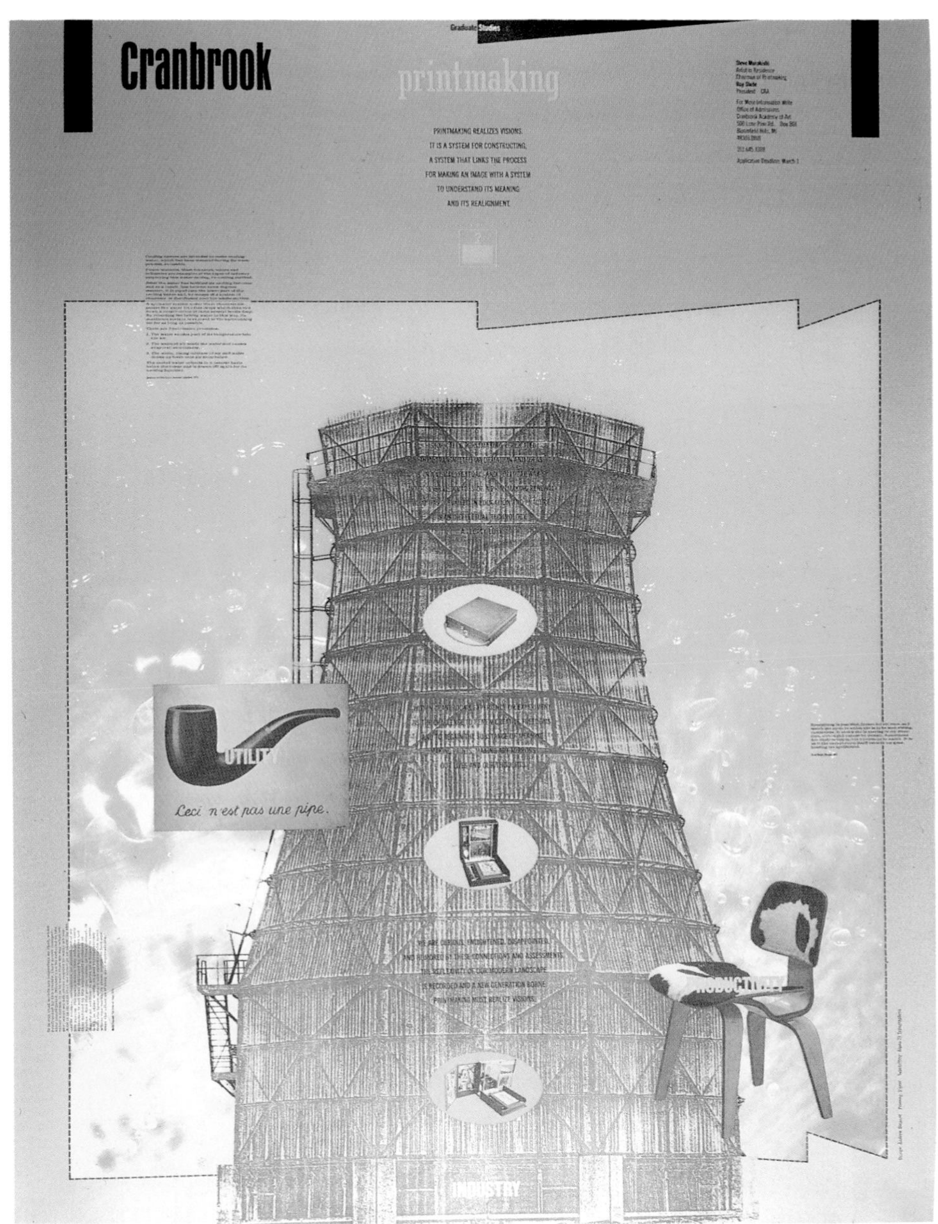

Graduate Studies
Cranbrook
printmaking
PRINTMAKING REALIZES VISIONS.
IT IS A SYSTEM FOR CONSTRUCTING,
A SYSTEM THAT LINKS THE PROCESS
FOR MAKING AN IMAGE WITH A SYSTEM
TO UNDERSTAND ITS MEANING
AND ITS REALIGNMENT.
UTILITY
Ceci n'est pas une pipe.
PRODUCTIVITY
INDUSTRY

Cranbrook Printmaking Poster
1987
Andrew Blauvelt, designer; Cranbrook Studio project; Cranbrook Academy of Art, client and publisher.
Production and replication are the subjects of this promotional poster. A cooling tower, oil and water, and works by Marcel Duchamp and Charles Eames relate production, industry, and utility to the printmaking process.

GRADUATE STUDIES IN Fiber
Cranbrook
GERHARDT KNODEL
Artist in Residence and Head of the Fiber Department
ROY SLADE
President, Cranbrook Academy of Art
For INFORMATION:
Office of the Registrar, Cranbrook Academy of Art
500 Lone Pine Road P.O. Box 801
Bloomfield Hills, Michigan 48013
We intend to alter the definition of our field called Fibers through our work.
Well-formed
questions may be more
useful
than well-formed
answers
You may be interested in joining us!

Cranbrook Fiber Poster 1989
Lisa Anderson, designer; Cranbrook Studio project; Cranbrook Academy of Art, client and publisher.
Images from nature and weaving traditions are overlaid by a provocative text about the goals of this department's investigations.

JAMES SURLS
recent
work

James Surls Exhibition Poster 1987

David Frej, designer; Cranbrook Studio project; Cranbrook Academy of Art Museum, client and publisher.

The spirit of surrealistic play in James Surls's large-scale sculpture is captured in the skewed composition and typography.

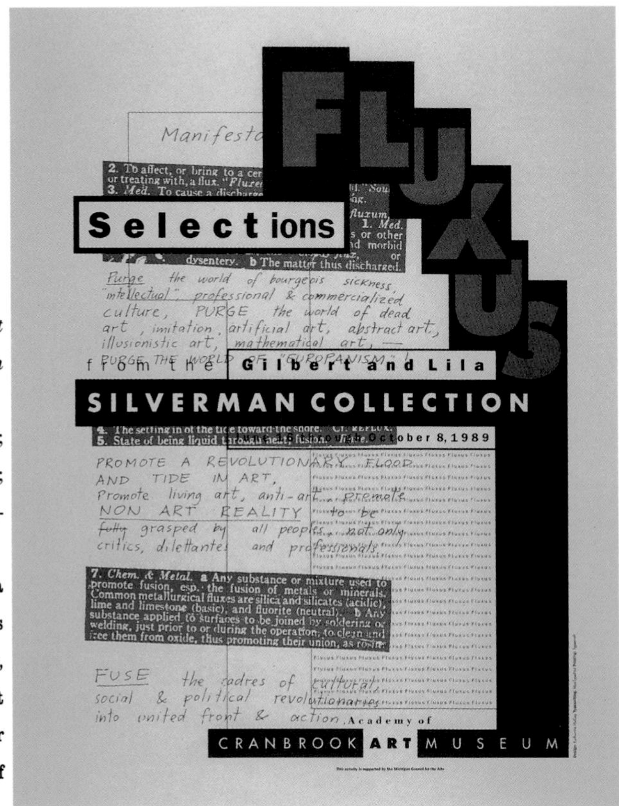
FLUXUS
Selections
from the Gilbert and Lila
SILVERMAN COLLECTION
Manifesto
CRANBROOK ART MUSEUM

Fluxus Selections from the Gilbert and Lia Silverman Collection Exhibition Poster 1989

Katherine McCoy, designer; Cranbrook Faculty project; Cranbrook Academy of Art Museum, client and publisher.

This poster's structure refers to a diagram of the history of Fluxus by the movement's founder, George Maciunas. The bright colors of cheap printing and paper are in the provocative spirit of Fluxus.

ETC.

Fluxus Etc. Exhibition Catalog 1981
Katherine McCoy, designer; Lori Barnett, Lynnette Silarski, and Kenneth Windsor, assistants; Cranbrook Faculty project; Cranbrook Academy of Art Museum, client and publisher.
This extensive low-budget catalog on a provocative art movement materializes its grid and graphic-arts processes for both visual expression and economy. An unorthodox use of the traditional Swiss-school grid both refers to a chart of the movement featured in the exhibition and saves space.

Viewpoint 86: Painting and the Third Dimension Exhibition Catalog 1986
David Frej, designer; Cranbrook Studio project; Cranbrook Academy of Art Museum, client and publisher.
A die-cut fold-out cover reveals elements of paintings in the exhibition, emphasizing their differing visions of space and depth. Elements on the interior pages are superimposed on an abstracted cone of vision that grows from left to right across each spread.

Vortex III, 1984
Acrylic on canvas
84 x 84 inches
Courtesy of André Emmerich Gallery, New York, New York
(Photo courtesy of André Emmerich Gallery, New York, New York)
The First Circle, 1985
Acrylic on canvas
60 x 198 inches
Courtesy of André Emmerich Gallery, New York, New York
Born in 1928 in Brooklyn, New York.
Studied at the Art Students League of New York, New York, New York (1948-1949) and the Académie de la Grande Chaumière, Paris, France (1950-1953).
Taught at Yale University, School of Art and Architecture, New Haven, Connecticut (1962-1980).
HELD
Viewpoint
86
Painting and the Third Dimension
Cranbrook Academy of Art Museum November 11, 1986-January 18, 1987

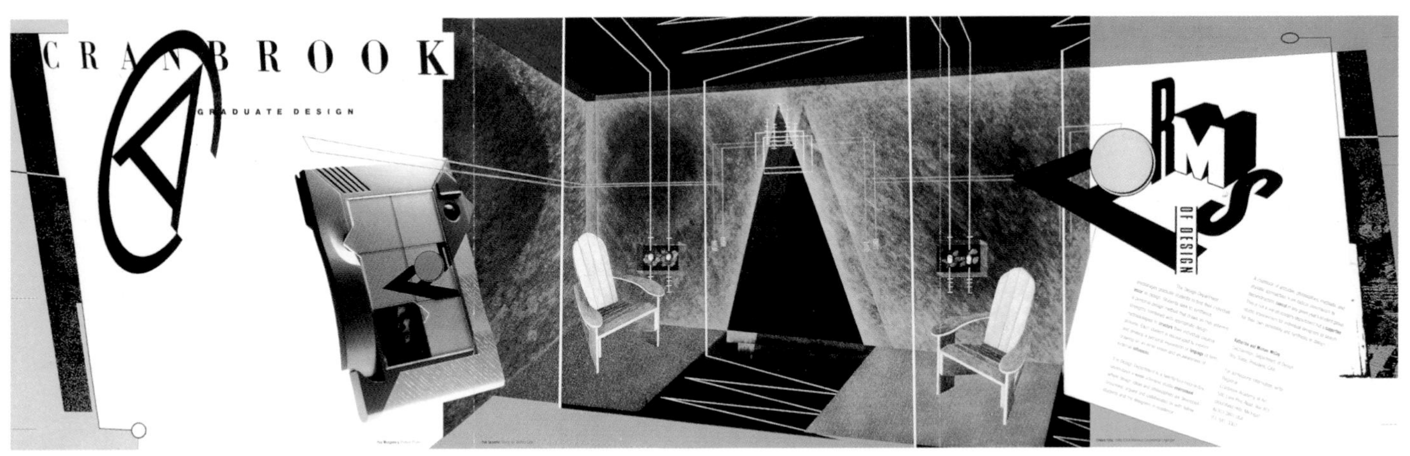
CRANBROOK
GRADUATE DESIGN
FORMS
OF DESIGN

Cranbrook Graduate Design
Brochure 1987
Glenn Suokko, designer; Cranbrook Studio project; Cranbrook Academy of Art, client and publisher.
Elements of the school's general catalog are warped in space, and student projects are combined in collage form to suggest the interaction of two- and three-dimensional design concerns.

CRANBROOK
GRADUATE DESIGN

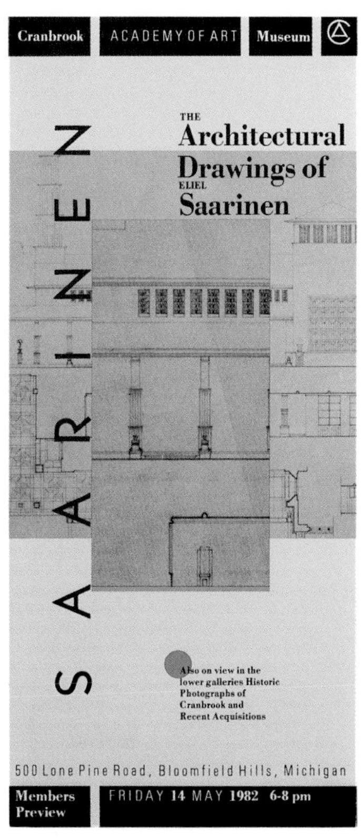
Cranbrook
ACADEMY OF ART
Museum
THE
Architectural
Drawings of
ELIEL
Saarinen
SAARINEN
Also on view in the
lower galleries Historic
Photographs of
Cranbrook and
Recent Acquisitions
500 Lone Pine Road, Bloomfield Hills, Michigan
Members
Preview
FRIDAY 14 MAY 1982 6-8 pm

Cranbrook
ACADEMY OF ART
Museum
STUDENT
Degree
Shows
April 15-25
April 29-May 7
500 Lone Pine Road, Bloomfield Hills, Michigan
Members
Previews
THURSDAY 15 APRIL 1982 5-7 pm
THURSDAY 29 APRIL 1982 5-7 pm

Cranbrook
ACADEMY OF ART
Museum
STUDENT
Summer
Show
500 Lone Pine Road, Bloomfield Hills, Michigan
Members
Preview
FRIDAY 14 MAY 1982 6-8 pm

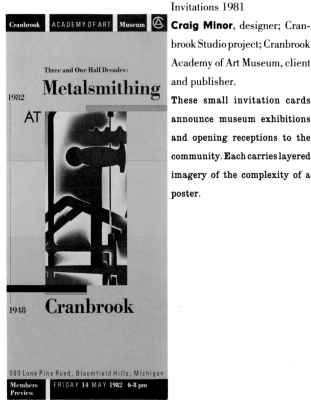

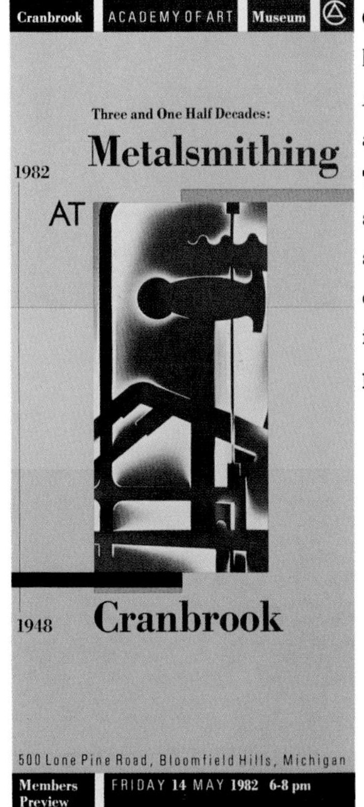
Cranbrook
ACADEMY OF ART
Museum
Three and One Half Decades:
Metalsmithing
1982
AT
1948
Cranbrook
500 Lone Pine Road, Bloomfield Hills, Michigan
Members
Preview
FRIDAY 14 MAY 1982 6-8 pm

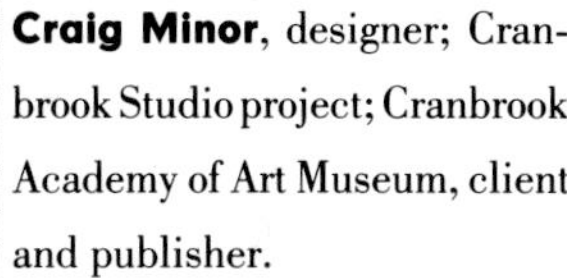

Cranbrook Museum Exhibition Invitations 1981

Craig Minor, designer; Cranbrook Studio project; Cranbrook Academy of Art Museum, client and publisher.

These small invitation cards announce museum exhibitions and opening receptions to the community. Each carries layered imagery of the complexity of a poster.

CRANBROOK

ACADEMY

OF

ART

CATALOGUE

CRANBROOK
ACADEMY OF ART
GRADUATE STUDIOS CATALOGUE
ARTISTS IN RESIDENCE
DESIGN

Cranbrook Academy of Art Catalog 1982

Katherine McCoy, designer; Constance Birdsall, design assistant; Cranbrook Faculty project; Cranbrook Academy of Art, client and publisher.

To celebrate the Academy's fiftieth anniversary, the cover abstracts and translates a frankly decorative Eliel Saarinen pattern from the Academy's first catalog cover. The cover pattern establishes the interior grid structure of the catalog, and elements of the pattern reappear in varying amounts throughout.

Cranbrook Academy of Art Catalog 1987

Katherine McCoy / Andrew Blauvelt, catalog designers; Andrew Blauvelt, cover photography; Glenn Suokko, Design section montage photography; Cranbrook Faculty project; Cranbrook Academy of Art, client and publisher.

Open windows, typical of Cranbrook, are a metaphor for expanding viewpoints. A photographic montage combines windows with a column, an image used repeatedly in past Cranbrook catalogs, and with graphic arts materials used to construct the catalog's interior.

Sequences Poster 1988
Katherine McCoy, designer; McCoy & McCoy project; Richard Hirneisen, photographer; Simpson Lee Paper Company, client and publisher.
A rear-view mirror advances toward the viewer, reflecting a historical progression of communications devices. The ubiquitous statement found on every car mirror, Objects in mirror are closer than they appear, refers to the role these machines play in culture, mirroring our values, simulating reality, and replacing primary experience.

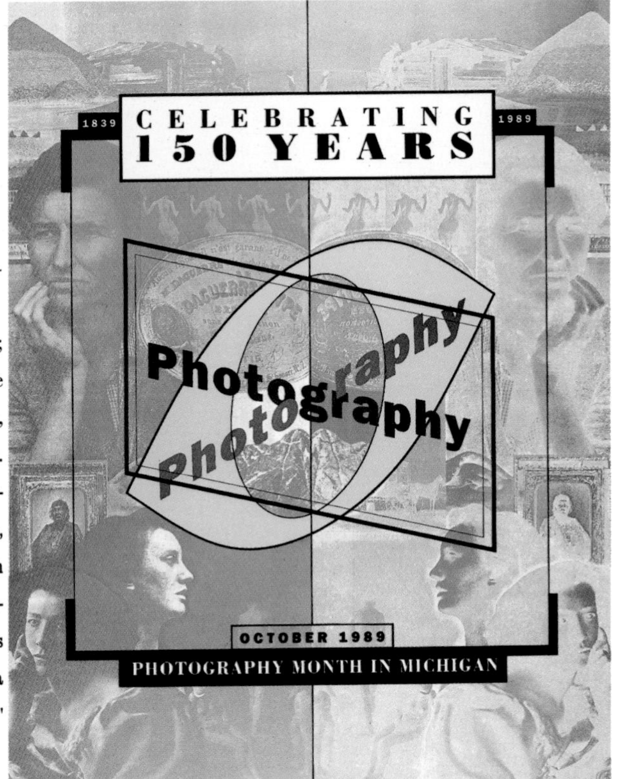
1839
CELEBRATING
150 YEARS
1989
Photography
Photography
OCTOBER 1989
PHOTOGRAPHY MONTH IN MICHIGAN

Photography Month in Michigan Poster 1989
Katherine McCoy, designer; McCoy & McCoy project; The Detroit Institute of Arts, Detroit, Michigan, client and publisher.
To celebrate the 150th anniversary of photography's invention, an abstracted eye is reflected in the transparent plane of photography and simultaneously sees through it. The background is a montage of photographic "icons" in our cultural memories.

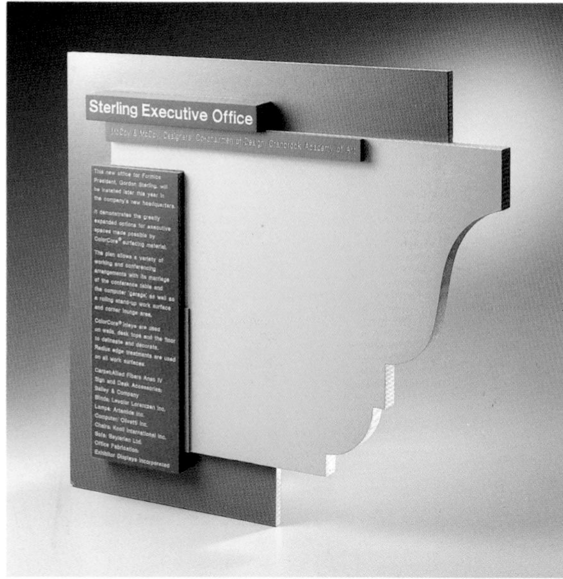
Sterling Executive Office

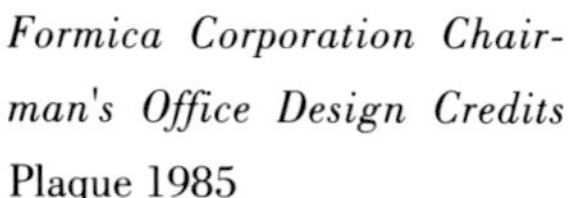

Formica Corporation Chairman's Office Design Credits Plaque 1985
Katherine McCoy, designer; McCoy & McCoy project; Formica Corporation, Wayne, New Jersey, client and fabricator.
Three-dimensional forms of the Sterling Office interior are flattened and abstracted into a bas-relief configuration fabricated in sandwiched layers of Formica's ColorCore product.

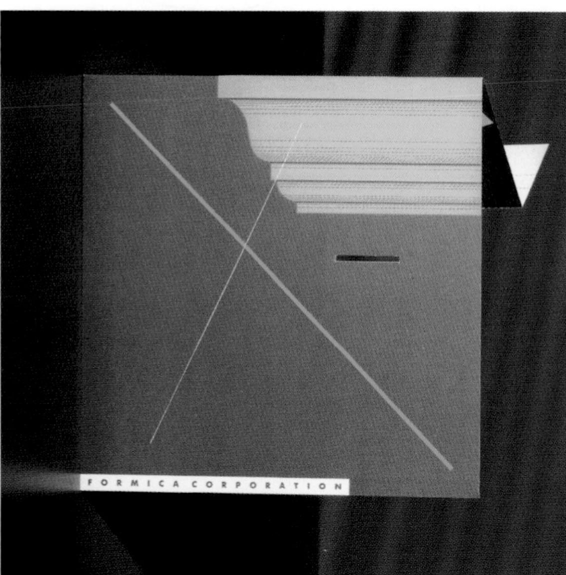
FORMICA CORPORATION

Formica Corporation Chairman's Office Reception Invitation 1985
Katherine McCoy, designer; McCoy & McCoy project; Formica Corporation, Wayne, New Jersey, client and publisher.
Three-dimensional forms of the Sterling Office interior are flattened and abstracted and combined with die-cuts taken from the McCoy & McCoy studio brochure.

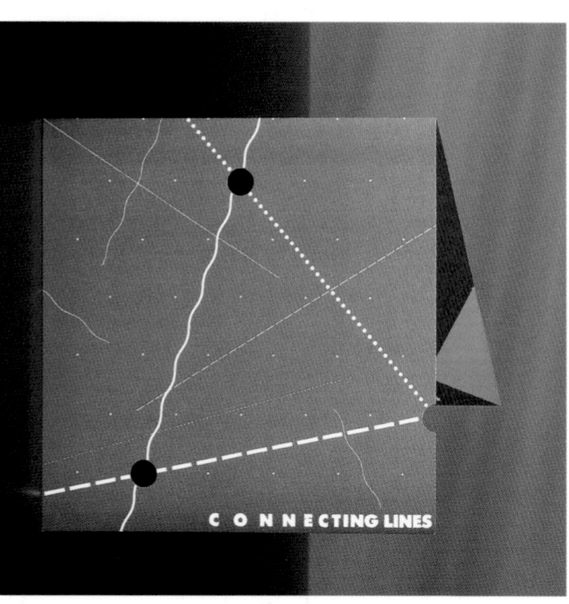
CONNECTING LINES

Connecting Lines Designers Saturday Reception Invitation 1987
Katherine McCoy, designer; McCoy & McCoy project; Krueger International, New York, New York, client.
Three die-cuts, three primary colors, and three networks of lines refer to three interior-design installations by three design studios using three electronic desk systems that carry three types of cables - telephone, electrical, and digital.

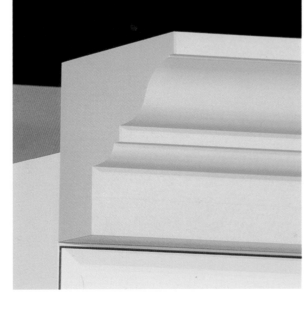

Formica Corporation Chairman's Office Interior, Wayne, New Jersey 1985

Michael and Katherine McCoy, McCoy & McCoy, Bloomfield Hills, Michigan, designers; Formica Corporation, Wayne, New Jersey, client.

A working office that reflects, in its plan and detailing, the working patterns and preferences of its occupant. The material, ColorCore, is used as an inlaid notational system, denoting active and passive areas and working patterns.

Office of the Year Interiors Initiative Project Installation, New York 1984

Michael McCoy, McCoy & McCoy, Bloomfield Hills, Michigan, designers; *Interiors* magazine, New York, Formica Corporation, Wayne, New Jersey, and Beylerian Inc., New York, clients.

This demonstration office for an aerospace executive explores the use of imagery that symbolically connects the space to the activity going on within it.

Casa Aperta Installation, Chicago, Illinois 1989

Michael and Katherine McCoy, McCoy & McCoy, Bloomfield Hills, Michigan, designers; Assopiastrelle, Association of Italian Tile Manufacturers, New York, and Mapei Corporation, Tempe, Arizona, clients.

Casa Aperta ("open house") is a tile-covered structure that is dissected to reveal psychological aspects of "house": protection, symbolized by the castle tower, and nurturing, inferred by the milk carton.

American Tatami Showroom Installation, New York 1987

Michael and Katherine McCoy, McCoy & McCoy, Bloomfield Hills, Michigan, designers; Krueger International, New York, client.

The space makes cross-cultural references to American and Japanese proportioning systems. The walls are internally illuminated air mattresses – human-scale mats, like the tatami – kept aloft by internal blowers.

Creel Morrell Offices Interior, Austin, Texas 1987

Michael and Katherine McCoy, McCoy & McCoy, Bloomfield Hills, Michigan, designers; Creel Morrell, Austin, Texas, client.

Offices for an architectural graphic-design firm that refer to the process of transforming two-dimensional figures into three-dimensional form. The doors to the conference room pivot around turned elements which are emblematic of the transformative process.

Eyes Nightclub Interior, Kansas City, Missouri 1987

Thomas Lehn and Kathleen Kelly, Kelly and Lehn, Kansas City, Missouri, designers; Eyes Nightclub, Kansas City, Missouri, client.

The space is a "city" of individual and diverse forms held together by a framework of industrial materials and exaggerated finishes. The club becomes a direct reflection of the urban life around it.

San Marco Shoe Store Interior, Seattle, Washington 1988
Thomas Lehn and Kathleen Kelly, Kelly and Lehn, Kansas City, Missouri, designers; San Marco Shoe Store, Seattle, Washington, client.

The store presents a range of images derived from the aquatic environment of the Northwest. It presents the real and surreal in ways that blur the boundaries between them.

GRAPHIC DESIGN IN AMERICA

GRAPHIC DESIGN IN AMERICA
A VISUAL LANGUAGE HISTORY

Walker Art Center
5 November through 21 January

Images of America Catalog and Product Brochures 1988-1989
Scott Santoro, Worksight, New York, designer; Images of America, Inc., Thomasville, North Carolina, client and publisher.
A contract-furniture manufacturer's program of product materials directed to interior designers and architects contrasts the factory environment with its highly refined products.

IMAGES
OF
A M E R I C A

Graphic Design in America: A Visual Language History Book 1989
Glenn Suokko, Walker Art Center Graphic Design, Minneapolis, Minnesota, designer; Walker Art Center, Minneapolis, Minnesota, client and publisher.
This first major book on American graphic design employs two early wood typefaces for its cover in an abstract reference to American vernacular typography.

IMAGES

IMAGES

PRODUCT: PROJECT 'N SKETCH

DESIGN LOGIC INC

CHICAGO

THE NEW AMERICAN FRONTIER

IT'S THE THING TO BE THESE DAYS.
PRODUCT DESIGNERS.
INDUSTRIAL DESIGNERS.
THE PEOPLE WHO BRING TO THE WORLD
ALL SHAPE
AND SIZE
AND MATERIAL
FOR EVERY FACET OF OUR LIVES.

THE ARBITERS OF TASTE AND STYLE.

THE NEW INTERPRETERS OF
ART AND LEADING EDGE CREATIVITY.

THE LENS
THROUGH WHICH WE VIEW
THE CONTINUALLY CHANGING TERRAIN
OF TECHNOLOGY AND OUR RELATIONSHIP
TO IT.

NOW IMAGINE THIS. A BARREN SCENE IN THE HEART
OF THE COUNTRY. A LANDSCAPE MADE UP
OF PLASTIC AND METAL AND NEON AND OPTICAL
FIBERS AND COMPUTER CHIPS. NOT A SOUL
TO BE FOUND
FOR MILES AROUND.

SUDDENLY, FROM OUT OF NOWHERE THE MOST SPECTACULAR
VEHICLE YOU'VE EVER LAID EYES ON FLOATS TO THE
GROUND. AND FROM IT EMERGES A TEAM

WITH TALENT AND IDEAS SO FRESH
IT DEFIES EXPECTATION.

A TEAM WITH INSIGHT AND VISION
AND INSTINCT.

A TEAM
DESTINED TO REDEFINE THE AMERICAN FRONTIER
OF PRODUCT DESIGN.

DESIGN LOGIC.

PROJECT 'N SKETCH

PLATFORM
835
835 BUSH STREET SUITE 15
SAN FRANCISCO, CA. 94108
(415) 928-0452

Platform Logotype and Stationery 1988
David Frej, Influx, Chicago, Illinois, designer; Platform, San Francisco, California, client and publisher.
A logotype and letterhead for a new industrial-design studio emphasize the unconventional quality of the studio's name.

Design Logic Capability Brochure and Logotype 1988
David Frej, Influx, Chicago, Illinois, designer; Design Logic, Chicago, Illinois, client and publisher.
This brochure binder for a cutting-edge industrial-design studio recalls office materials of an earlier era, as do the tough "industrial" typefaces of the logotype. The sepia-toned photographic details of avant-garde, high-tech electronic products in the interior play the memory of historic heavy industry against post-industrial electronics.

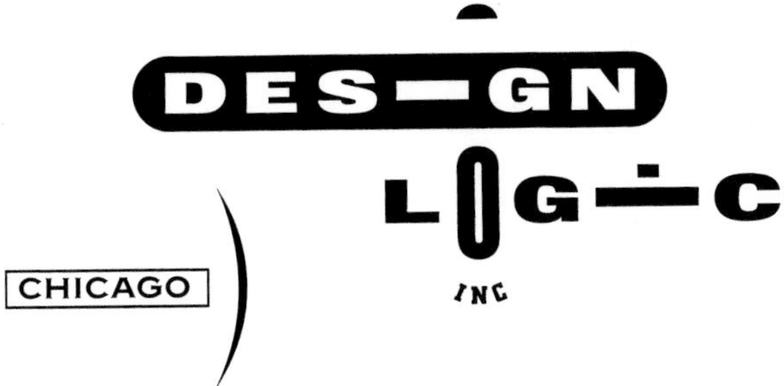
DESIGN
LOGIC
INC
CHICAGO

Holiday Greeting Card 1988
Edward Fella, Valencia, California, designer and publisher.
This business card-sized "Christmas card" uses vernacular "quickie printer" typography and printing. The ordinary form belies the complex message which makes sly reference to the religious aspect of Christmas through the words "see son" and to the designer's new residence in southern California through the words "sea sun." A variety of readings are made through alternate reading order of "greetings" and "ah ha."

EMILIO AMBASZ
The Poetics Of The Pragmatic
Architecture, Exhibit, Industrial And Graphic Design
Essays By
Mario Bellini
Alessandro Mendini
Michael Sorkin
Ettore Sottsass
Rizzoli

Lucille Halsell Conservatory
San Antonio, Texas

Emilio Ambasz: The Poetics of the Pragmatic Book 1989
Bradford P. Collins, Group C, New Haven, Connecticut, designers; Rizzoli International, New York, client and publisher.
The subtle tension between the typography and the photographic layout of this monograph echoes the tension between the classical nature of Ambasz' vision and the modern technology which allows its realization.

Mask of Medusa Book 1985
Lorraine Wild, Los Angeles, California, designer; Rizzoli International, New York, client and publisher.
This book on the architecture and writing of John Hejduk defies convention with its monotone cover and subtly complex interior typography.

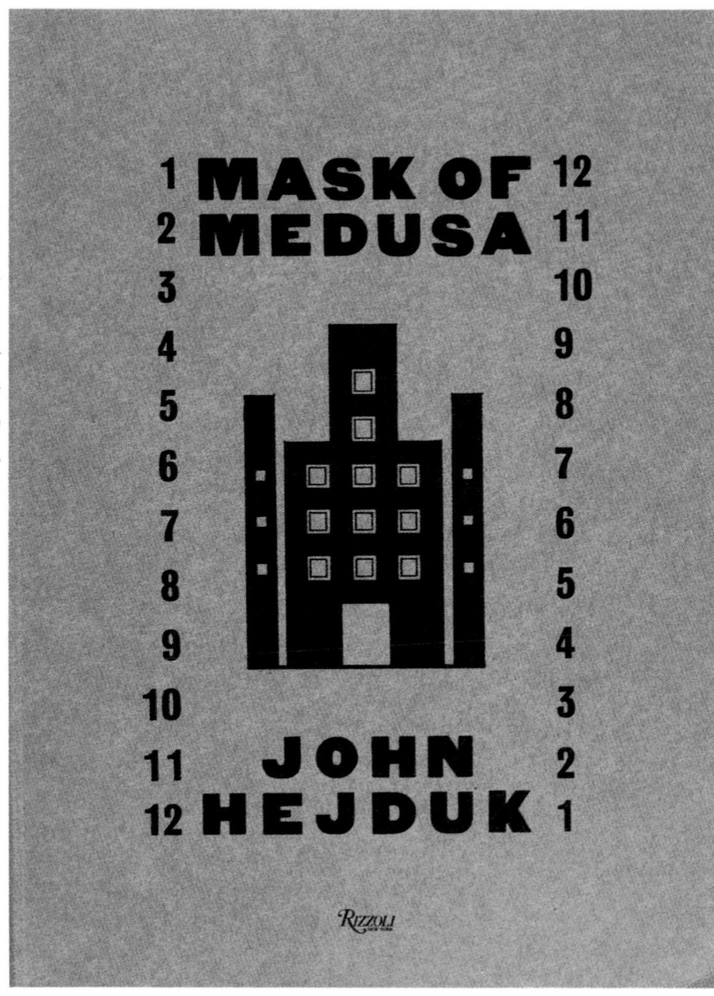

MASK OF
MEDUSA
1 2 3 4 5 6 7 8 9 10 11 12
12 11 10 9 8 7 6 5 4 3 2 1
JOHN
HEJDUK
RIZZOLI

Victims Book 1986
Lorraine Wild, Los Angeles, California, designer; Architectural Association, London, England, client and publisher.
This book on architecture draws on opposing traditions of classical handcrafted books and the Swiss school of graphic design.

VICTIMS

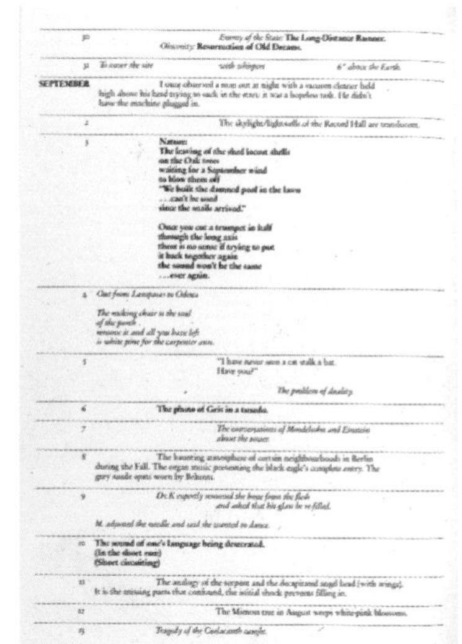

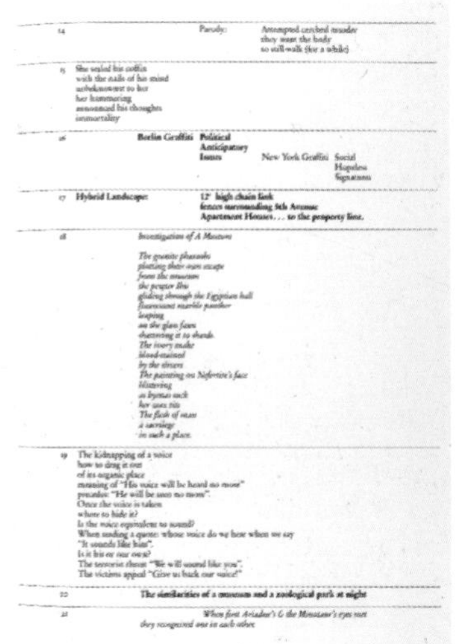

California Institute of the Arts

Visual Communication

For almost two decades CalArts has encouraged a conceptual approach to the study of design, recognizing the necessity for professional competence without being limited by it.

AT A TIME WHEN BOTH CULTURAL CONTEXT AND TECHNOLOGICAL POTENTIAL ARE RAPIDLY CHANGING THE FIELD OF DESIGN, THE GRADUATE PROGRAM IN Visual Communication continues its commitment to an advanced exploration of practice and theory.

In studios, seminars, and independent study projects, issues of critical theory, history, and design methodology inform the development of a personal direction within the public context of VISUAL COMMUNICATION.

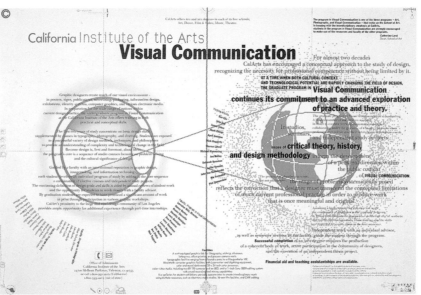

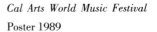

Visual Communications Poster 1986

Jeffery Keedy / Lorraine Wild, Los Angeles, California, designers; California Institute of the Arts, Valencia, California, client and publisher.

Unconventional text compositions become part of this poster's imagery, extending the meaning of the twin circles of eye and globe to create a visual/verbal text/image message on visual communications.

CALARTS
WORLD
MUSIC
FESTIVAL

Cal Arts World Music Festival Poster 1989

Caryn Aono, California Institute of the Arts Office of Public Affairs, designer; California Institute of the Arts, Valencia, California, client and publisher.

Abstracted musical instruments in copper ink announce a music festival sponsored by the School of Music.

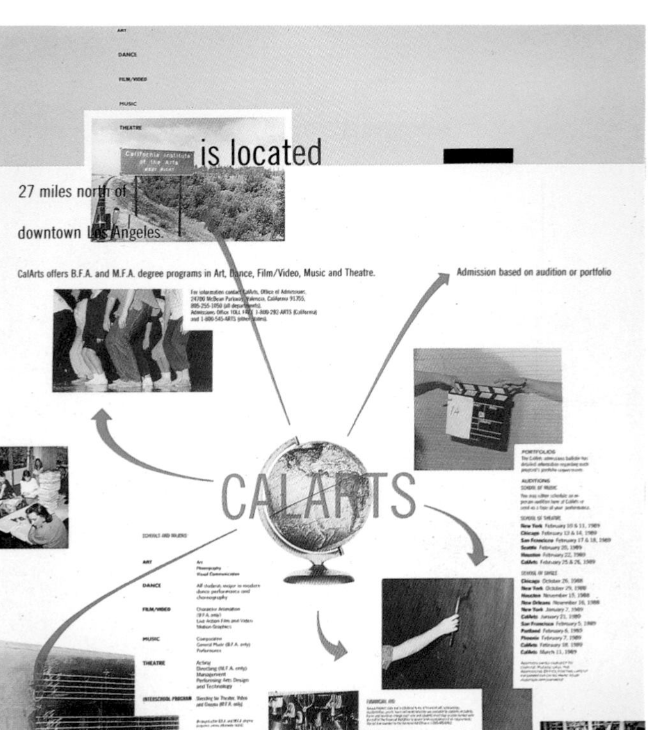
is located
27 miles north of
downtown Los Angeles.
CalArts offers B.F.A. and M.F.A. degree programs in Art, Dance, Film/Video, Music and Theatre.
Admission based on audition or portfolio
CALARTS

California Institute of the Arts Poster 1988

Edward Fella / Jeffery Keedy / Lorraine Wild, Agenda, Los Angeles, California, designers; California Institute of the Arts, Valencia, California, client and publisher.

This recruitment poster utilizes imagery from its companion piece, the Cal Arts academic catalog.

California Institute of the Arts
Academic Catalog 1988
Edward Fella / Jeffery Keedy / Lorraine Wild, Agenda, Los Angeles, California, designers; California Institute of the Arts, Valencia, California, client and publisher.
A die-cut cover reveals a photograph of the freeway exit to this school. A stable "classic" page structure counters the color distortions in the photographic imagery about this avant-garde art school.

DANCE

SCHOOL OF DANCE

California Institute of the Arts
Postcard 1986-1987
Jeffery Keedy, Los Angeles, California, designer; California Institute of the Arts, Valencia, California, client and publisher.
Symbols appropriated from vernacular sources talk about being, thinking, and working creatively in each of these recruiting postcards for an art college that stresses the avant-garde.

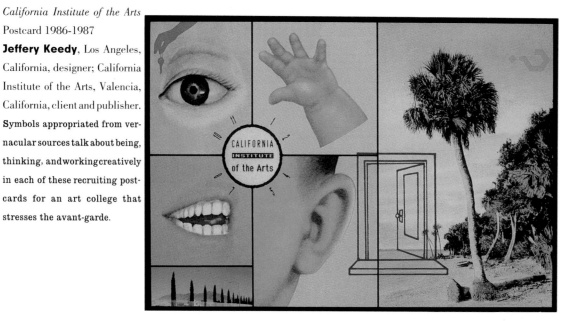

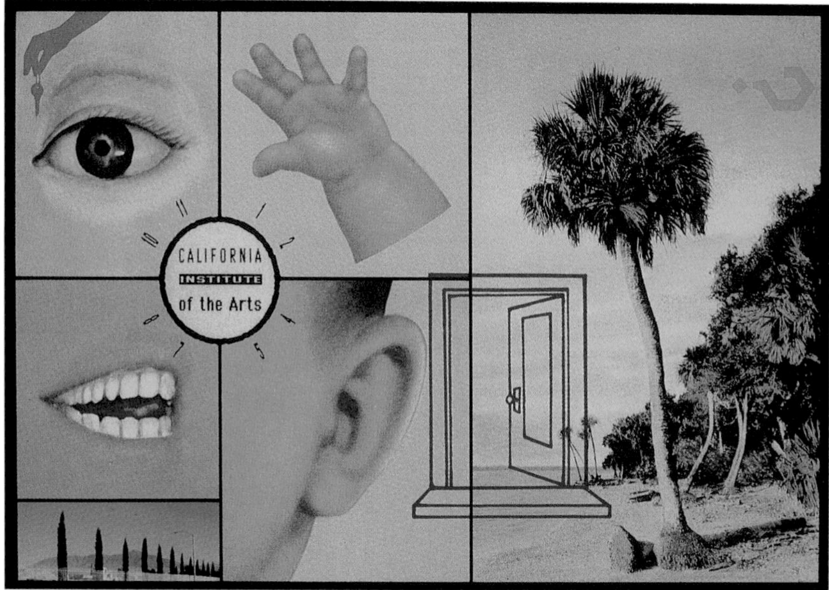
CALIFORNIA
INSTITUTE
of the Arts

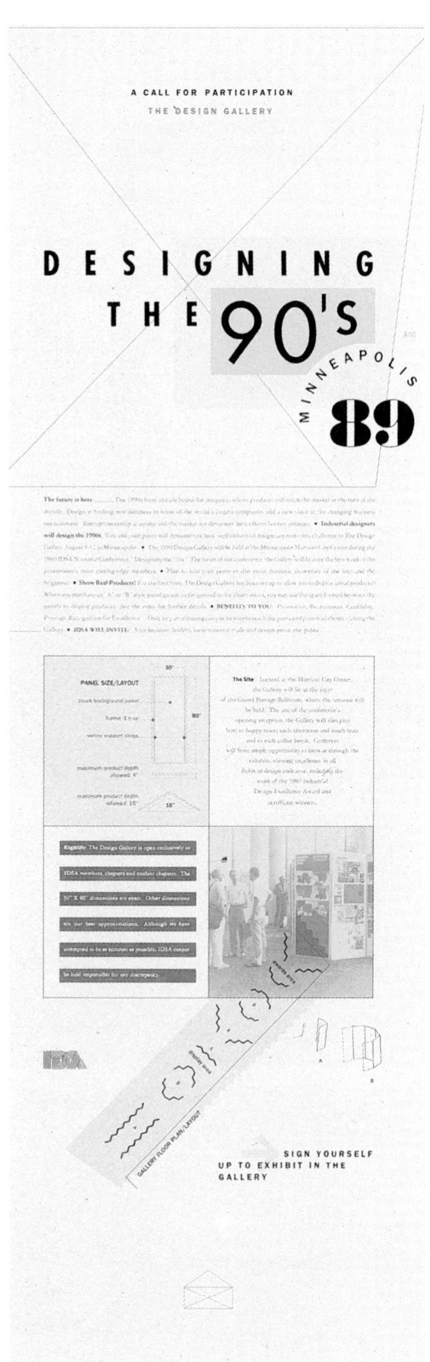
A CALL FOR PARTICIPATION
THE DESIGN GALLERY
DESIGNING
THE 90'S
MINNEAPOLIS
89
IDSA
SIGN YOURSELF
UP TO EXHIBIT IN THE
GALLERY

Designing the 90's Poster 1989

Jan Marcus Jancourt, Minneapolis, Minnesota, designer; Industrial Designers Society of America, Great Falls, Virginia, client and publisher.

This poster announces the 1989 IDSA conference.

AN
EVENING
OF
DANCE
CRANBROOK/
KINGSWOOD DANCERS
MAY
19 20 21
Director
Jessica Sinclair
8 O'CLOCK
CRANBROOK
P.A.C.
$2 Students,
$3 All Others
850 Lone Pine Road

An Evening of Dance Poster 1989

Edward McDonald, Ann Arbor, Michigan, designer; Cranbrook Kingswood School, Bloomfield Hills, Michigan, client and publisher.

A poster full of unconventional energy announces a dance performance.

artWORKS
YOUR NAME
170 S. LA BREA AVE.
(213)934·2205
ca. 90036
LOS ANGELES
STAMP

Artworks Postcard 1988

Jeffery Keedy, Los Angeles, California, designer; Artworks Artists' Books, Los Angeles, California, client and publisher.

This postcard transforms a familiar commercial printing paper stock with refined, vernacular typography.

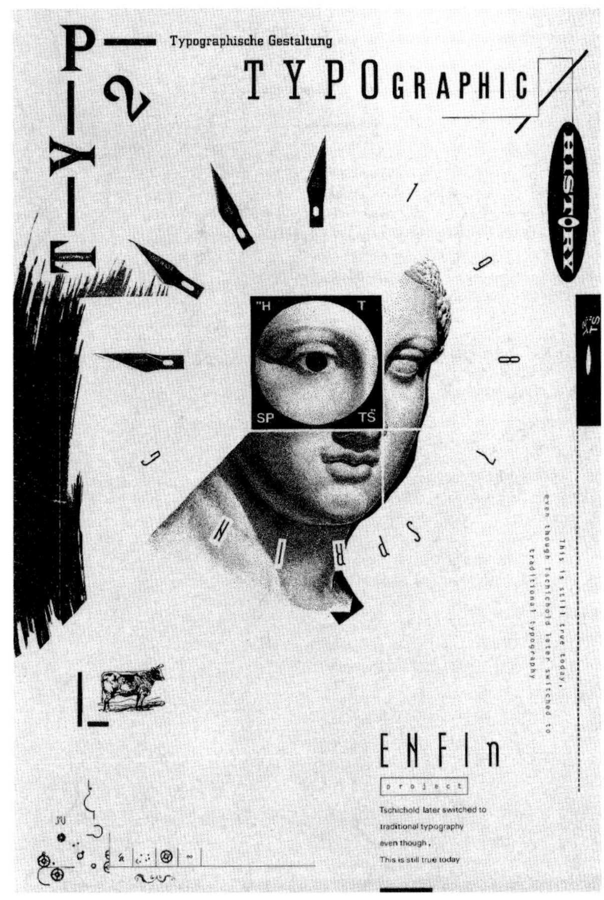
Typographische Gestaltung
TYPOGRAPHIC
HISTORY
This is still true today,
even though Tschichold later switched to
traditional typography
ENFIn
project
Tschichold later switched to
traditional typography
even though,
This is still true today

TYPIS COMPUTERUS
VISION
READING
Once upon a time, it was widely believed that typography was a type of language unto itself, that runs parallel to the written word. The specific significance of the signs of this typographic language were regulated by the craftsmen who practiced the typographic arts. Therefore, they alone could accurately evaluate the use/value of the art. However as language use multiplied and expanded through time, typography expanded far beyond the reaches of the craftsman. Now typography is straining at the farthest edge of language. Keep on reading into the shadow of language.
PERSONAL VISION
PHILOSOPHY
THEORY
PROPAGANDA
DIGITAL POETICS
CULTURAL CRITIQUE
PRACTICE
AESTHETICS

Typographic History Course Poster 1987

Jan Marcus Jancourt, Minneapolis, Minnesota, designer; Minneapolis College of Art and Design, Minneapolis, Minnesota, client and publisher.

This poster blends typography and imagery to form diagrammatic symbols to announce a design history course.

Vision and Reading Magazine Page 1989

Jeffery Keedy, Los Angeles, California, designer; *Emigré* magazine, Berkeley, California, client and publisher.

This page in an experimental culture-and-design magazine discusses both visually and verbally the interaction of these two processes in the construction of meaning. It seeks to provoke the reader to reassess what is possible in graphic design.

JANUARY
EXHIBITIONS LOS ANGELES CONTEMPORARY
LACE
one

LACE Broadside 1989

Jeffery Keedy, Los Angeles, California, designer; Los Angeles Contemporary Exhibitions, Los Angeles, California, client and publisher.

This broadside employs pseudosymbolic techno-forms generated on a Macintosh computer for a cooperative avant-garde exhibition space.

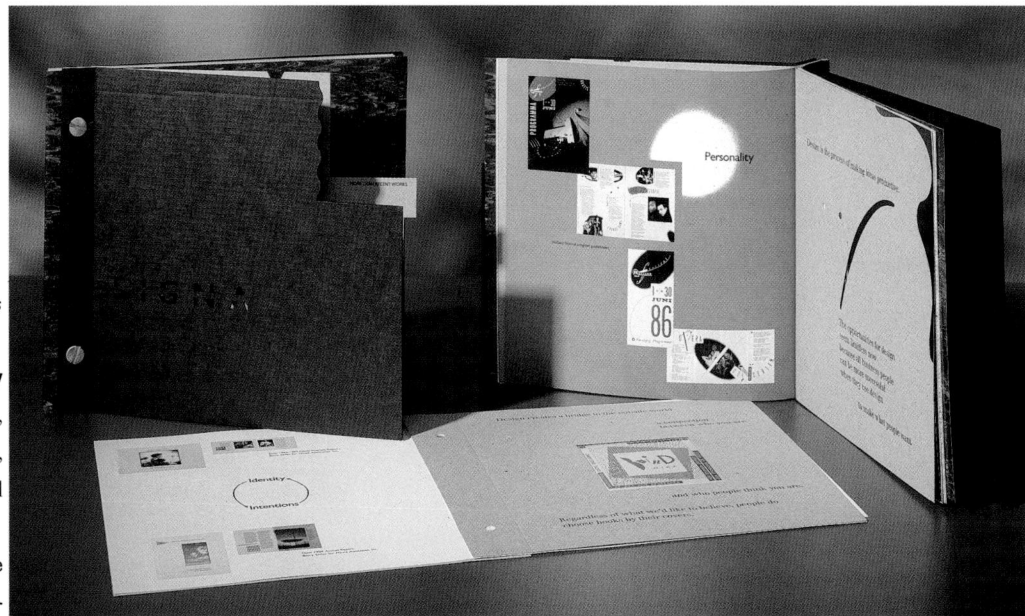
Personality
Identity
Intentions

Signa: More Than Recent Works Capabilities Brochure 1987

Edward McDonald / Barry Seifert, Signa, Ann Arbor, Michigan, designers; Signa, Inc., Ann Arbor, Michigan, client and publisher.

This small book combines a wide variety of paper stocks and editorial content in a refreshingly subjective approach to describing design services to prospective clients.

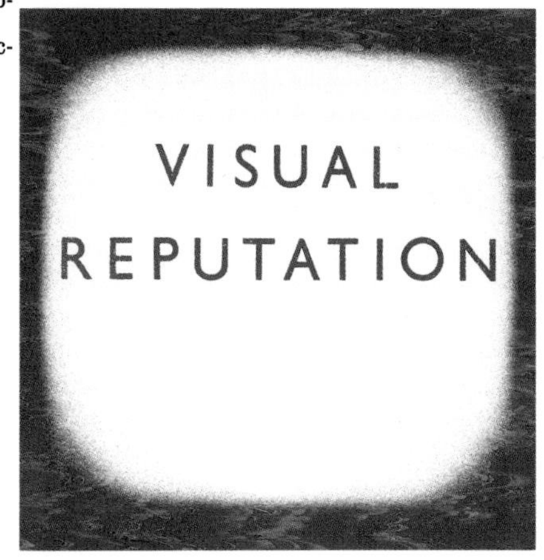
VISUAL
REPUTATION

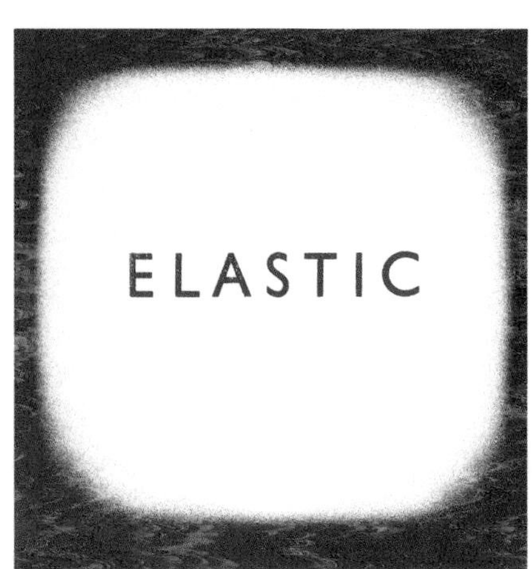
ELASTIC

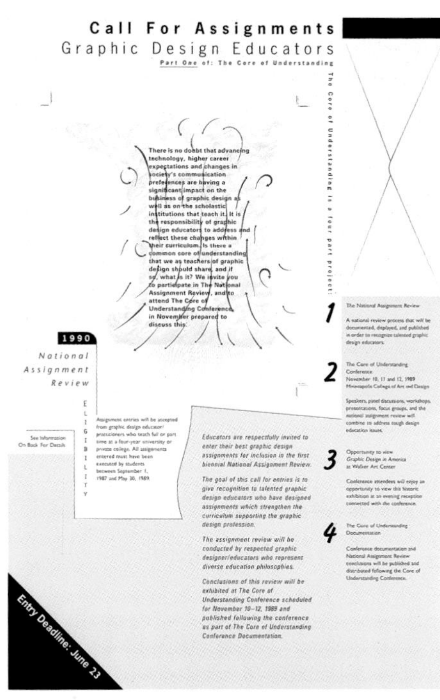
Call For Assignments
Graphic Design Educators
Part One of: The Core of Understanding
The Core of Understanding is a four part project:
There is no doubt that advancing technology, higher career expectations and changes in society's communication preferences are having a significant impact on the business of graphic design as well as on the scholastic institutions that teach it. It is the responsibility of graphic design educators to address and reflect these changes within their curriculum. Is there a common core of understanding that we as teachers of graphic design should share, and if so, what is it? We invite you to participate in The National Assignment Review, and to attend The Core of Understanding Conference in November prepared to discuss this.
1990
National
Assignment
Review
ELIGIBILITY
1
2
3
4
Entry Deadline: June 23

Core of Understanding Poster, 1989

Jan Marcus Jancourt, designer; Minneapolis College of Art and Design, Minneapolis, Minnesota, client and publisher.

A poster to announce a review of effective assignments was sent to North American graphic-design educators.

QUADRIO
F960/L F960/R
Artifort

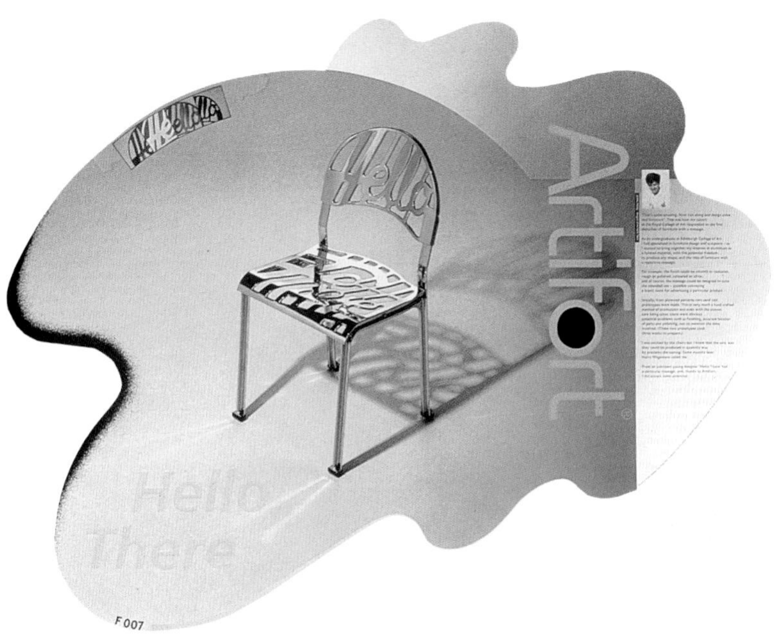
Artifort
Hello There
F007

Artifort Furniture Poster Series
1986
Jan Marcus Jancourt with Studio Dumbar, Den Haag, The Netherlands, designers; Artifort Company, Maastrict, The Netherlands, client and publisher.
Four posters feature works of contemporary furniture and their designers by a Dutch manufacturer. The die-cut posters' inventive sense of graphic space questions the normal assumption of the flat picture plane.

EC II Phone 1989
Eric Chan, ECCO, New York, designer; Becker Company, Connecticut, client and manufacturer.
The ergonomic profile of the handset offers the best angle for hearing and speaking. The curve of the base expresses the rhythm and smoothness of information flow.

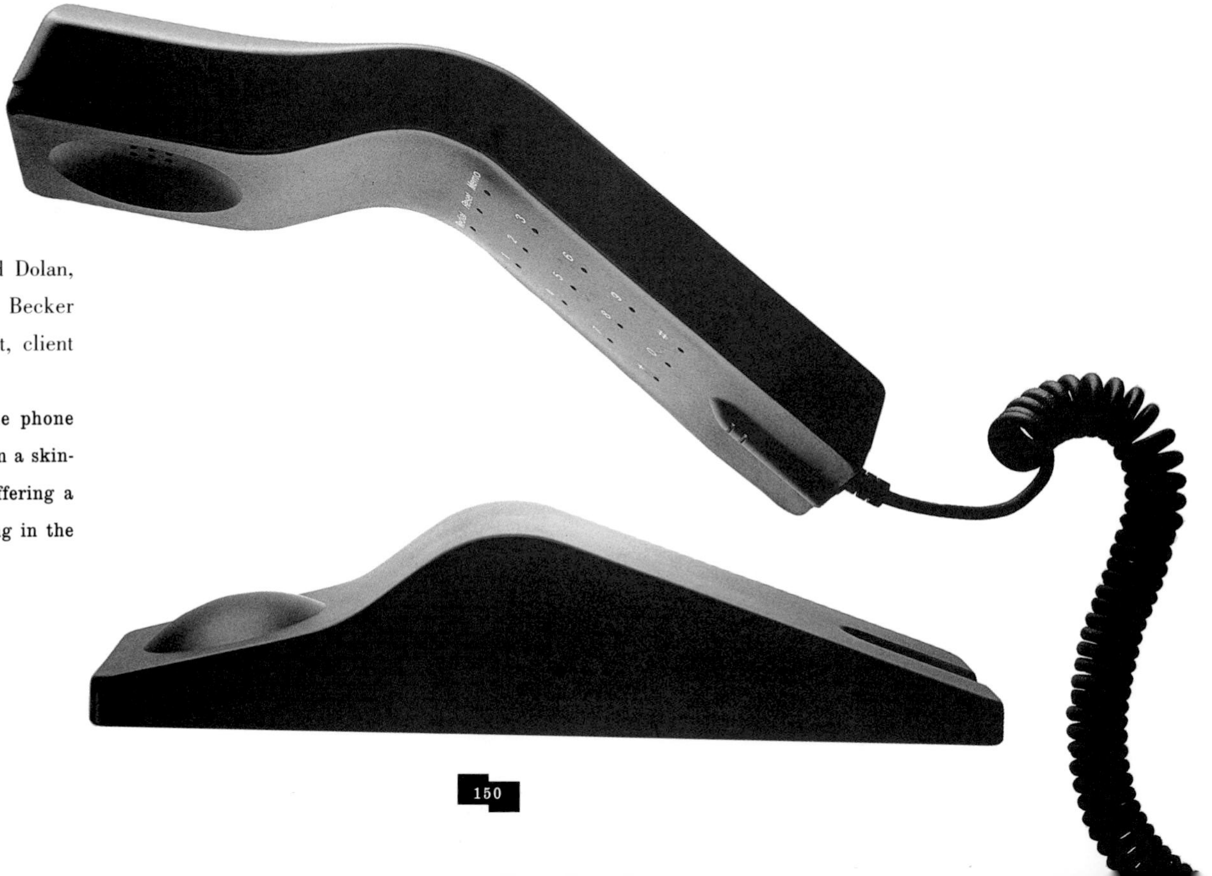

EC Phone 1987
Eric Chan, Chan and Dolan, New York, designer; Becker Company, Connecticut, client and manufacturer.
The soft curves of the phone handset are rendered in a skin-like resilient rubber offering a very comfortable feeling in the hand.

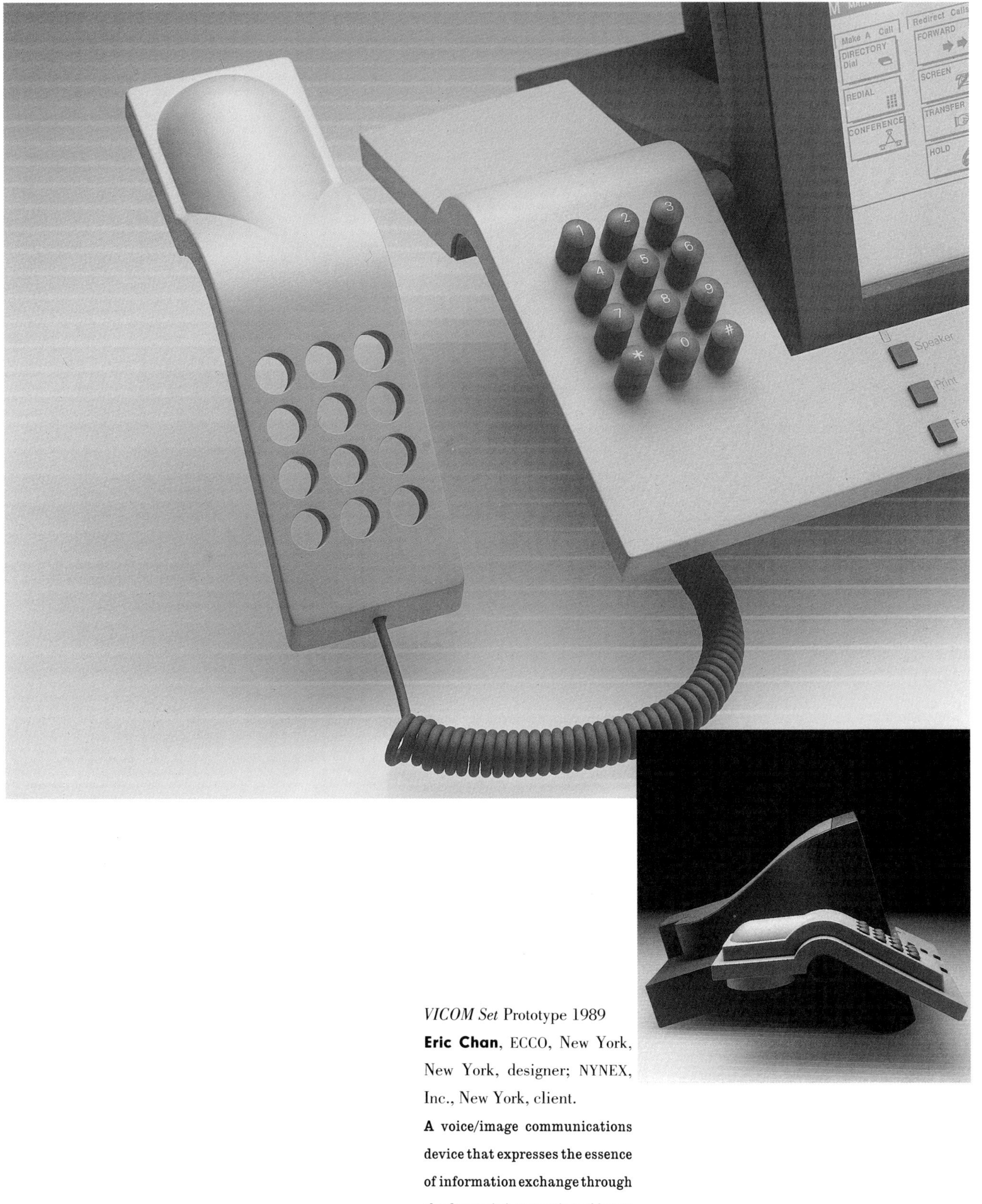
Make A Call
Redirect Calls
DIRECTORY
Dial
FORWARD
REDIAL
SCREEN
TRANSFER
CONFERENCE
HOLD
Speaker
Print

VICOM Set Prototype 1989
Eric Chan, ECCO, New York, New York, designer; NYNEX, Inc., New York, client.
A voice/image communications device that expresses the essence of information exchange through the dynamic integration of forms and surfaces.

Viewmaster Book Reader 1987
David Gresham and Martin Thaler, Design Logic, Chicago, Illinois, designers; Viewmaster Corporation, New York, client and manufacturer.
The book reader reads aloud while the child turns the pages. The playful form conjures up images of musical instruments and sound-making devices.

Look, sir. Look, sir.
Mr. Knox, sir.
Let's do tricks with
bricks and blocks, sir.
Let's do tricks with
chicks and clocks, sir.
Chicks with bricks come.
Chicks with blocks come.
Chicks with bricks and
blocks and clocks come.
8

Viewmaster Project 'n Sketch 1987
David Gresham and Martin Thaler, Design Logic, Chicago, Illinois, designers; Viewmaster Corporation, New York, client and manufacturer.
A children's drawing toy invoking playful images of the machine age. The image to be traced is projected onto a drawing pad surrounded by a picture frame .

Viewmaster Slide Viewer 1986
David Gresham and Martin Thaler, Design Logic, Chicago, Illinois, designers; Viewmaster Corporation, New York, client and manufacturer.
To celebrate the 50th anniversary of Viewmaster, the viewer was redesigned with a clear front panel, making the inner workings of the device visible while allowing light through the lens.

yellow

Workstation Terminal 1987

David Gresham and Martin Thaler, Design Logic, Chicago, Illinois, designers; RC Corporation, Ballerup, Denmark, client and manufacturer.

The display is presented as a simple facade with a complex composition of forms in back. The assemblage of forms behind allows the housing to grow to accept larger picture tubes without expensive retooling.

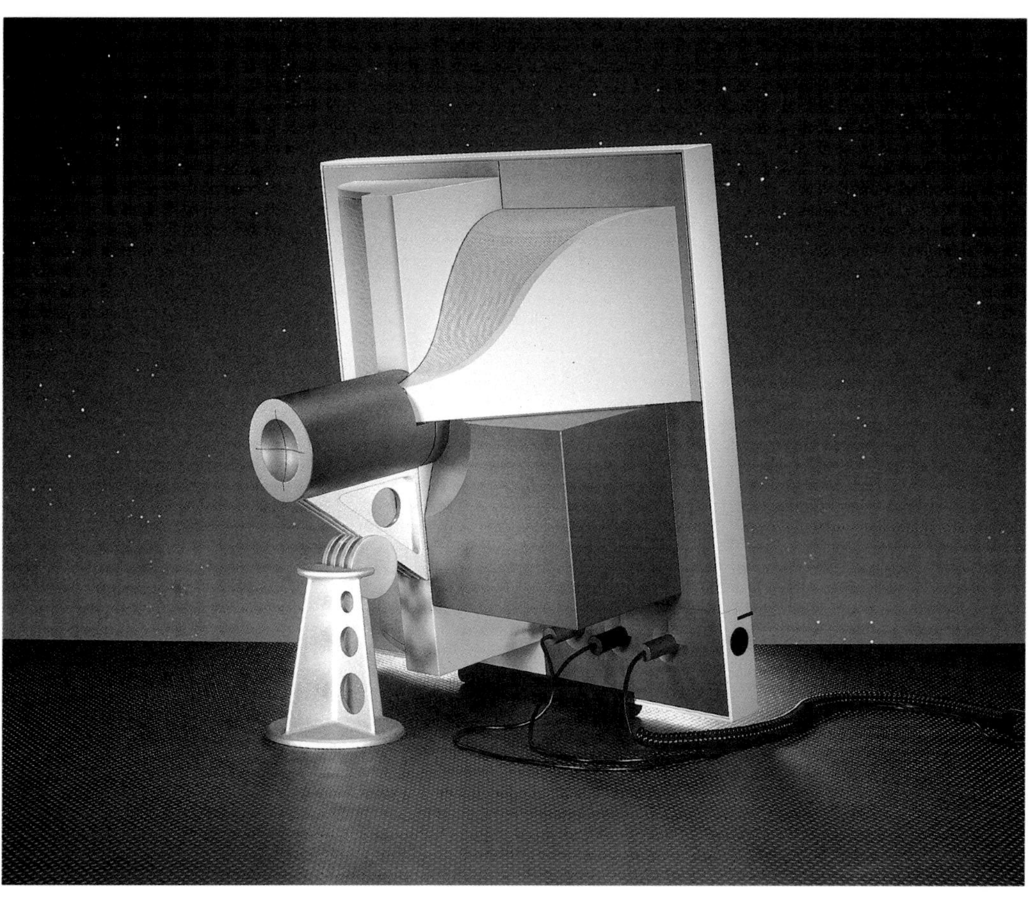

Workstation Terminal 1986

David Gresham and Martin Thaler, Design Logic, Chicago, Illinois, designers; RC Corporation, Ballerup, Denmark, client and manufacturer.

The gridded form of the monitor housing evokes the idea of the rational circuitry within.

L
R
signal: green
overload: red
load impedance adjust
(rear panel)
Apt Corporation
Cambridge, Massachusetts
Power Amplifier 1

Power Amplifier 1 1980

Charles Rozier, Charles Rozier Design, New York, designer; Apt Corporation, Cambridge, Massachusetts, client and manufacturer.

Only the essential modal information is present in this radically minimal power amplifier.

ADCOM
FM 102.5
balance
bass
treble
ADCOM

Adcom 500 Series Audio Components 1985

Charles Rozier, Charles Rozier Design, New York, designer; Adcom, East Brunswick, New Jersey, client and manufacturer.

Controls evoking the sensual feeling of early Bakelite radio knobs are contrasted with a minimalist, rational facade.

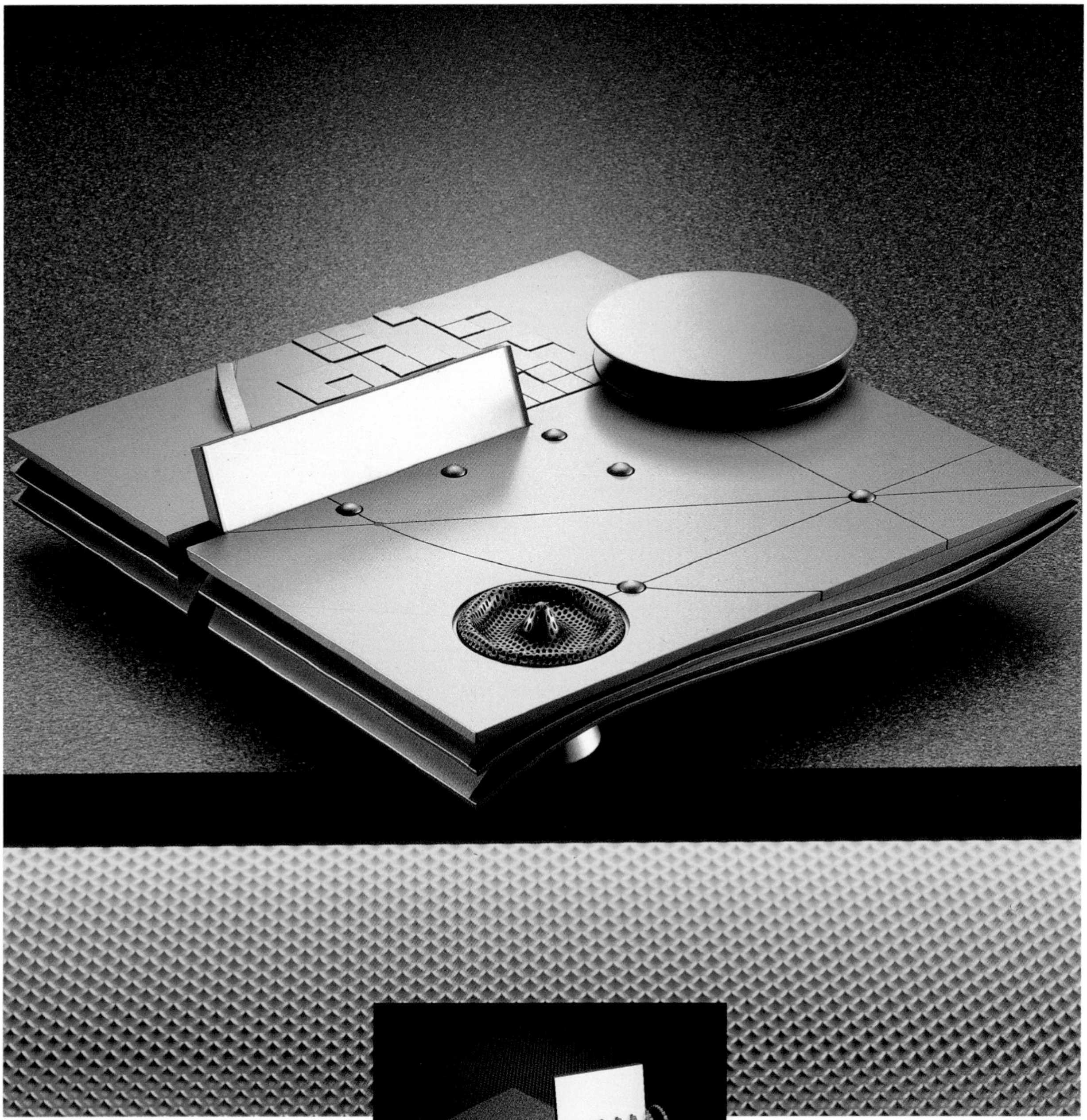

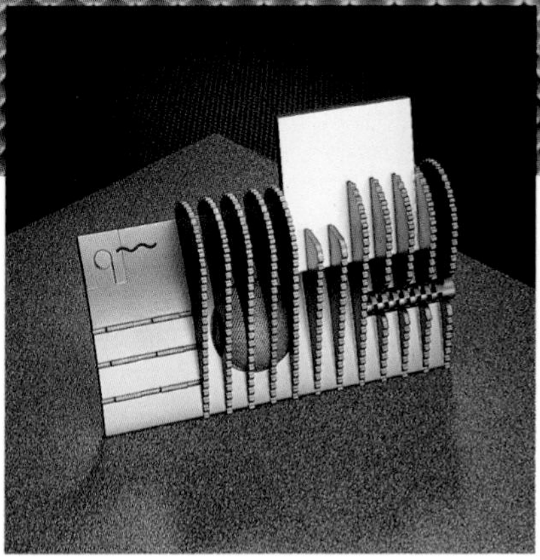

Dictaphone Models 1987
David Gresham and Martin Thaler, Design Logic, Chicago, Illinois, designers; Dictaphone Corporation, Rye, New York, client.

A series of studies for telephone answering machine designs. The machine is symbolically presented as a personal "mailbox," as a "head," and as "layers" of messages or information.

Corey & Company Greeting Cards 1986-1988
Scott Nash, Corey McPherson Nash, Watertown, Massachusetts, designer; Corey & Company, Watertown, Massachusetts, client and publisher.
These four studio promotion cards combine illustration, photography, and appropriated printed images in collage form.

NASTY SURPRISES in 2D
oh no!
oh no!
Z

Innova Postcards 1987
Craig Minor, Minor Design Associates, Houston, Texas, designer; Innova, Houston, Texas, client and publisher.
These postcards publicize a building of contract-furniture showrooms to the architecture and interior design professional community.

Swain School of Design Academic Catalog Cover 1986
Scott Nash, Corey McPherson Nash, Watertown, Massachusetts, designer; Swain School of Design, New Bedford, Massachusetts, client and publisher.
An abstracted eye interacts with water and materials to introduce the programs of this art-and-design college.

CATALOG 1986-87
EST. 1881
SWAIN SCHOOL OF DESIGN

I N N O V A
I N N O V A

American Style
White

The Soft Touch

American Style Magazine Covers and Interior Spreads 1987
Terri Ducay, Whittle Communications, Knoxville, Tennessee, designer; Whittle Communications, Knoxville, Tennessee, client and publisher.
A cover and interior format design for a magazine on American life-style trends featuring interior design, beauty, and fashion editorial matter.

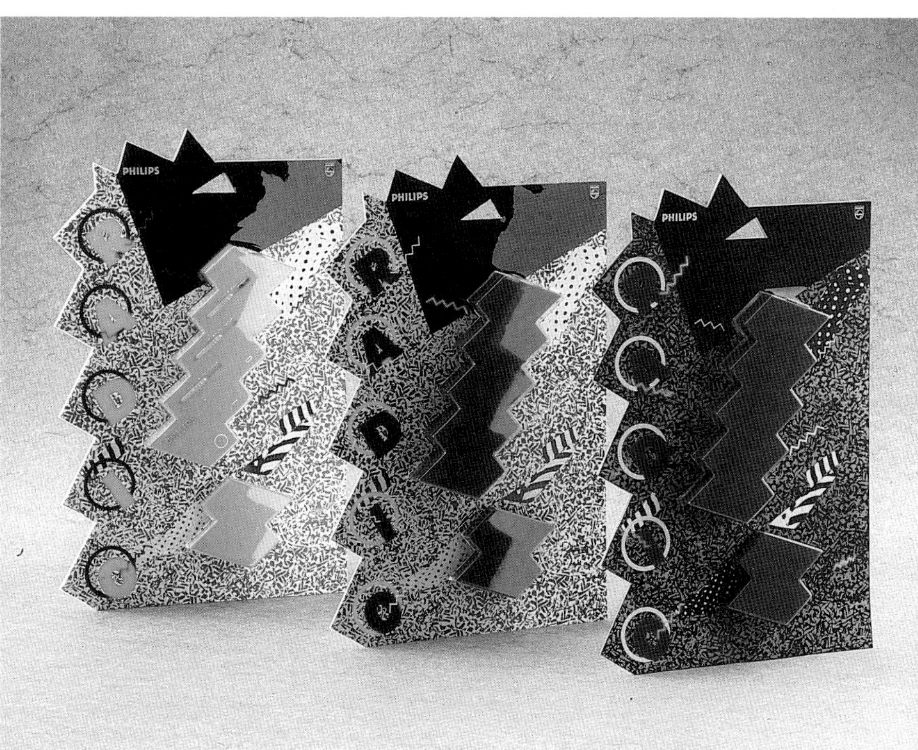
PHILIPS
PHILIPS
PHILIPS

Transistor Radio Package 1986
Terri Ducay, Philips Corporate Industrial Design, Eindhoven, The Netherlands, designer; N.V.Philips Company, Eindhoven, The Netherlands, client.
A package design solution for a small personal stereo/radio designed as pop jewelry for the youth market. The graphic designer collaborated with a product designer to place a consumer electronics product in a fashion environment.

Alle prijzen zijn inclusief servicekosten. Plaatsbespreken tot 31 augustus door overmaking op onze postgiro 316700 van de abonnementsgelden onder vermelding van de verlangde serie(s). Vanaf 13 september aan de zaal Diligentia van 10.00-14.00 uur en telefonisch van 10.00-15.00 uur (behalve op zondag en maandag). Telefoon 651851.
1988•89 SERIE D
16 okt 88 Hakon Austbö
Claude Helffer
06 nov 88 Jeremy Menuhin
11 dec 88 Imogen Cooper
26 dec 88 2e Kerstdag
Daniël Wayenberg
01 jan 89 Nieuwjaarsdag
Theo Bruins
15 jan 89 Eliane Rodrigues
12 feb 89 Bella Davidovich
12 maart 89 Malcolm Frager
Losse kaarten resp. ƒ 25,-/ ƒ 30,-* ƒ 15,-/ ƒ 17,50* * afhankelijk van de pianist
Zondag aanvang 14.30 uur
Abonnement
CJP, jongeren tot 21 jaar, studenten Conservatorium
SERIE D
Diligentia
SEIZOEN
1988•89
SERIE
D 8 Internationale Pianorecitals

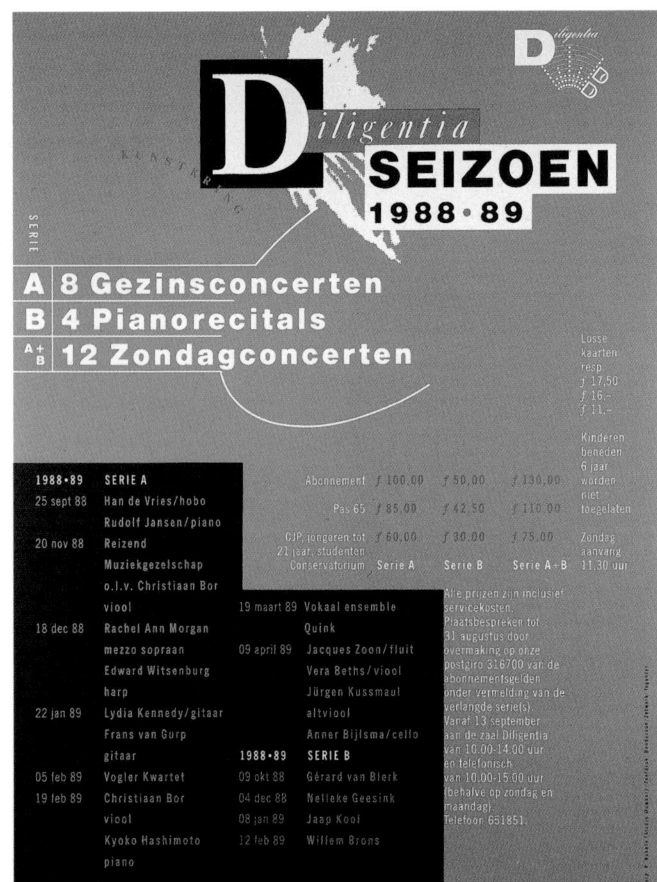
Diligentia
KUNSTKRING
SEIZOEN
1988•89
SERIE
A 8 Gezinsconcerten
B 4 Pianorecitals
A+B 12 Zondagconcerten
Losse kaarten resp. ƒ 17,50 ƒ 16,- ƒ 11,-
Kinderen beneden 6 jaar worden niet toegelaten
Zondag aanvang 11.30 uur
Abonnement ƒ 100,00 ƒ 50,00 ƒ 130,00
Pas 65 ƒ 85,00 ƒ 42,50 ƒ 110,00
CJP, jongeren tot 21 jaar, studenten Conservatorium ƒ 60,00 ƒ 30,00 ƒ 75,00
Serie A Serie B Serie A+B
1988•89 SERIE A
25 sept 88 Han de Vries/hobo
Rudolf Jansen/piano
20 nov 88 Reizend Muziekgezelschap o.l.v. Christiaan Bor viool
18 dec 88 Rachel Ann Morgan mezzo sopraan
Edward Witsenburg harp
22 jan 89 Lydia Kennedy/gitaar
Frans van Gurp gitaar
05 feb 89 Vogler Kwartet
19 feb 89 Christiaan Bor viool
Kyoko Hashimoto piano
19 maart 89 Vokaal ensemble Quink
09 april 89 Jacques Zoon/fluit
Vera Beths/viool
Jürgen Kussmaul altviool
Anner Bijlsma/cello
1988•89 SERIE B
09 okt 88 Gérard van Blerk
04 dec 88 Nelleke Geesink
08 jan 89 Jaap Kool
12 feb 89 Willem Brons
Alle prijzen zijn inclusief servicekosten. Plaatsbespreken tot 31 augustus door overmaking op onze postgiro 316700 van de abonnementsgelden onder vermelding van de verlangde serie(s). Vanaf 13 september aan de zaal Diligentia van 10.00-14.00 uur en telefonisch van 10.00-15.00 uur (behalve op zondag en maandag). Telefoon 651851.

Diligentia Posters 1988
Robert Nakata, Studio Dumbar, Den Haag, The Netherlands, designer; Kunstkring Diligentia, Den Haag, The Netherlands, client and publisher.
Two posters of a series publicizing classical music performances.

Diligentia Logotype 1988
Robert Nakata, Studio Dumbar, Den Haag, The Netherlands, designer; Kunstkring Diligentia, Den Haag, The Netherlands, client and publisher.
This logotype for a theater offering plays, variety shows, and classical music abstracts theater seating with a playful reference to musical stanzas and sound waves.

Diligentia

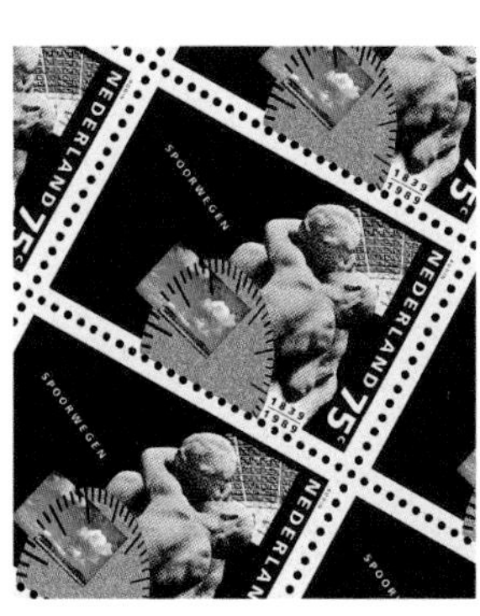
NEDERLAND
SPOORWEGEN
75

75-cent Postage Stamp 1989
Robert Nakata, Studio Dumbar, Den Haag, The Netherlands, designer; Netherlands Postal Authority, Den Haag, The Netherlands, client and publisher.
A postage stamp to commemorate the 150th anniversary of the Nederlandse Spoorwegen, the Dutch national railway. The familiar Rodin sculpture, "The Kiss," playfully refers to the greetings and farewells that accompany the arriving and departing of trains.

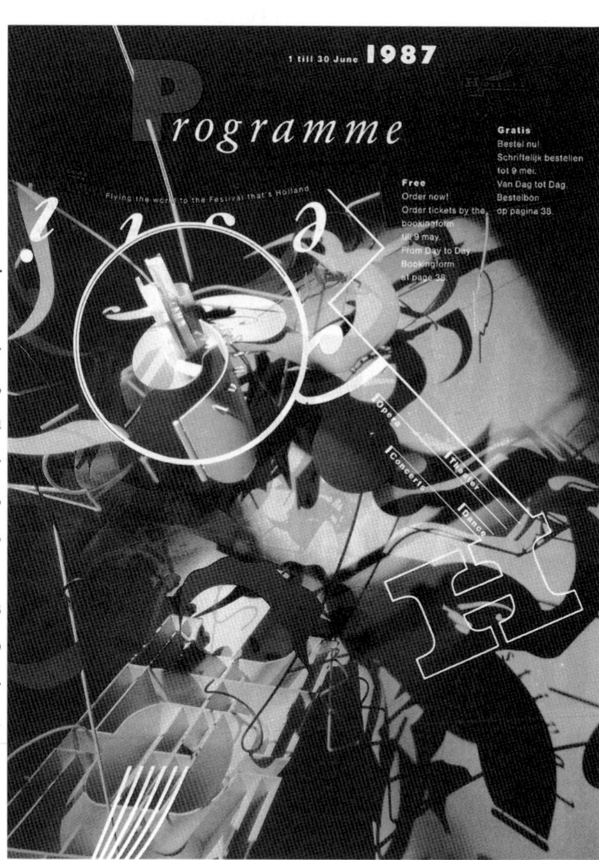
1 till 30 June 1987
Programme
Gratis
Bestel nu!
Schriftelijk bestellen
tot 9 mei.
Van Dag tot Dag.
Bestelbon
op pagina 38.
Free
Order now!
Order tickets by the
bookingform
till 9 may.
From Day to Day
Bookingform
at page 38.
Opera
Concert
Theater
Dance

Holland Festival Program Cover 1987
Robert Nakata, Studio Dumbar, Den Haag, The Netherlands, designer; Lex van Peterson, Den Haag, The Netherlands, photographer; The Holland Festival, Amsterdam, The Netherlands, client and publisher.
A staged photograph interplays with typographic elements to create an energetic festive attitude for an annual cultural event.

Fort Asperen Logotype 1988
Robert Nakata, Studio Dumbar, Den Haag, The Netherlands, designer; Fort Asperen, Acquoy, The Netherlands, client and publisher.
This logotype for a sixteenth-century Dutch fortress recently converted to an art museum refers to its historical flooding to resist invaders in wartime.

FORT ASPEREN

Theater Krasnaja Presjna/
De Meeuw
Het Litouws Theater
van de Jeugd/Oom Vanja
Theater van de Jonge
Toeschouwers/Hondehart
15/16
JUNI
19/20
JUNI
THEATER UIT DE
SOVJET
UNIE
Holland Festival

Holland Festival Poster 1989
Robert Nakata, Studio Dumbar, Den Haag, The Netherlands, designer; Lex van Peterson and Gert Dumbar, Den Haag, The Netherlands, photographers; The Holland Festival, Amsterdam, The Netherlands, client and publisher.
To announce a series of cultural events featuring Russian music, theater, and dance, a staged photograph interacts with typographic elements.

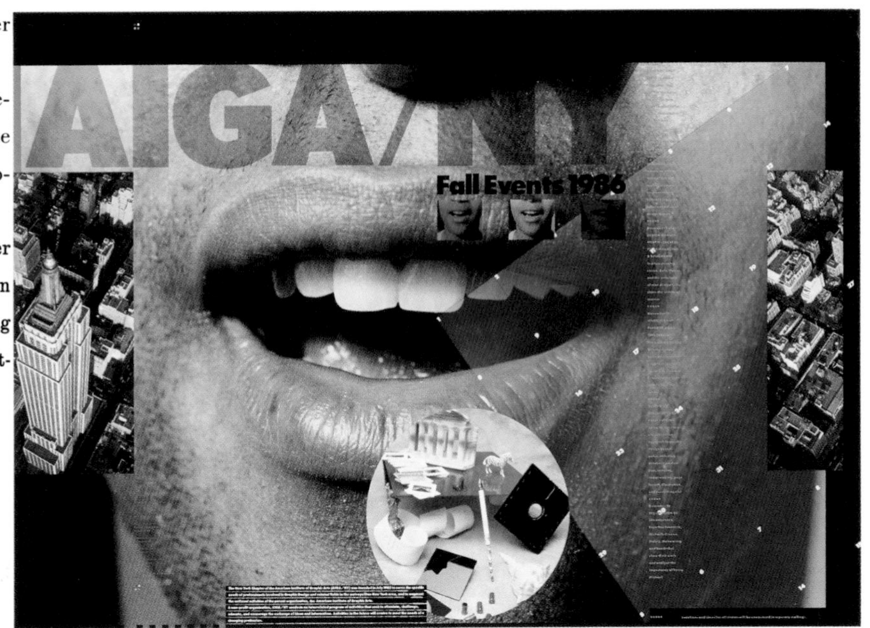
AIGA/NY
Fall Events 1986

AIGA/NY Fall Events Poster 1986

Richelle Huff, New York, designer; The American Institute of Graphic Arts New York Chapter, client and publisher.

The open mouth on this poster for a professional organization of graphic designers is calling everyone to come to the meetings.

FIFTH
ANNUAL
INTERNATIONAL
FURNITURE
Progressive Architecture
COMPETITION

International Furniture Competition Poster 1985

Richelle Huff, *Progressive Architecture* magazine, Stamford, Connecticut, designer; *Progressive Architecture* magazine, Stamford, Connecticut, client and publisher.

This poster montages images, geometric forms, and materials to announce the exhibition of the fifth furniture competition sponsored by Progressive Architecture magazine.

Dutch Graphic Design Exhibition Poster 1987
Lucille Tenazas, Tenazas Design, San Francisco, California, designer; The American Institute of Graphic Arts San Francisco Chapter, client and publisher.
To announce an exhibition on recent Dutch graphic design, images of the Netherlands have been presented in an irreverent collage in the spirit of the Dutch work.

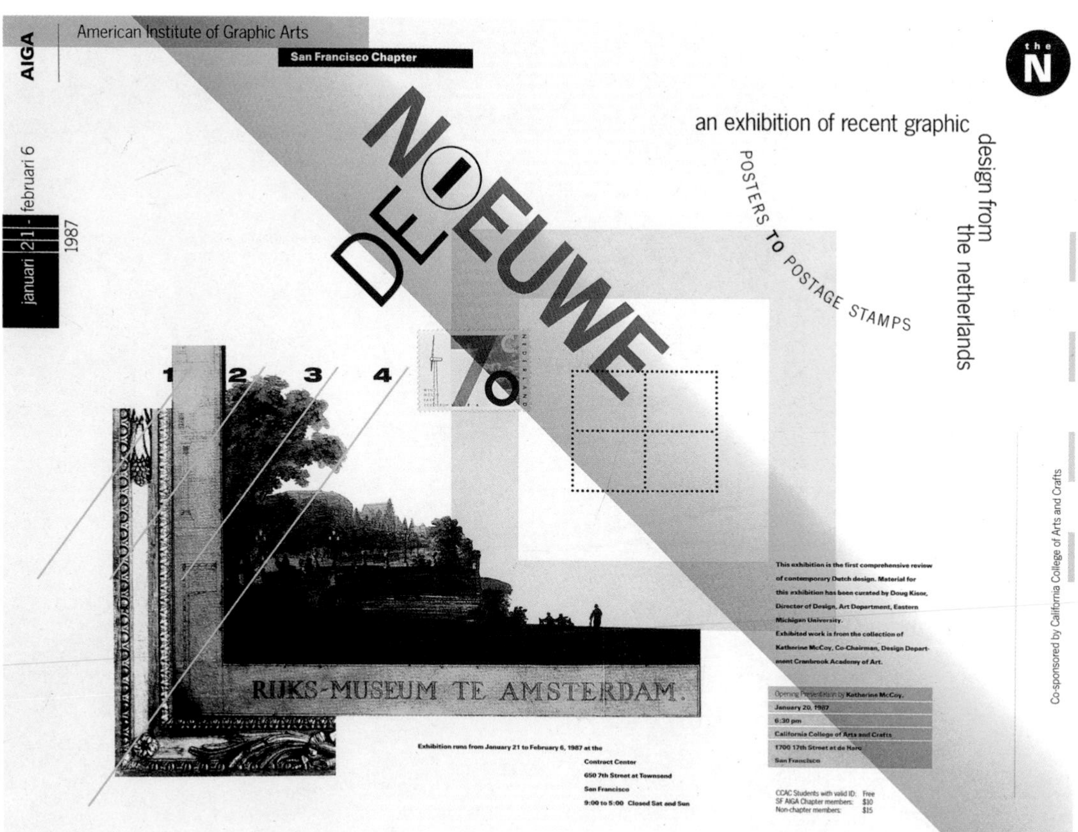

AIGA
American Institute of Graphic Arts
San Francisco Chapter
januari 21 - februari 6 1987
DE NIEUWE
an exhibition of recent graphic design from the netherlands
POSTERS TO POSTAGE STAMPS
1 2 3 4
RIJKS-MUSEUM TE AMSTERDAM.
This exhibition is the first comprehensive review of contemporary Dutch design. Material for this exhibition has been curated by Doug Kisor, Director of Design, Art Department, Eastern Michigan University.
Exhibited work is from the collection of Katherine McCoy, Co-Chairman, Design Department Cranbrook Academy of Art.
Opening Presentation by Katherine McCoy.
January 20, 1987
6:30 pm
California College of Arts and Crafts
1700 17th Street at de Haro
San Francisco
Exhibition runs from January 21 to February 6, 1987 at the
Contract Center
650 7th Street at Townsend
San Francisco
9:00 to 5:00 Closed Sat and Sun
CCAC Students with valid ID: Free
SF AIGA Chapter members: $10
Non-chapter members: $15
Co-sponsored by California College of Arts and Crafts

Progressive Architecture Magazine Poster Series 1985
Richelle Huff, *Progressive Architecture* magazine, Stamford, Connecticut, designer; Michael Geiger, New York, photographer; *Progressive Architecture* magazine, Stamford, Connecticut, client and publisher.
This poster series employs staged photography by an important American photographer to suggest the context in which architecture is created.

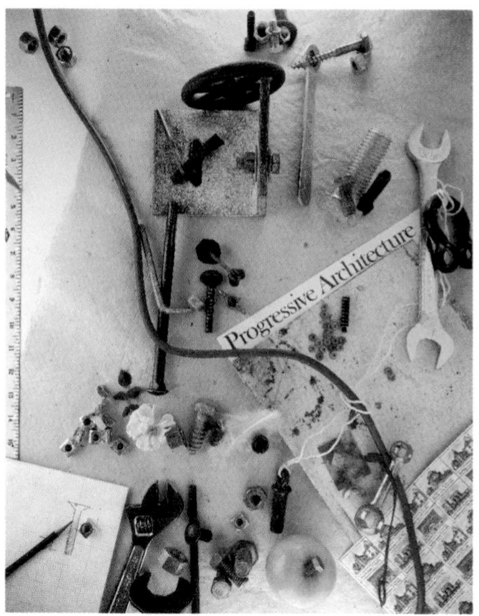

Progressive Architecture

Progressive Architecture

MIES
AALTO
Progressive Architecture

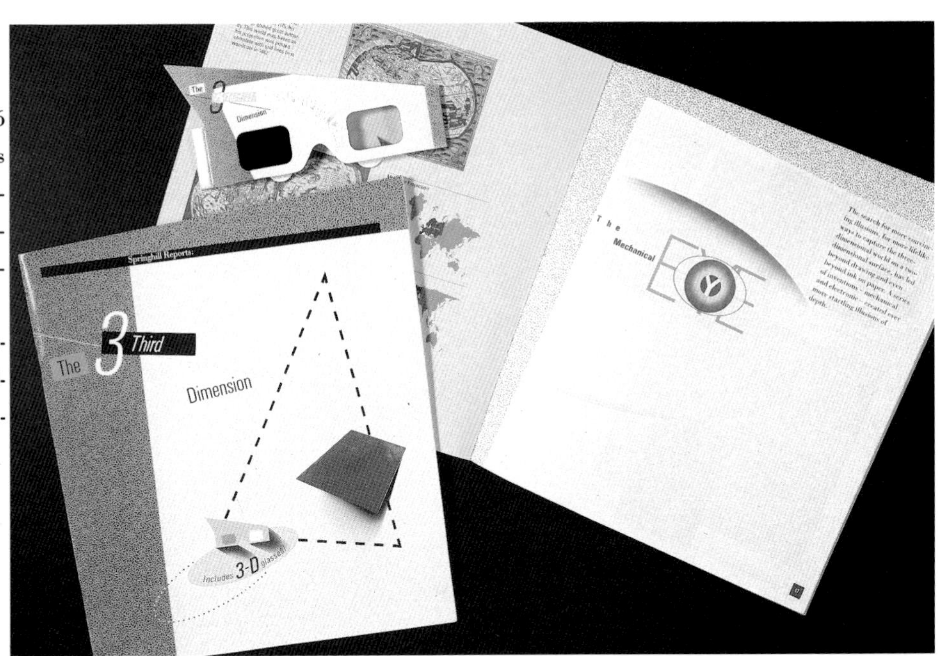
Springhill Reports:
The
3
Third
Dimension
Includes 3-D glasses
The
Mechanical

Third Dimension Brochure 1986
Lucille Tenazas, Tenazas Design, San Francisco, California, designer; International Paper Company, Knoxville, Tennessee, client and publisher.
This brochure explores the phenomena of three-dimensional illusions on paper for a paper-company promotion.

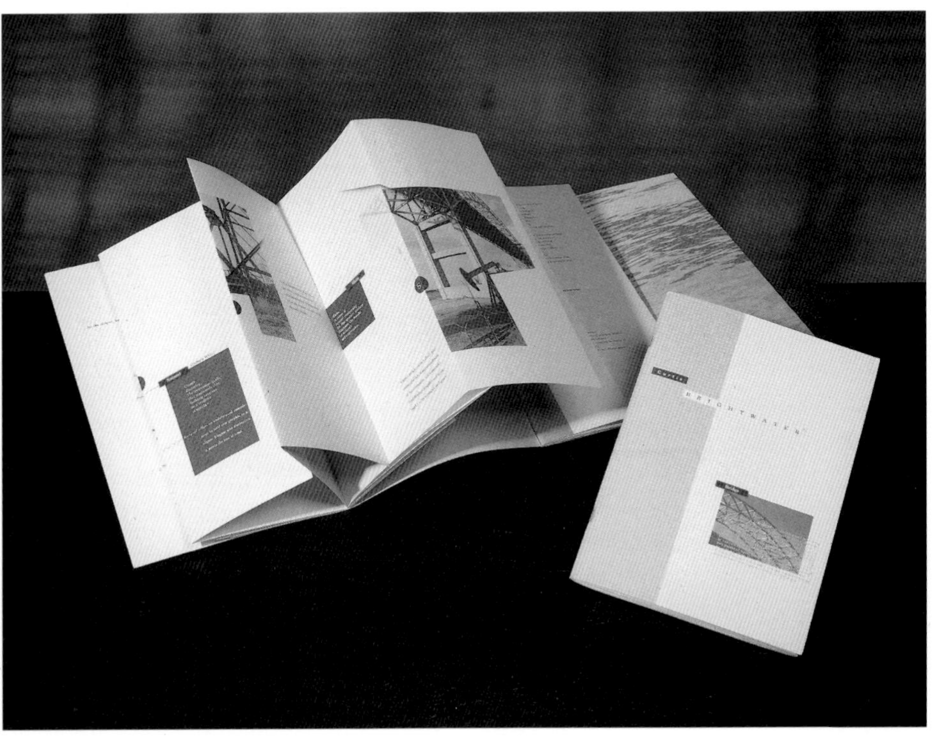

Curtis Brightwater Bridge Brochure 1989
Lucille Tenazas, Tenazas Design, San Francisco, California, designer; Richard Barnes, San Francisco, California, photographer; James River Paper, Southampton, Pennsylvania, client and publisher.
The metaphor of "bridge" suggests that paper links communications, concept to execution. A variety of printing papers is assembled in an unconventional double binding.

INTERNATIONAL
Printing Week

International Printing Week Poster 1986
Christopher Ozubko with W. Joseph Gagnon, Ozubko Design, Seattle, Washington, designers; Washington Alaska Printing Industries of America and Seattle Club of Printing House Craftsmen, Seattle, Washington, clients and publishers.
A photographic and graphic-arts process montage demonstrates a wide range of sophisticated printing techniques in a celebration of the state of the craft.

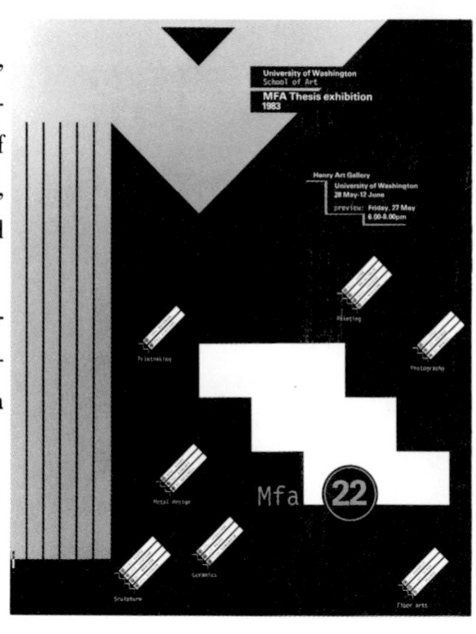
University of Washington
School of Art
MFA Thesis exhibition
1983
Mfa
22

MFA Thesis Exhibition Poster 1983
Christopher Ozubko, Ozubko Design, Seattle, Washington, designer; University of Washington Department of Art, Seattle, Washington, client and publisher.
This poster employs a playful diagrammatic typographic composition to announce an exhibition of fine art.

מעגל

Ma'agal Poster 1988
Kenneth Windsor, Metamark International, Tel Aviv, Israel, designer; Israel Electric Company, Tel Aviv, Israel, client and publisher.
"Circuit" is the English-language translation for this large poster announcing the opening of an alternative artists' space in the Israel Electric Company. Hebrew characters are abstracted and layered with notated architectural forms.

DESIGN IN
The Cranbrook Vision 1925~1950
AMERICA

R. CRAIG MILLER
5
INTERIOR DESIGN
AND FURNITURE

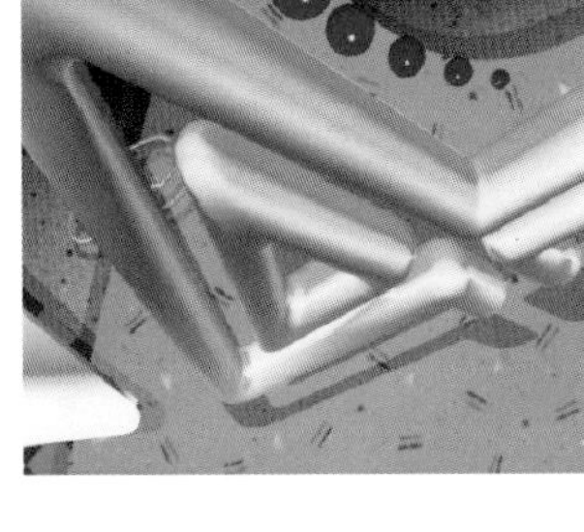

Design in America: The Cranbrook Vision 1929-1950 Book 1983
Kenneth Windsor, Design Department, Harry N. Abrams, Inc., New York, designer; Harry N. Abrams, Inc., New York, client and publisher.
A book on the historical work and significance of Cranbrook Academy of Art.

WDIV-TV Station Identification Computer Animation 1985
James A. Houff, WDIV-TV Design Department, Detroit, Michigan, design director; WDIV-TV, Detroit, Michigan, client and publisher.
Typography, materials, shapes, and light flow through space and time to build a graphic identity for Channel 4, the Detroit NBC-affiliate television station.

TOGETHER

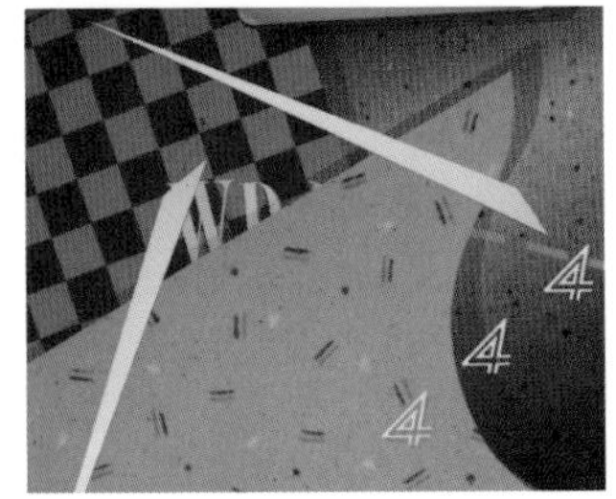

WDIV

Broadcast Designers Annual Conference Posters 1987-1989
James A. Houff, WDIV-TV Design Department, Detroit, Michigan, designer; Broadcast Designers Association, Inc., San Francisco, California, client and publisher.
These limited-edition silkscreen posters employ complex layering of photographic and typographic imagery to evoke the character of the location of each year's conference. The eye is a recurring theme in the posters for Los Angeles and Detroit.

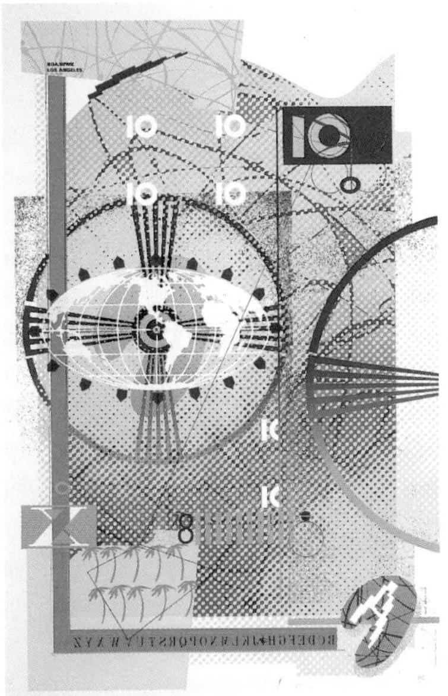

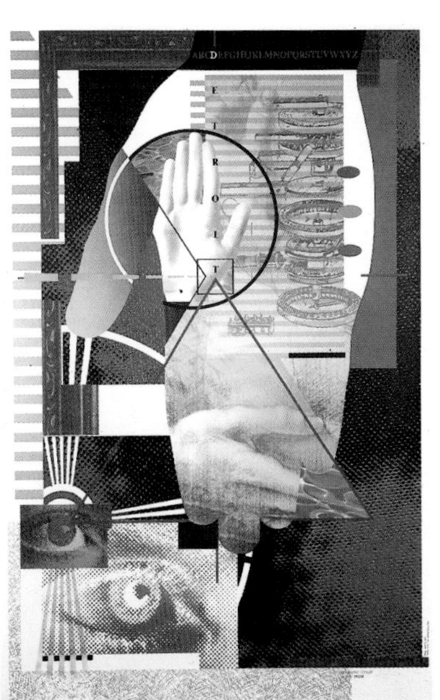

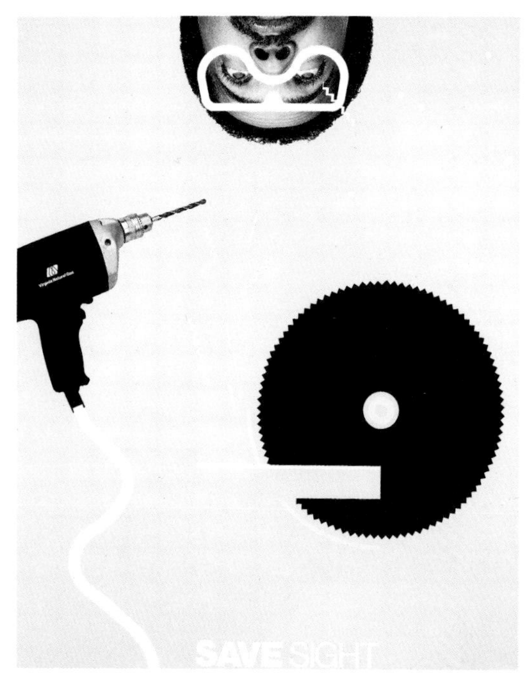
SAVE SIGHT

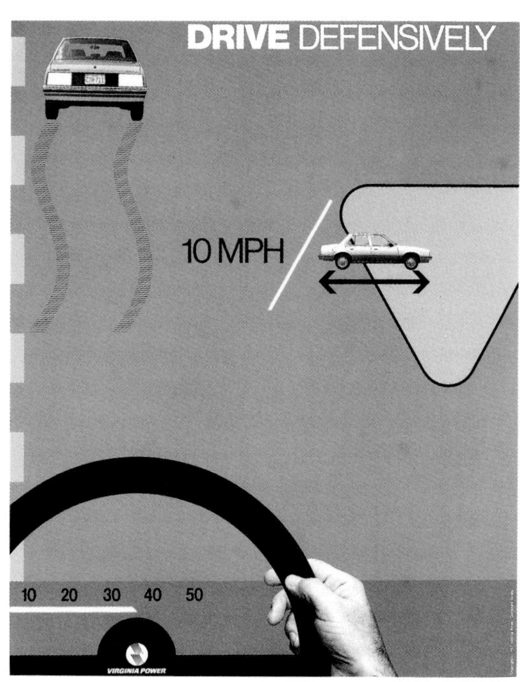
DRIVE DEFENSIVELY
10 MPH
10 20 30 40 50
VIRGINIA POWER

Virginia Power Public Safety Posters 1987

Kevin Cahill / Meredith Davis / Robert Meganck, Communications Design, Richmond, Virginia, designers; Virginia Power Company, Richmond, Virginia, client and publisher.

Through a playful use of image and symbols, these posters communicate safety caution in daily life.

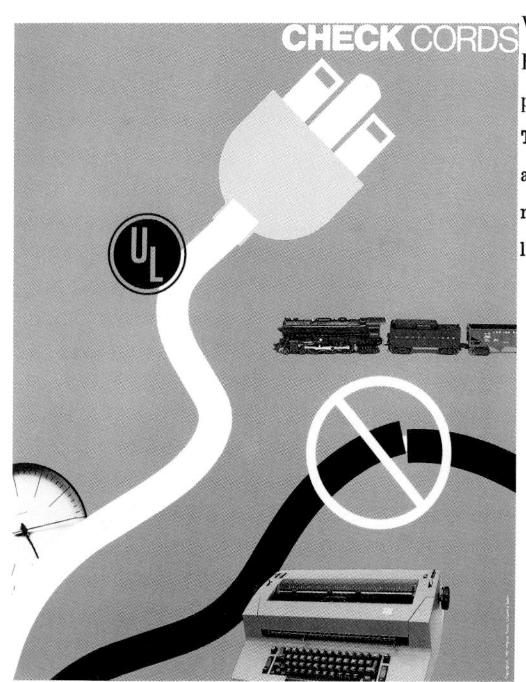
CHECK CORDS
UL

Canada
36

36-cent Postage Stamp 1987
Richard Kerr, Design Source, Toronto, Canada, designer; The Canada Post Corporation, client and publisher.
Engineering for electronics and industry is the subject of this Canadian postage stamp.

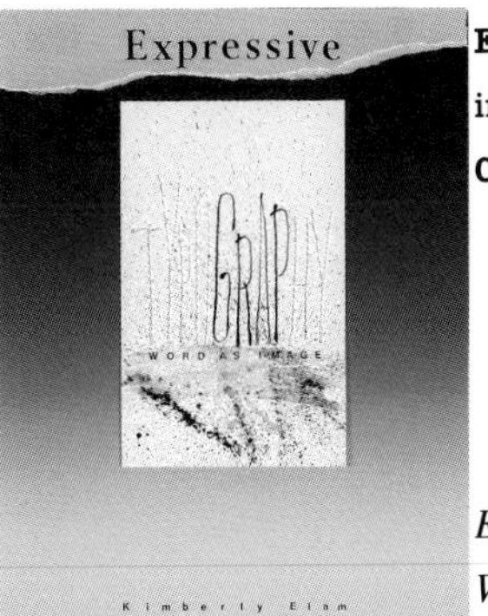
Expressive
WORD AS IMAGE
Kimberly Elam

Expressive Typography: The Word as Image Book 1989
Kimberly Elam, Columbus, Ohio, designer and author; Van Nostrand Reinhold, New York, client and publisher.
This book-cover design playfully communicates the expressive nature of typography.

Art in America Guide to Museums, Galleries and Artists 1989
Mary Sillman, *Art in America* Art Department, New York, designer; *Art in America*, New York, client and publisher.
A playful publication cover for an annual magazine supplement.

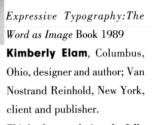

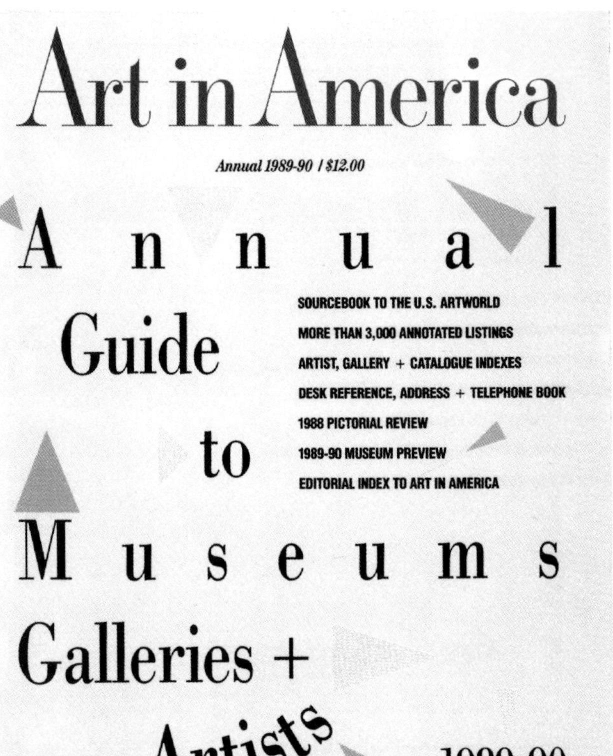
Art in America
Annual 1989-90 / $12.00
Annual
Guide
to
Museums
Galleries +
Artists
SOURCEBOOK TO THE U.S. ARTWORLD
MORE THAN 3,000 ANNOTATED LISTINGS
ARTIST, GALLERY + CATALOGUE INDEXES
DESK REFERENCE, ADDRESS + TELEPHONE BOOK
1988 PICTORIAL REVIEW
1989-90 MUSEUM PREVIEW
EDITORIAL INDEX TO ART IN AMERICA
1989-90

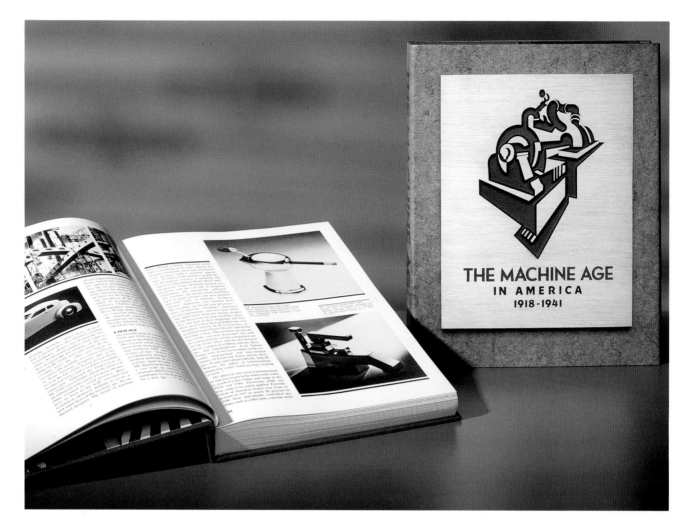

The Machine Age in America Book 1985

Michael Hentges, Harry N. Abrams, Inc., Design Department, New York, designer; Harry N. Abrams, Inc., New York, client and publisher.

This extensive book on early-twentieth-century American product design evokes the stylized geometry and elegant industrial materials of the era.

BankStreet
court

Bank Street Court Poster 1987

Mary Lou Hecht, Hecht Design, Philadelphia, Pennsylvania, designer; James B. Abbott, New York, photographer; The Rothschild Company, Philadelphia, Pennsylvania, client and publisher.

This poster employs photomontage to announce the completion of an adaptive reuse renovation in an urban setting.

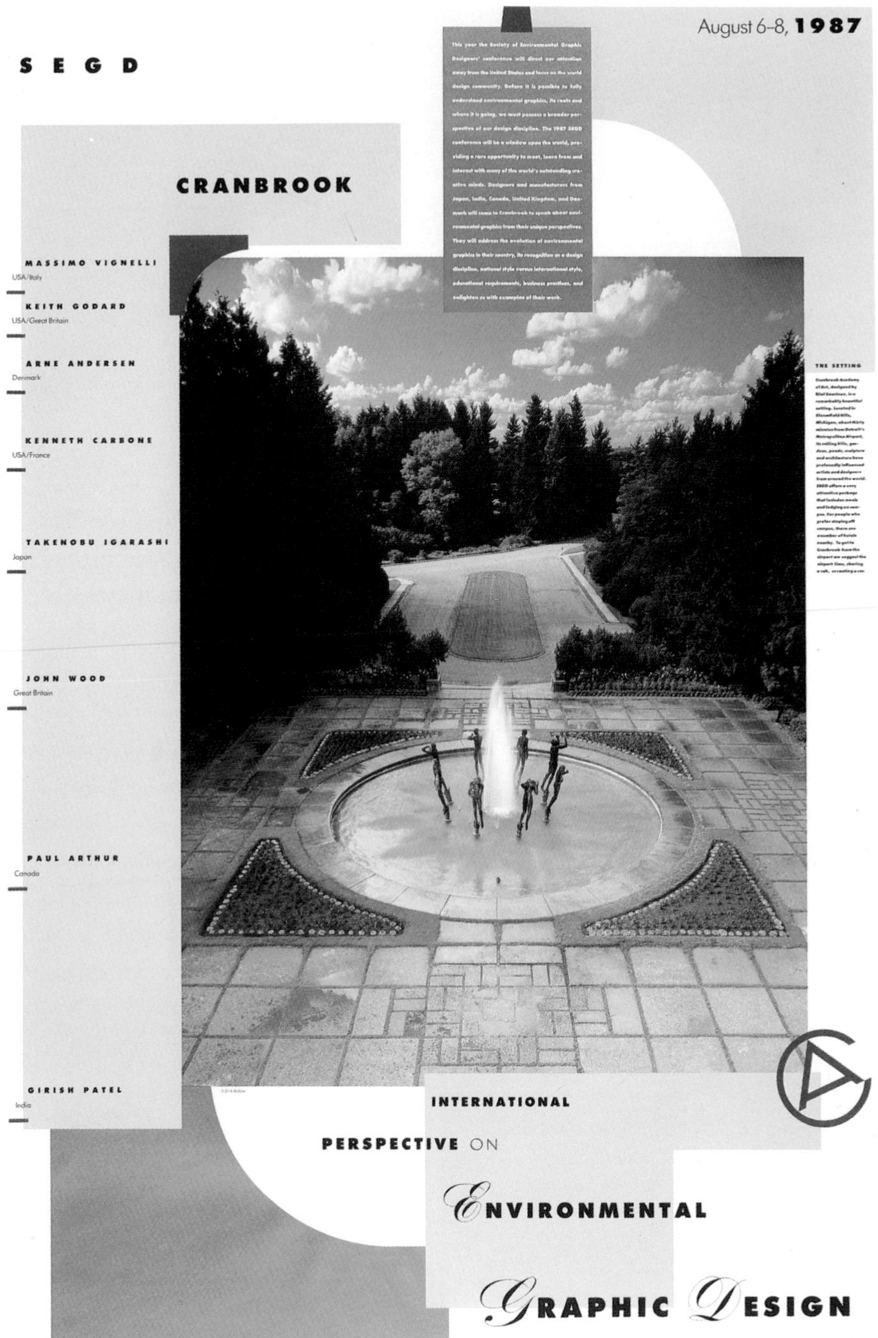
SEGD
August 6-8, 1987
This year the Society of Environmental Graphic Designers' conference will direct our attention away from the United States and focus on the world design community. Before it is possible to fully understand environmental graphics, its roots and where it is going, we must possess a broader perspective of our design discipline. The 1987 SEGD conference will be a window upon the world, providing a rare opportunity to meet, learn from and interact with many of the world's outstanding creative minds. Designers and manufacturers from Japan, India, Canada, United Kingdom, and Denmark will come to Cranbrook to speak about environmental graphics from their unique perspectives. They will address the evolution of environmental graphics in their country, its recognition as a design discipline, national style versus international style, educational requirements, business practices, and enlighten us with examples of their work.
CRANBROOK
MASSIMO VIGNELLI
USA/Italy
KEITH GODARD
USA/Great Britain
ARNE ANDERSEN
Denmark
KENNETH CARBONE
USA/France
TAKENOBU IGARASHI
Japan
JOHN WOOD
Great Britain
PAUL ARTHUR
Canada
GIRISH PATEL
India
THE SETTING
INTERNATIONAL
PERSPECTIVE ON
ENVIRONMENTAL
GRAPHIC DESIGN

International Perspective on Environmental Design Poster 1987
Alice Hecht, Hecht Design, Cambridge, Massachusetts, designer; Society of Environmental Graphic Designers, Boston, Massachusetts, client and publisher.
This poster announces the 1987 SEGD conference held annually on the Cranbrook campus.

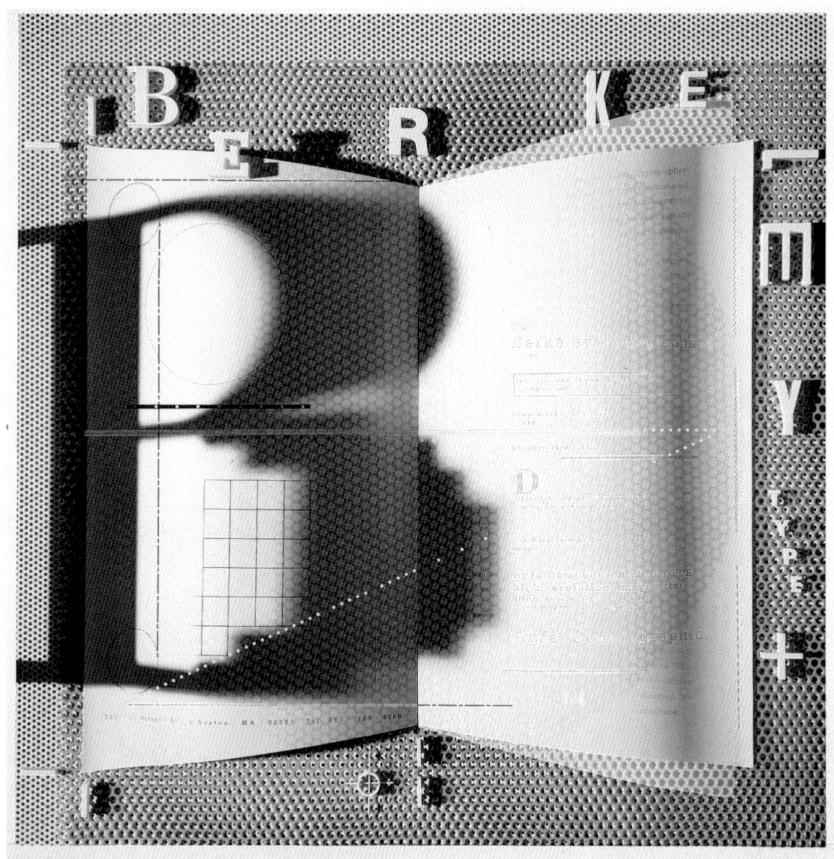

Berkeley Typographers Posters 1984-1990

Nancy Skolos / Thomas B. Wedell, Skolos / Wedell /Raynor, Charlestown, Massachusetts, designers and photographers; Berkeley Typographers, Boston, Massachusetts, client and publisher.

Three-dimensional typography is generated out of paper, multimedia constructions,and computer graphics to promote the services of this typesetter.

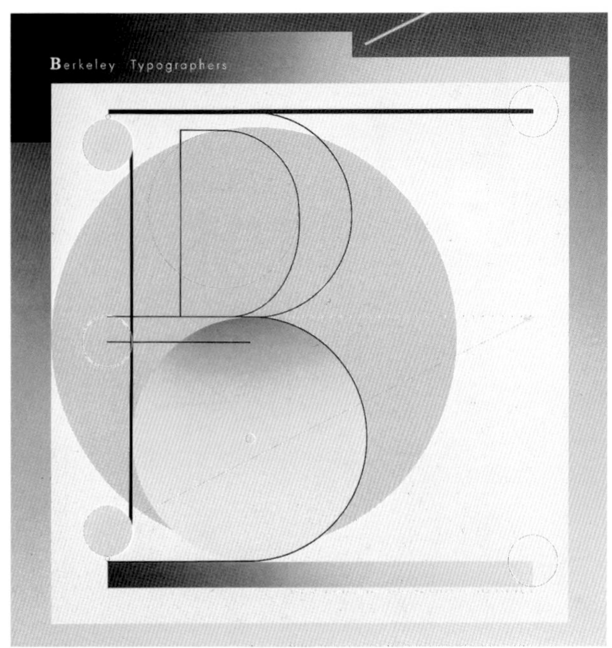
Berkeley Typographers

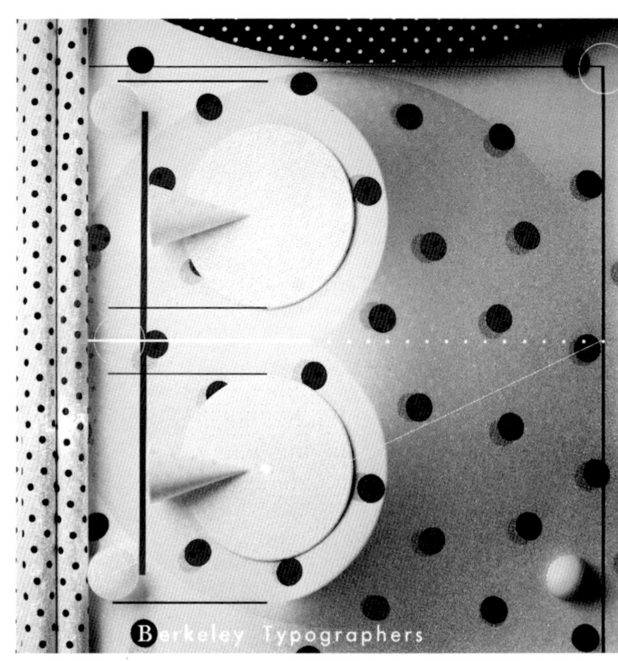
Berkeley Typographers

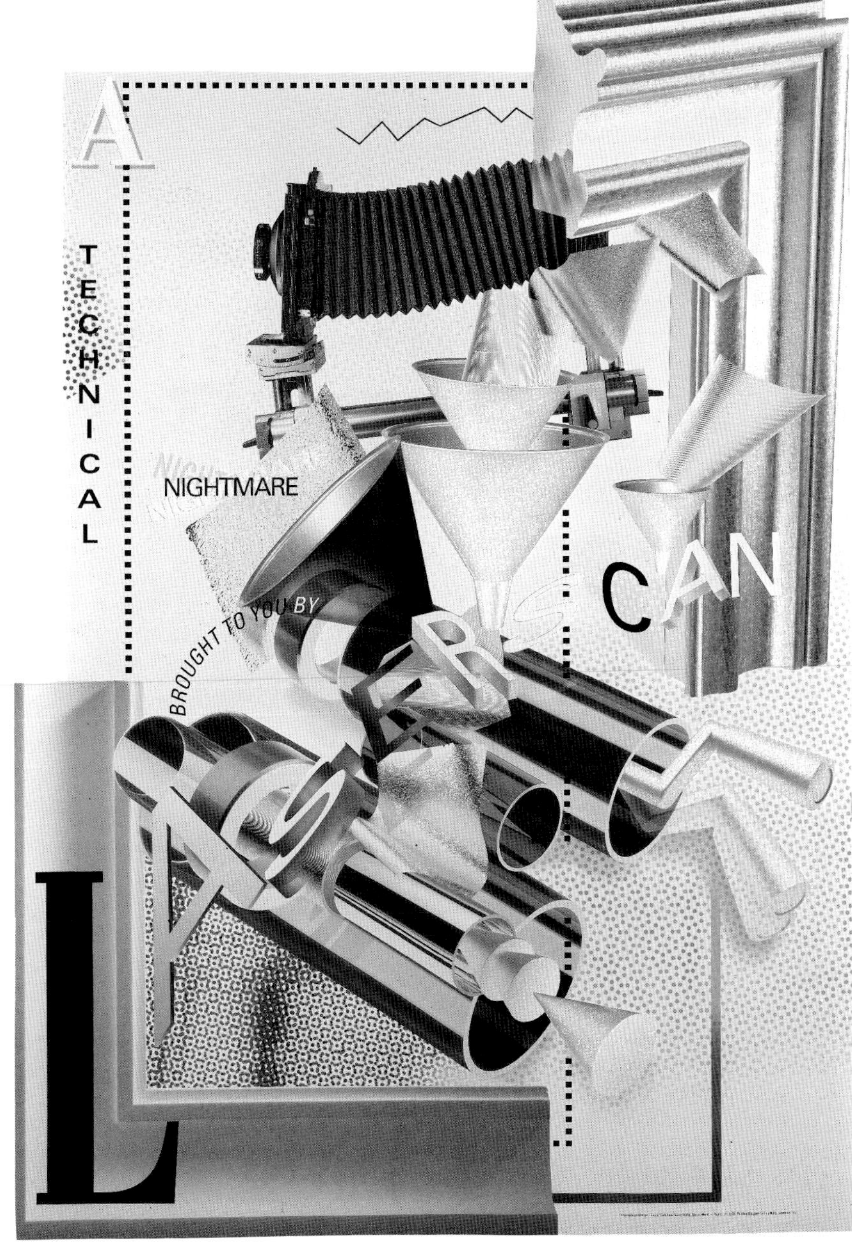
A
TECHNICAL
NIGHTMARE
BROUGHT TO YOU BY
CAN

Laserscan Poster 1989

Nancy Skolos / Thomas B. Wedell, Skolos / Wedell / Raynor, Charlestown, Massachusetts, designers and photographers; Laserscan, Phoenix, Arizona, client and publisher.

"A Technical Nightmare" is the subject of this complex pseudoinstrument constructed of photographed objects mixed with digitally generated typography, geometric forms, and effects.

Fonts Poster 1988

Nancy Skolos / Thomas B. Wedell, Skolos / Wedell / Raynor, Charlestown, Massachusetts, designers and photographers; Fonts, Boston, Massachusetts, client and publisher.

Three-dimensional typography, solid geometric forms, and type proofs are intermixed photographically and digitally with typography to confuse reality and illusion in a promotional poster for an ion typesetting system.

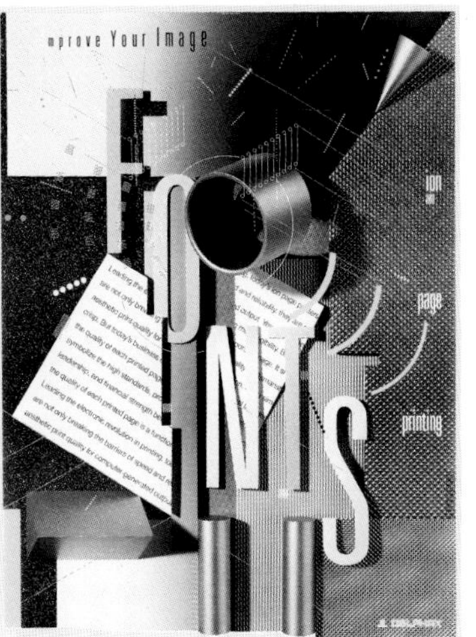
mprove Your Image
FONTS
ion
page
printing

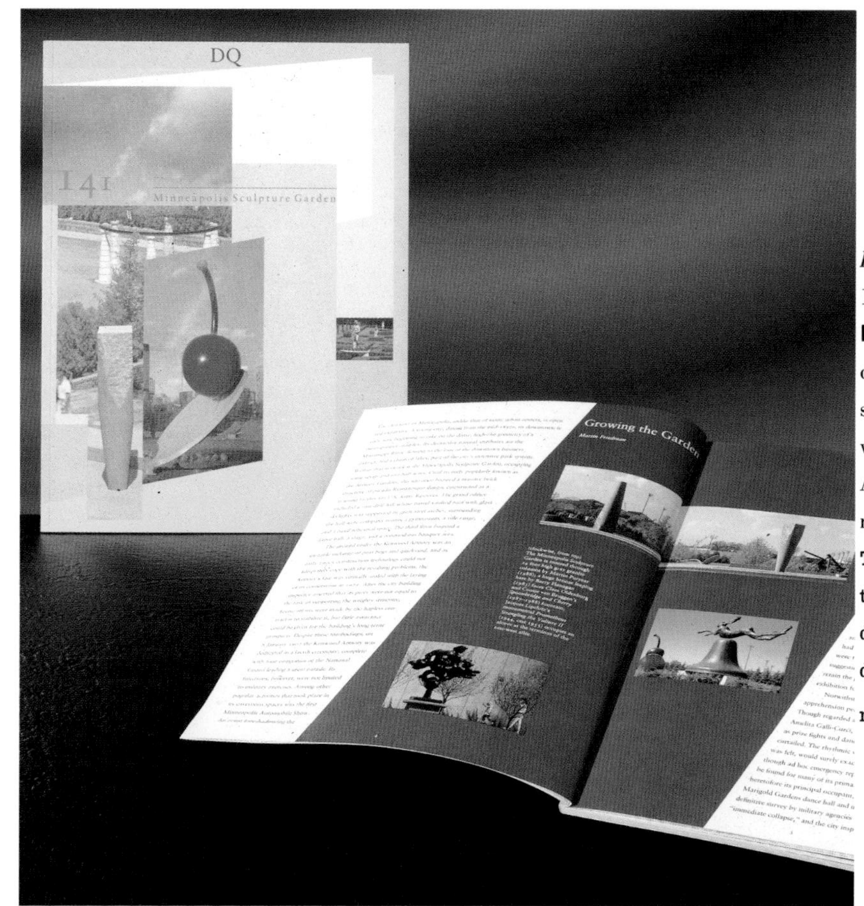
DQ
141
Minneapolis Sculpture Garden
Growing the Garden

Design Quarterly 141 Journal 1988
Nancy Skolos, Skolos / Wedell/Raynor, Charlestown, Massachusetts, designer; Glenn Halvorson, photographer; Walker Art Center, Minneapolis, Minnesota, client and publisher.
The photographic montage for this cover of a quarterly art-and-design journal suggests the three-dimensionality of the new Minneapolis Sculpture Garden.

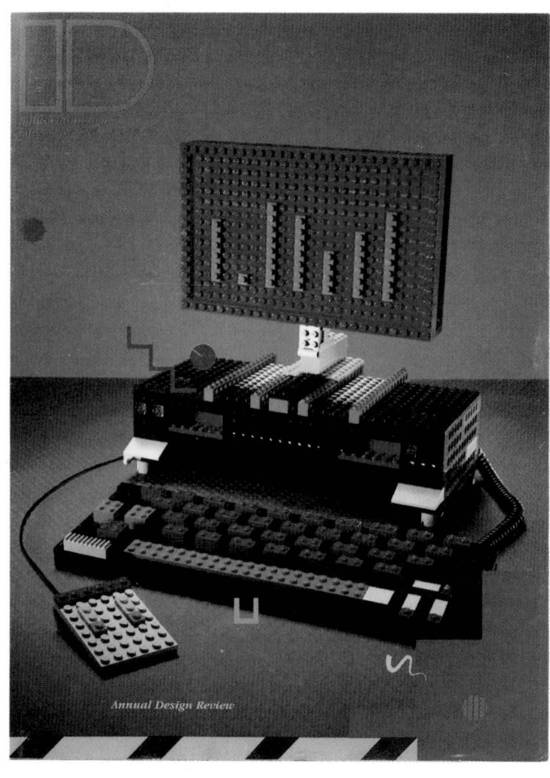
ID
Annual Design Review

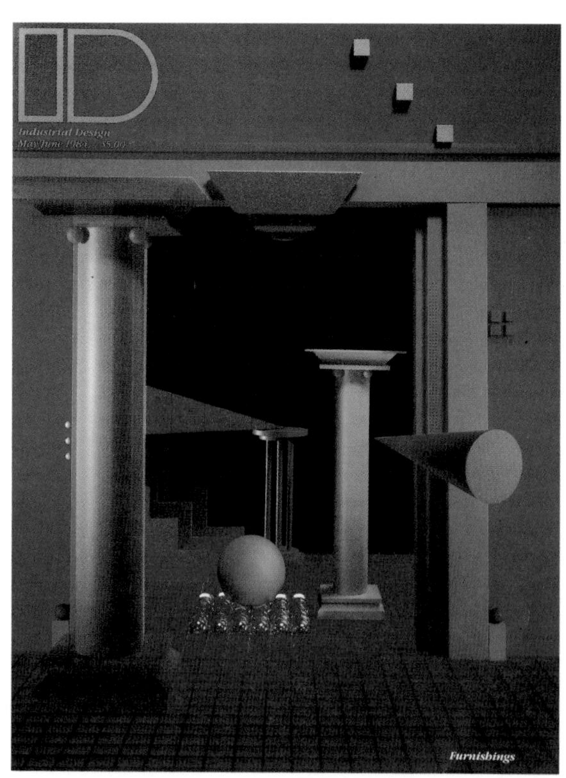
ID
Industrial Design
Furnishings

Skolos / Wedell / Raynor Poster 1982

Nancy Skolos / Thomas B. Wedell, Skolos / Wedell /Raynor, Charlestown, Massachusetts, designers and photographers; Skolos/Wedell/Raynor, Charlestown, Massachusetts, client and publisher.

Three-dimensional paper constructions are photographed and mixed with graphic arts elements in a poster to promote the services of this design and photography studio.

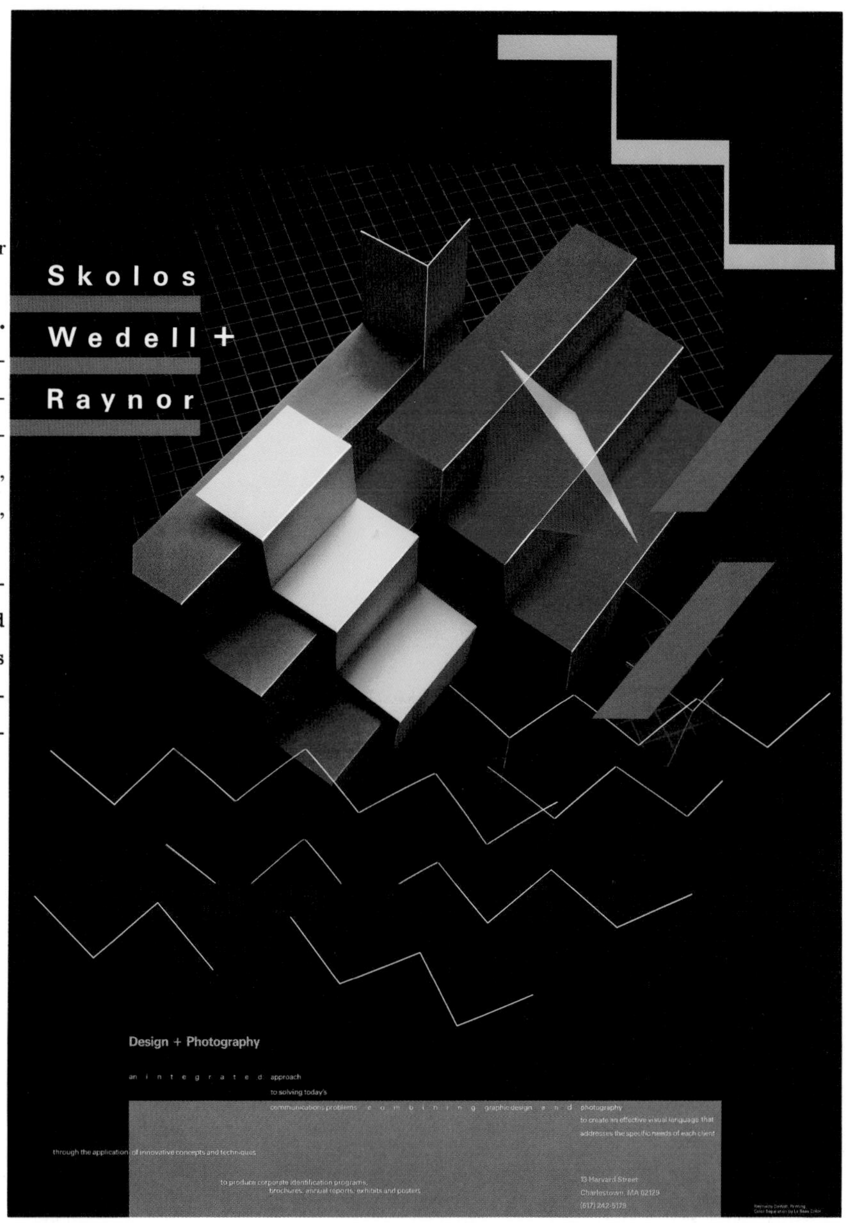
Skolos
Wedell +
Raynor
Design + Photography

ID Magazine Covers 1984

Thomas B. Wedell, Skolos / Wedell / Raynor, Charlestown, Massachusetts, designer and photographer; *ID* magazine, New York, client and publisher.

Staged photographs constructed by the photographer combine tangible and electronic materials including paper, plastic, Legos, and digital effects.

AIGA Boston Lectures and Exhibitions Poster 1985

Nancy Skolos / Thomas B. Wedell, Skolos / Wedell /Raynor, Charlestown, Massachusetts, designers and photographers; American Institute of Graphic Arts Boston, Boston, Massachusetts, client and publisher.

Three-dimensional geometric solids construct the name AIGA in a staged photograph mixed with graphic arts elements to announce the programs of this professional organization.

BOSTON
LECTURES

David Byrne Rei MOMO Poster 1990

Jane Kosstrin / David Sterling, Doublespace, Inc., New York, and David Byrne, designers; Kurigami, AP/Wide World Photos, New York, photographers; Warner Brothers Records, Los Angeles, client.

This poster shares its vocabulary of forms with compact disc and record album covers. Hearts and flowers, inner conflict and urban conflict mix in colorful layers that suggest the music's fresh interpretations of Latin rhythms.

DAVID
BYRNE
REI MOMO

Fetish Magazine Travel Issue Cover 1980

Jane Kosstrin / David Sterling / Terence Main, Doublespace, New York, designers and publishers; Richard Sferra, Minneapolis, Minnesota, photographer.

Staged photography creates a beckoning space populated with travel icons.

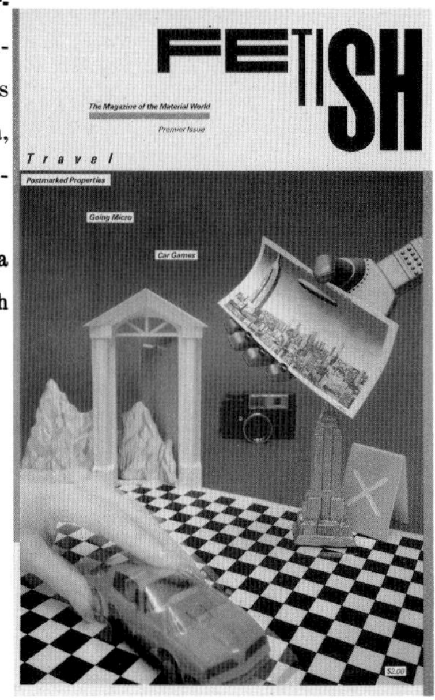
FETISH
Travel

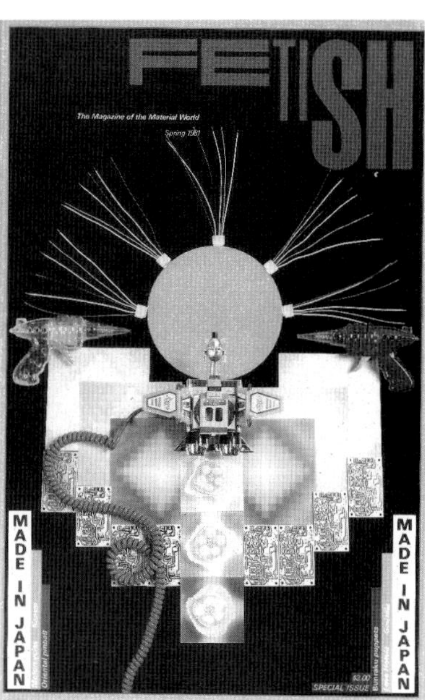
FETISH
MADE IN JAPAN
MADE IN JAPAN

Fetish Magazine Made in Japan Issue Cover 1980

Jane Kosstrin / David Sterling / Terence Main, Doublespace, Inc., New York, designers and publishers; Jere Cockrell, New York, photographer.

A composition of toys, electrical parts, and photographs becomes an abstracted robot in this cover for a magazine on contemporary material culture.

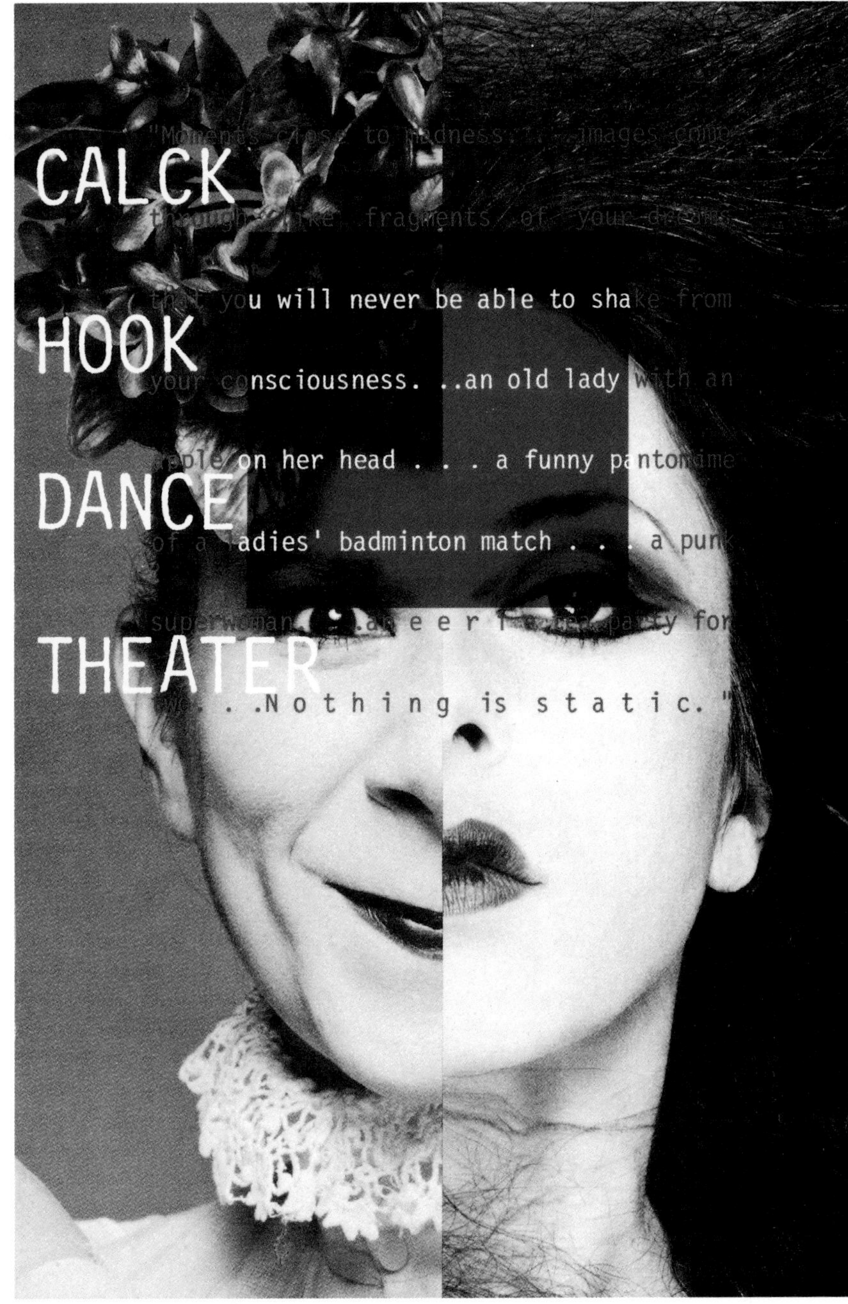
CALCK
HOOK
DANCE
THEATER
u will never be able to sha
nsciousness. ..an old lady
on her head . . . a funny pa
adies' badminton match . . . a
. . .Nothing is static."

Calck Hook Dance Theater Announcement Brochure 1985
Jane Kosstrin / David Sterling, Doublespace, Inc., New York, designers; Brooklyn Academy of Music, Brooklyn, New York, client and publisher.
To announce an avant-garde dance performance, the text reads, Nothing is static, on a brochure that folds and unfolds to reveal interchangeable combinations of faces and text.

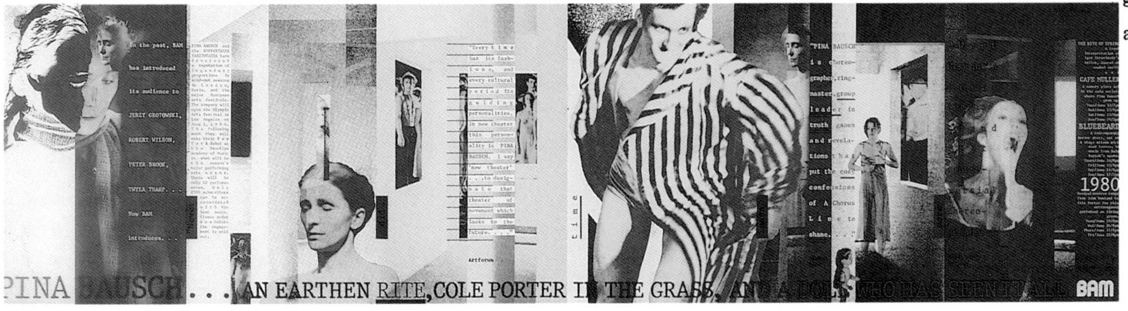
PINA BAUSCH . . . AN EARTHEN RITE, COLE PORTER IN THE GRASS,
BAM

Pina Bausch Tanztheater Wuppertal Performance Announcement 1984
Jane Kosstrin / David Sterling, Doublespace, Inc., New York, designers; Brooklyn Academy of Music, Brooklyn, New York, client and publisher.
Typewriter text is superimposed on photographic montages, suggesting the time and sequence of a theatrical dance performance.

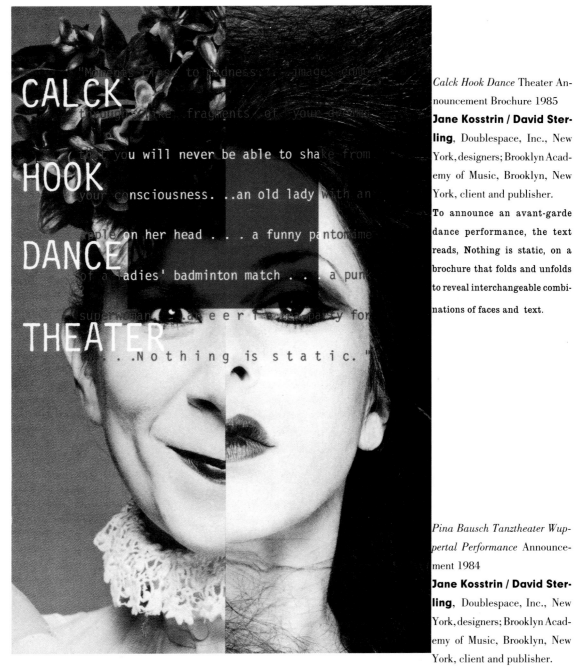

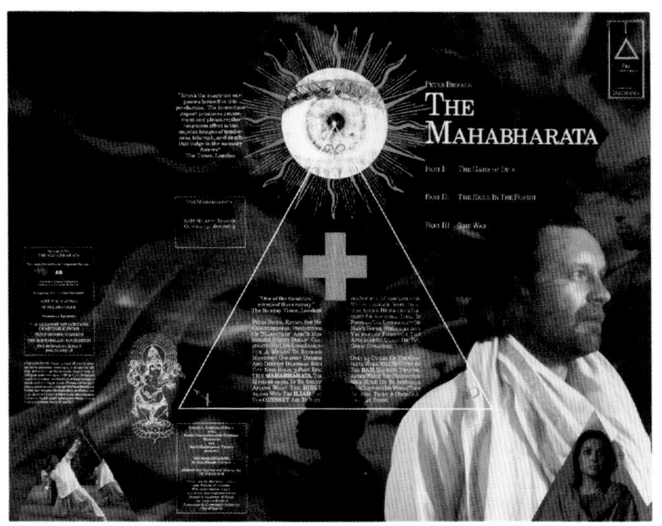
THE MAHABHARATA

ZANGEZI
NIXON IN CHINA
SWING
"L" TRAIN TO ELDORADO
SQUAT THEATRE

STEVE REICH
ELLIOTT SHARP AND CARBON
MEREDITH MONK
THE PETER ZUMMO ORCHESTRAS
HENRY THREADGILL AND ORCHESTRA

NINA WIENER AND DANCERS
ANNE TERESA DE KEERSMAEKER
MAGUY MARIN
BABEL, BABEL EDEN
KAROLE ARMITAGE
DAVID SALLE

Next Wave Festival Announcement Brochure Spreads 1987
Jane Kosstrin / David Sterling, Doublespace, Inc., New York, designers; Brooklyn Academy of Music, Brooklyn, New York, client and publisher.
Each of the spreads deals with symbols from alchemic themes, including "Fire/Creation," "Earth/The Material," "Air/The Judgment," and "Water/The Return."

"AN AVANT GARDE POWERHOUSE GROWS IN BROOKLYN."
NEW YORK MAGAZINE
NEXT WAVE
BROOKLYN ACADEMY OF MUSIC
FESTIVAL 1988
OCTOBER 19 - DECEMBER 17
STOP

Next Wave Festival Poster 1988
Jane Kosstrin / David Sterling, Doublespace, Inc., New York, designers; Brooklyn Academy of Music, Brooklyn, New York, client and publisher.
This poster announces avant-garde theater and music performances in an urban context.

Gaetano Pesce "Modern Times Again" Furniture and Architecture Exhibition Catalog 1988
Jane Kosstrin / David Sterling, Doublespace, Inc., New York, designers; Steelcase Design Partnership, New York, client and publisher.
This montage of photographs and text records the architect/designer's work in an accordion-fold brochure/poster.

End Table Prototype 1983
Ken Smith, designer; Cranbrook Studio project.
This table's geometric form was inspired by the Wiener Werkstätte.

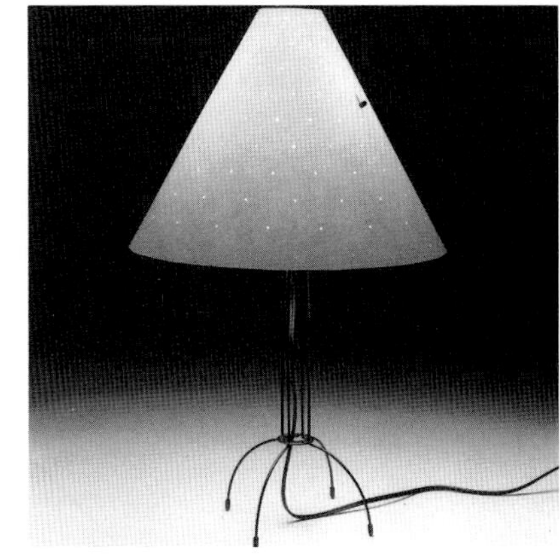

Crown Lamp 1989
Eric Williams, designer; Artemide, Milan, Italy, client.
Table lamp with perforated paper shade presents stance and scale of traditional table lamps without their mass.

Interior Space Study Models 1980
Helga Kahl, designer; Cranbrook Studio project.
Decompositions and recompositions of historic spatial and decorative models.

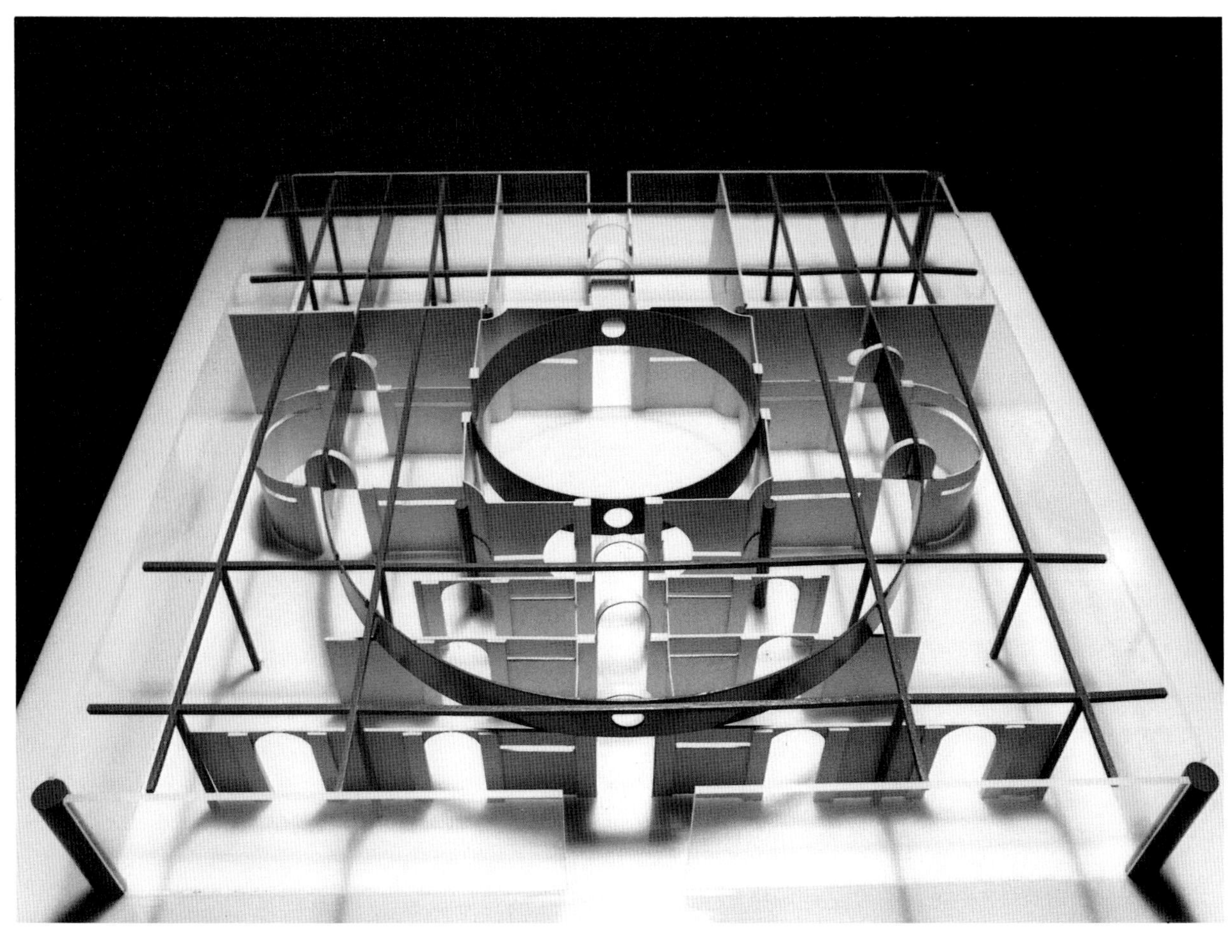

Perforated Metal Chair Prototype 1986
Andrew Fisher, designer; Cranbrook Studio project.
Die-cut magnetic decorative figures can be placed at random on the surface of this metal chair.

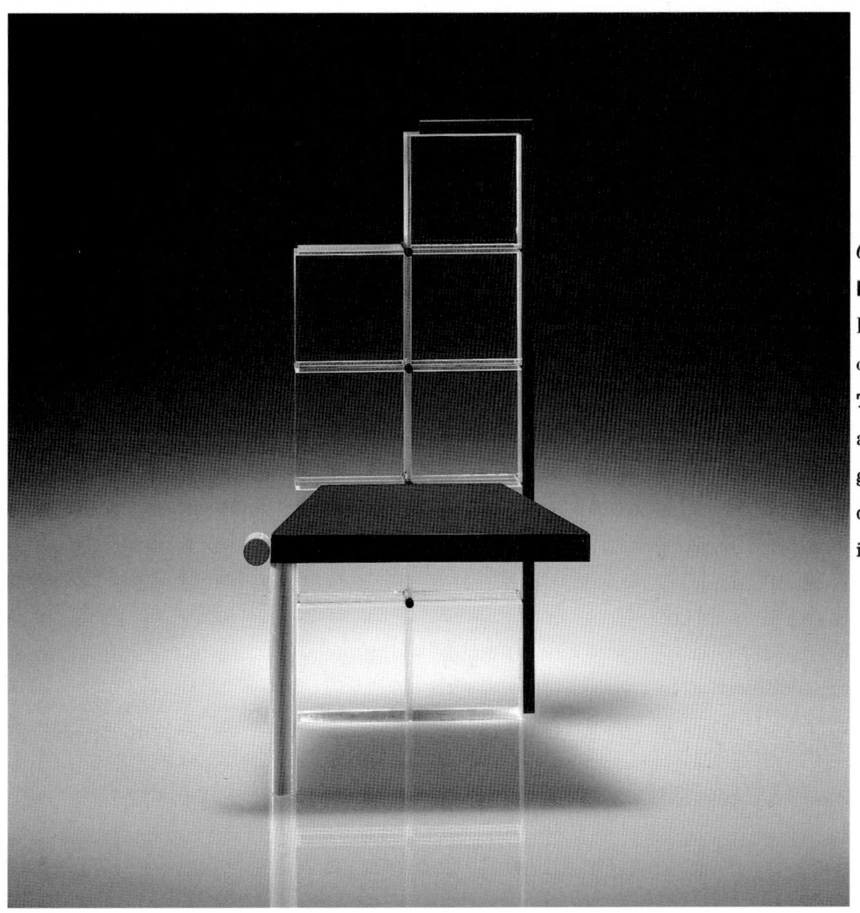

Crystal Chair Model 1983
Nancy Skolos, Skolos/Wedell/Raynor, Charlestown, Massachusetts, designer.
The window seat represented as a fragment of architecture. The glass blocks with inlaid rubber discs parody the presence of cushions and upholstery buttons.

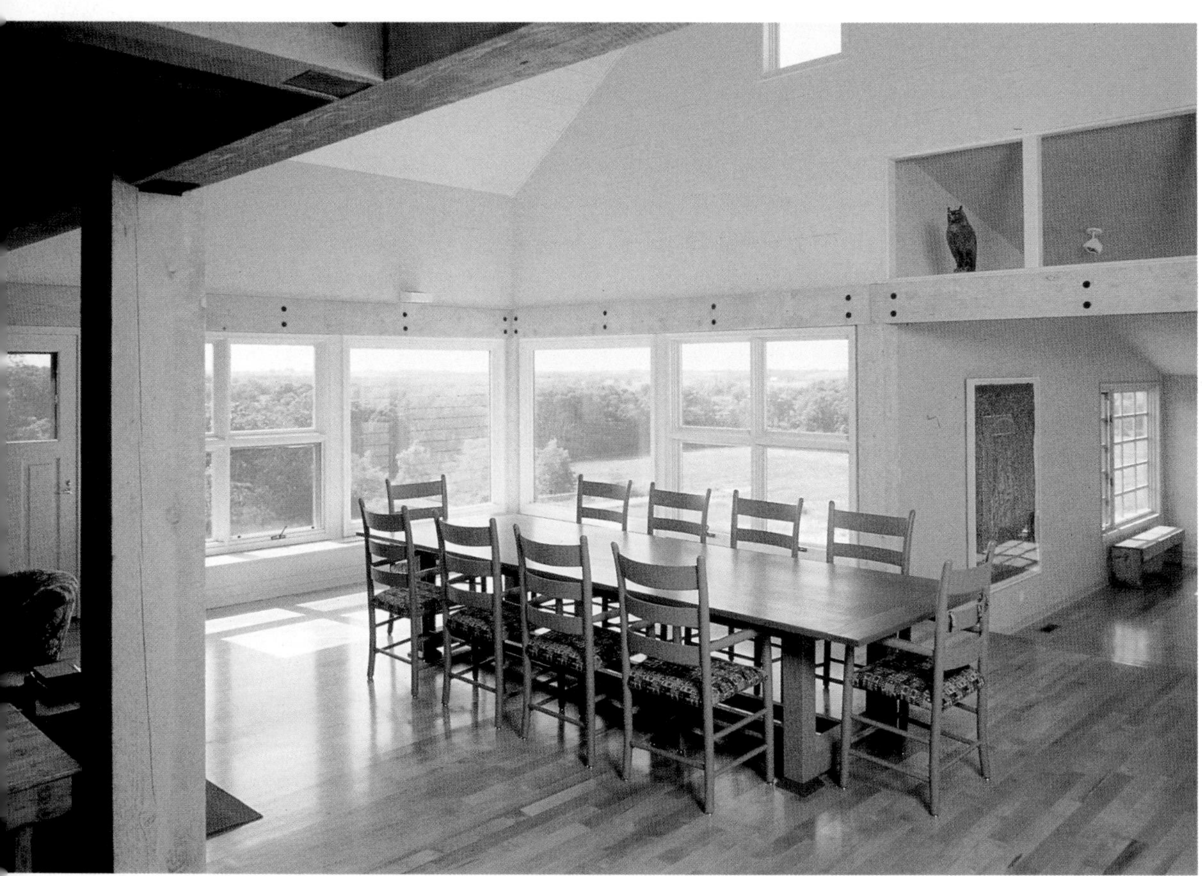

Von Blon Residence Interior 1987

Lynn Barnhouse, Meyer, Scherer & Rockcastle, interior designer, and Dan Cramer, furniture designer, Minneapolis, Minnesota; Von Blon Family, Minnetrista, Minnesota, client.

The lodge-sized dining room of this large but intimate house uses warm, traditional, and informal materials to welcome the visitor. The table, by Dan Cramer, has aluminum legs with interchangeable wooden feet under an antique barn-wood top.

Esprit Shop at Macy's, San Francisco, Interior 1986

Aura Oslapas, Esprit Company, store design director; Esprit Company, San Francisco, California, client.

This interior is representative of an extensive series of retail interiors for this notable American clothing manufacturer.

Par Ve Nu 1987

Jonathan Teasdale, designer; Cranbrook Studio project; Art et Industrie, New York, gallery.

A tea service that embodies many of the designer's concerns with the relationship of man to technology. Biomorphic forms are harnessed or contained.

Toilette 1989

Jonathan Teasdale, New York, designer; Art et Industrie, New York, gallery.

Toiletry stand constructed of nickel-, chrome-, and copper-plated steel, aluminum, rubber, and glass.

Garden Gate 1987

Jonathan Teasdale, designer; Cranbrook Studio project.

A gate, activated by infrared sensors, that presents technology and structure as servant.

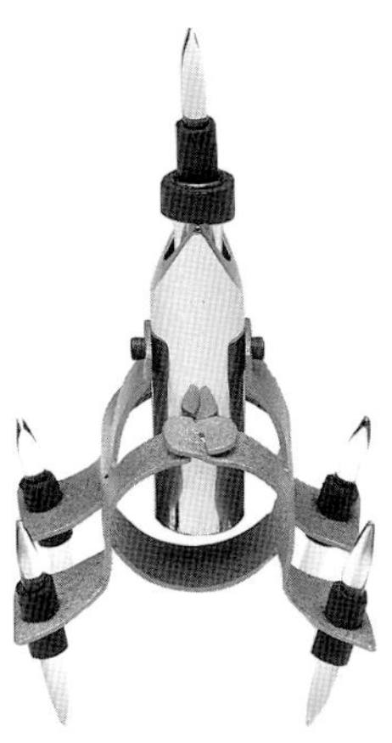

Toilette 1989

Jonathan Teasdale, New York, designer; Art et Industrie, New York, gallery.

Cologne container constructed of steel, rubber, and glass.

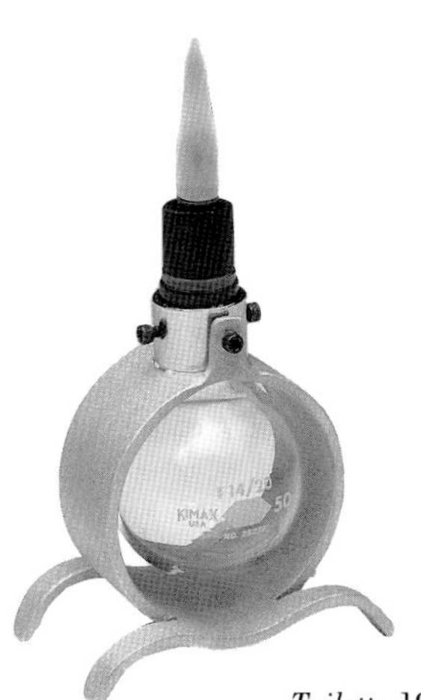

Toilette 1989

Jonathan Teasdale, New York, designer; Art et Industrie, New York, gallery.

Oil container constructed of aluminum, glass, and rubber.

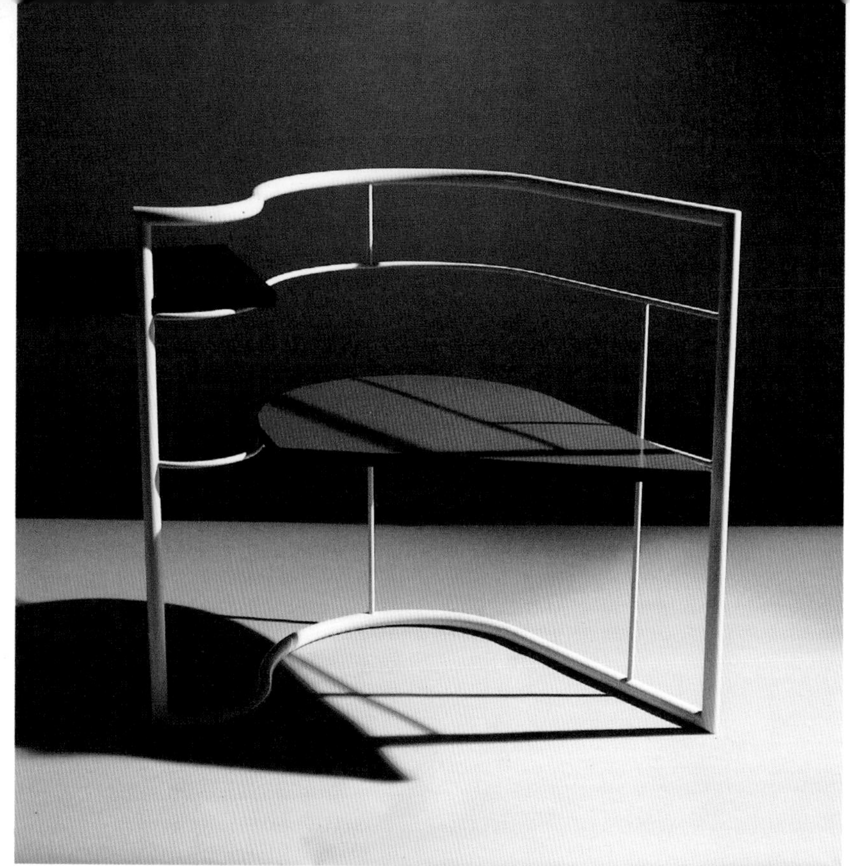

Homage to the Berlin Chair
Prototype 1982
Angela Wiegand, designer;
Cranbrook Studio project.
A transhistorical composition based on Rietveld's Berlin Chair.

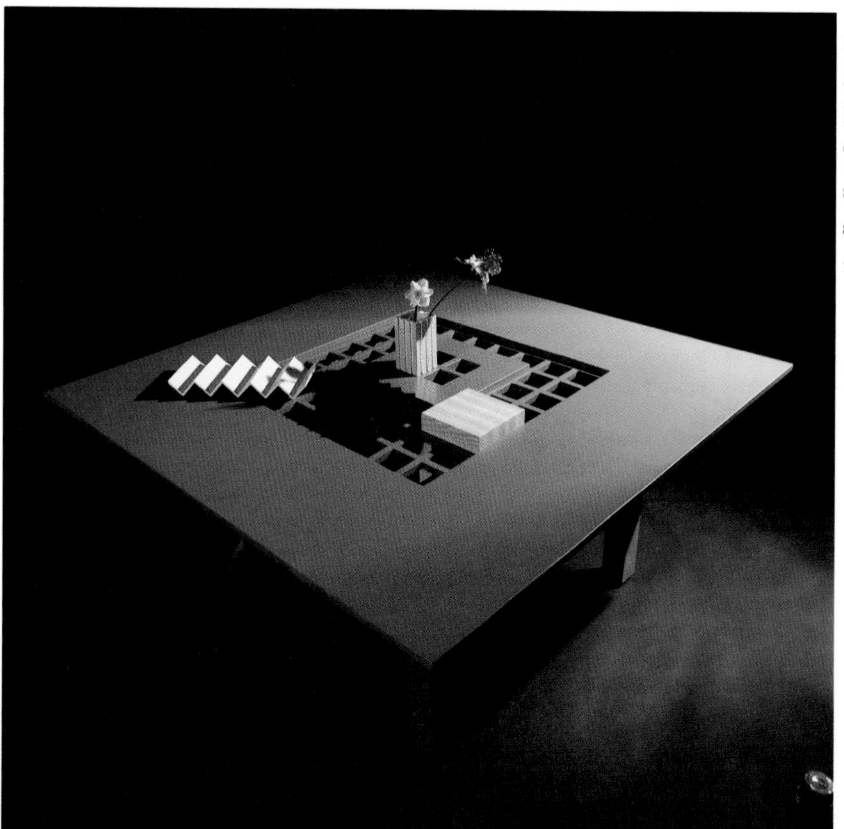

Table and Tablewares Prototypes 1983
Aura Oslapas, designer; Cranbrook Studio project.
The central open grid organizes specially designed ceramic, iron, and wood utensils for serving food.

Library Desk and Chair for Roland Barthes Prototypes 1987
Mike Scott, designer; Cranbrook Studio project.

At the front of the cast-concrete desk is a window, representing the framing effect of language, through which the library is viewed. The chair is dissected and its parts — seat, back, and leg structure — are presented as separate linguistic entities.

Queen Anne Queen Anne 1982
Terence Main and Laura Johnson, Main & Main, designers; Art et Industrie, New York, New York, gallery.
A chair emblematic of the repetition and simulation of history.

Primogeniture 1990
Terence Main, designer; Art et Industrie, New York, gallery.
A primitive iconography is evoked in this cast bronze chair.

Chair Prototype 1986

Greg Eitelman, designer;

Cranbrook Studio project.

A chair that reveals the coexistence of two objects within one figure, dissected by Cartesian space.

Furniture Prototypes 1986

Sheri Schumacher, designer;

Cranbrook Studio project.

Furniture based on the designer's interest in the relationships among the figure, dwelling, and furniture.

Lamp Prototype 1988

Marcy Stefura, designer;

Cranbrook Studio project.

The bowed support of this pewter-and-glass lamp refers to the bending of light through glass.

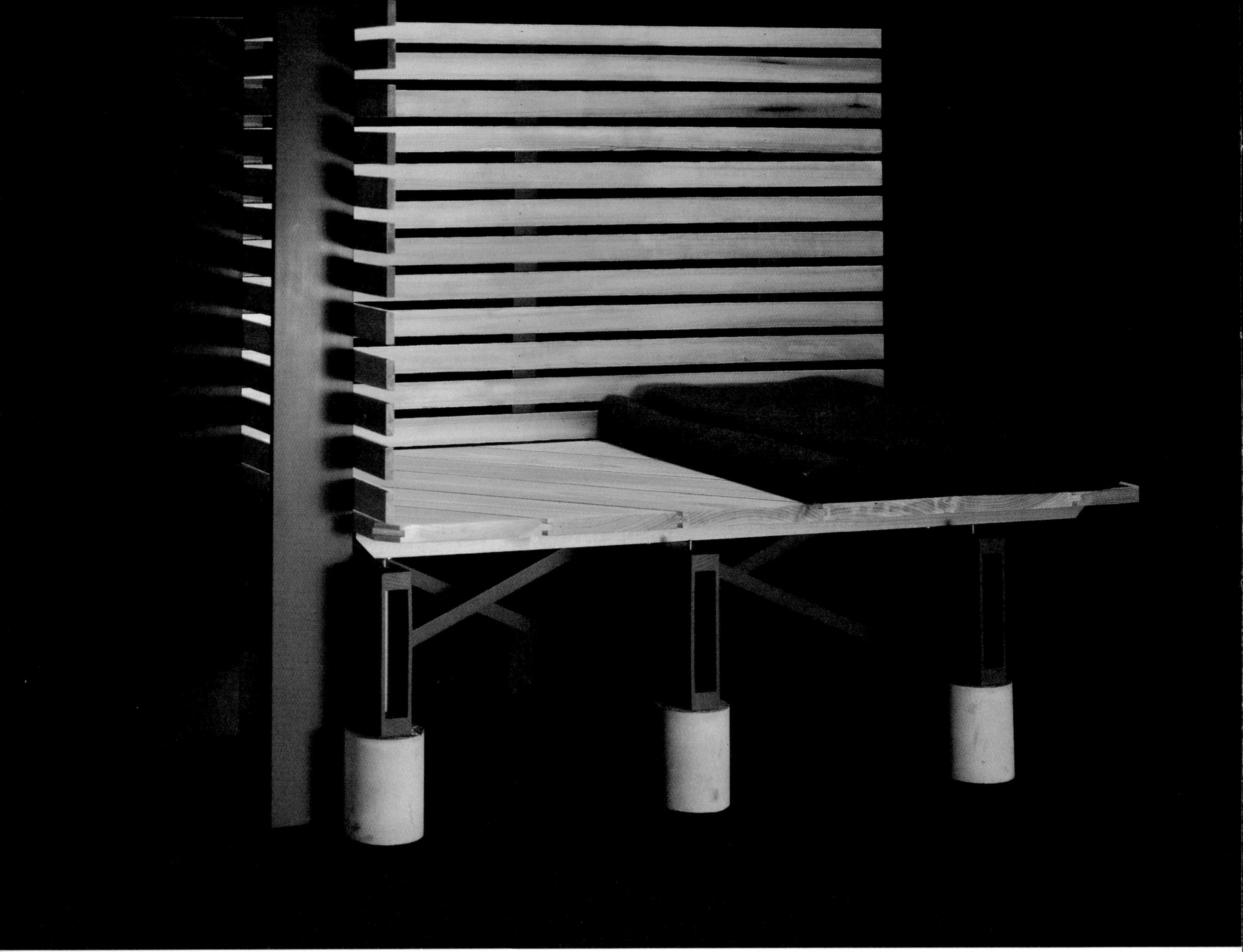

Bench Prototype 1987

Jim Hill, designer; Cranbrook Studio project.

The structure of the sofa represents the unseen structure of the house within which it resides.

Table Prototype 1987

Jim Hill, designer; Cranbrook Studio project.

The table's structure is an acknowledgment of the structure and dynamics of the house around it – the framing of the wall, the swing of the door.

Triangle Table Prototype 1983
Martin Linder, designer; Cranbrook Studio project.
The table is supported on one end by a large spring, structurally ambiguous as to its flexibility or rigidity.

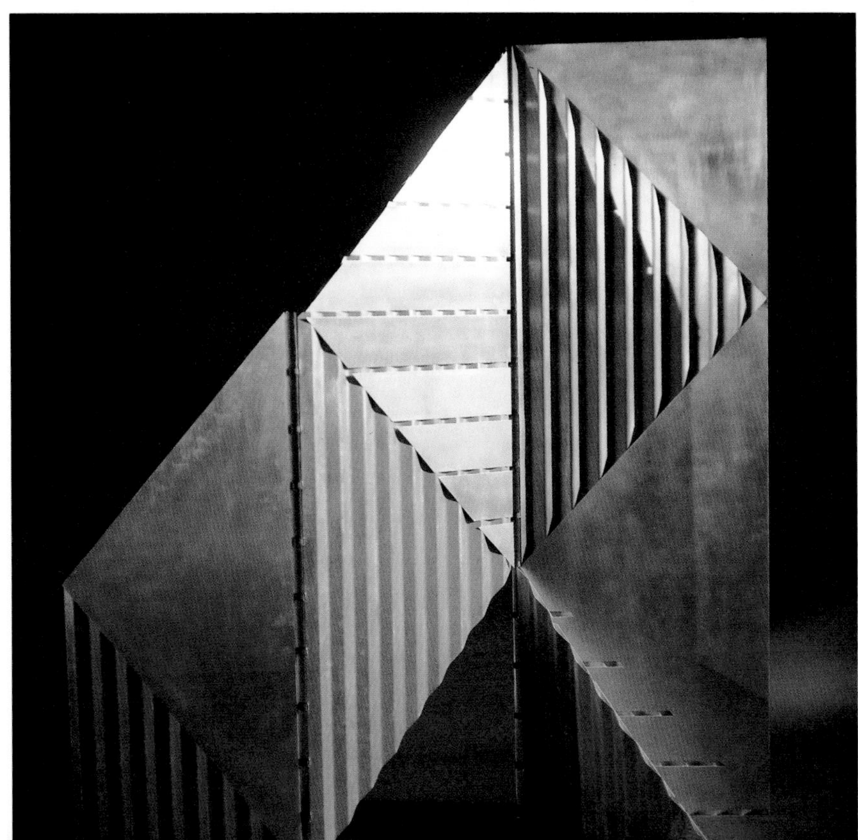

Room Divider Prototype 1983
David Burkholder, designer; Cranbrook Studio project.
A composition in galvanized and corrugated steel that divides space with a rigorous geometry.

Nami Desktop Accessories Prototype 1988

Tadao Shimizu, Studio Tad, Tokyo, Japan, designer.

Progressive waves of laser-cut, color-anodized aluminum form storage units for papers, pens, and other desktop items.

Wheelchair for interior use Model 1986

Tadao Shimizu, Studio Tad, Tokyo, Japan, designer.

This wheelchair uses soft, biomorphic forms to make it friendlier and more comfortable to use.

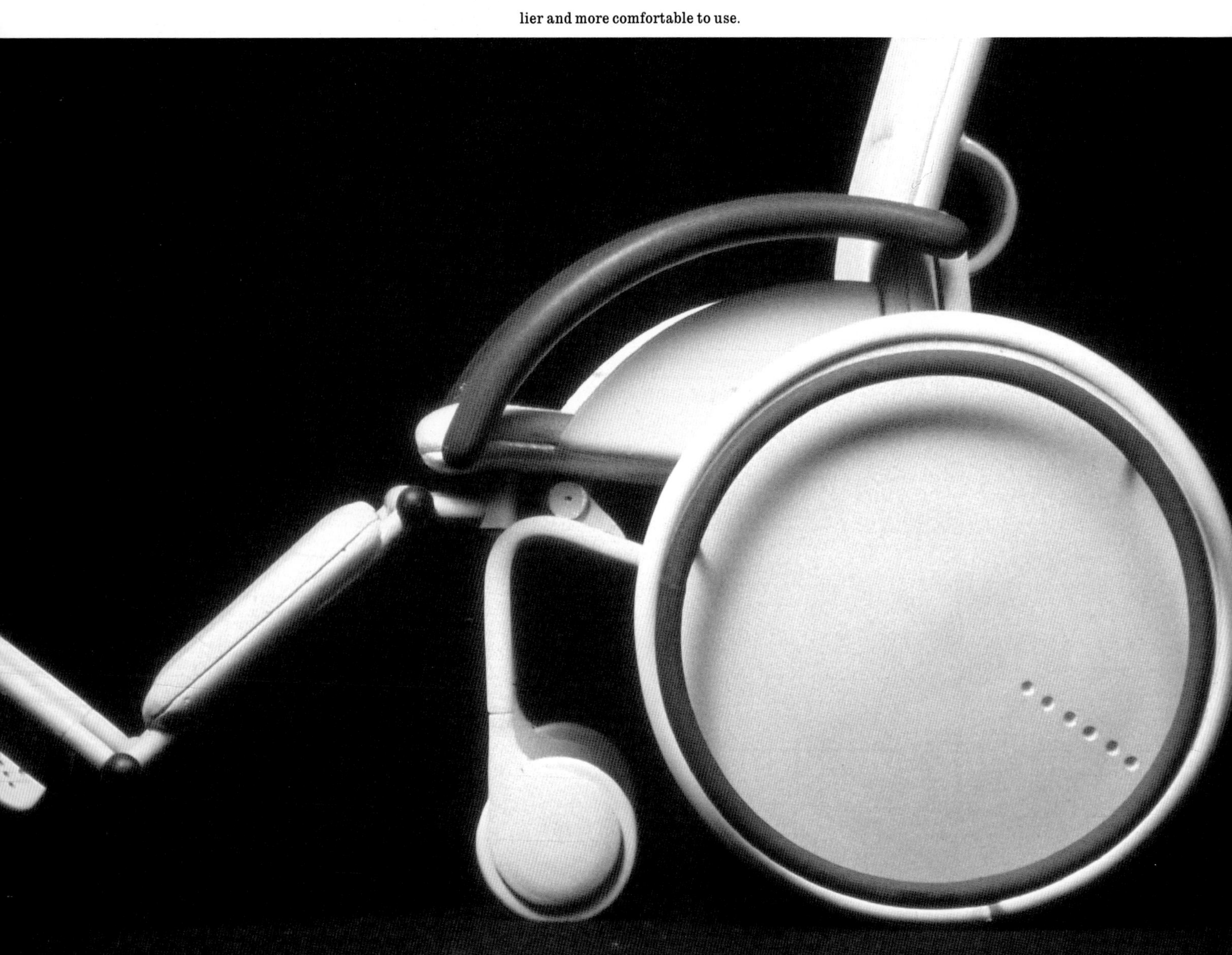

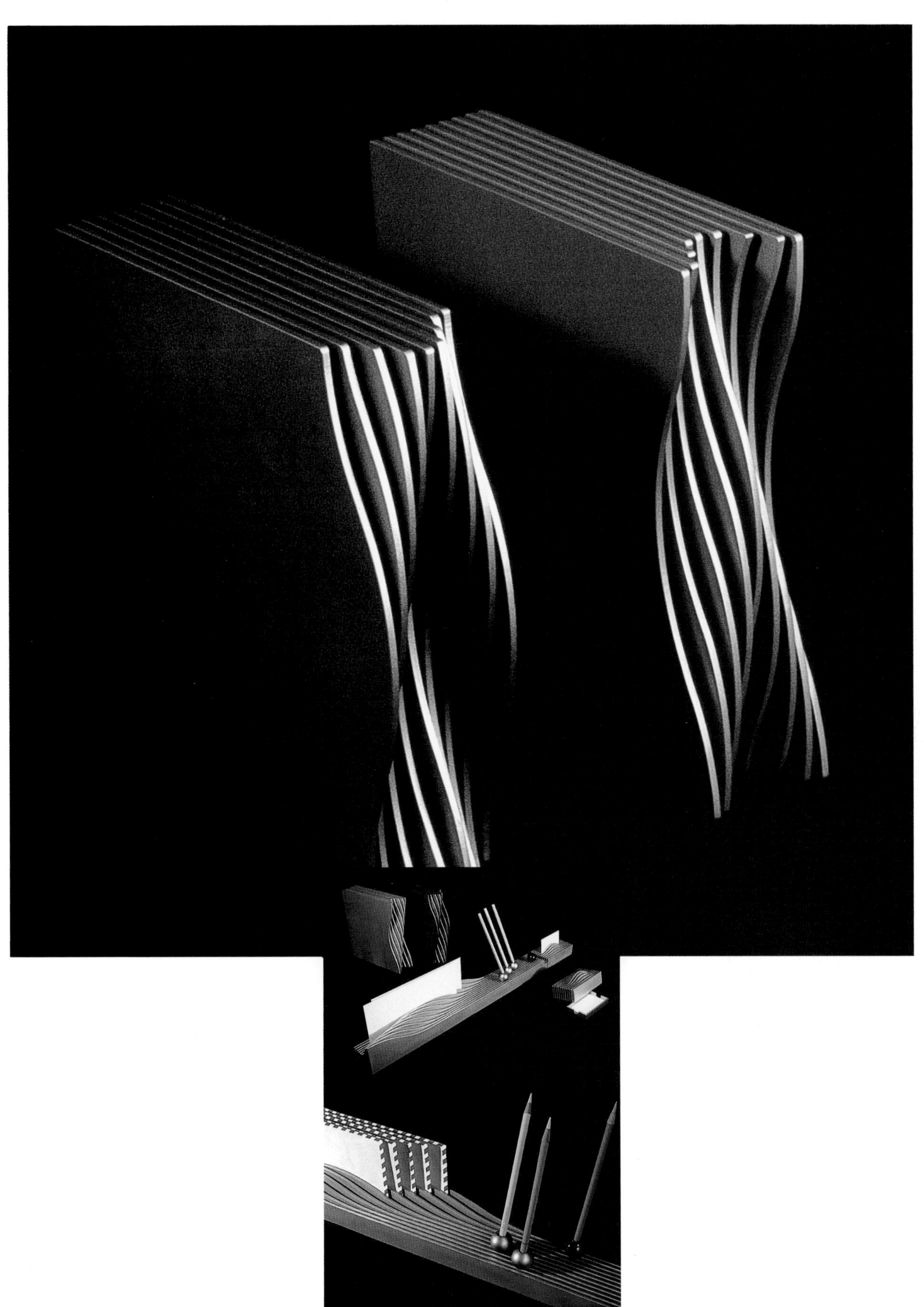

Philips HES Home Entertainment Center Model 1987
Michael McCoy and Dale Fahnstrom with David Vanden-Branden, Fahnstrom/McCoy, Chicago, Illinois, designers; N.V. Philips, Eindhoven, The Netherlands, client.
The 19-inch square modules of this home-entertainment center are only two inches thick and can be stacked edge to edge to form electronic walls of different shapes and sizes. The functions, including CD player and videocassette, are indicated by bas-relief icons on the surface of the wall.

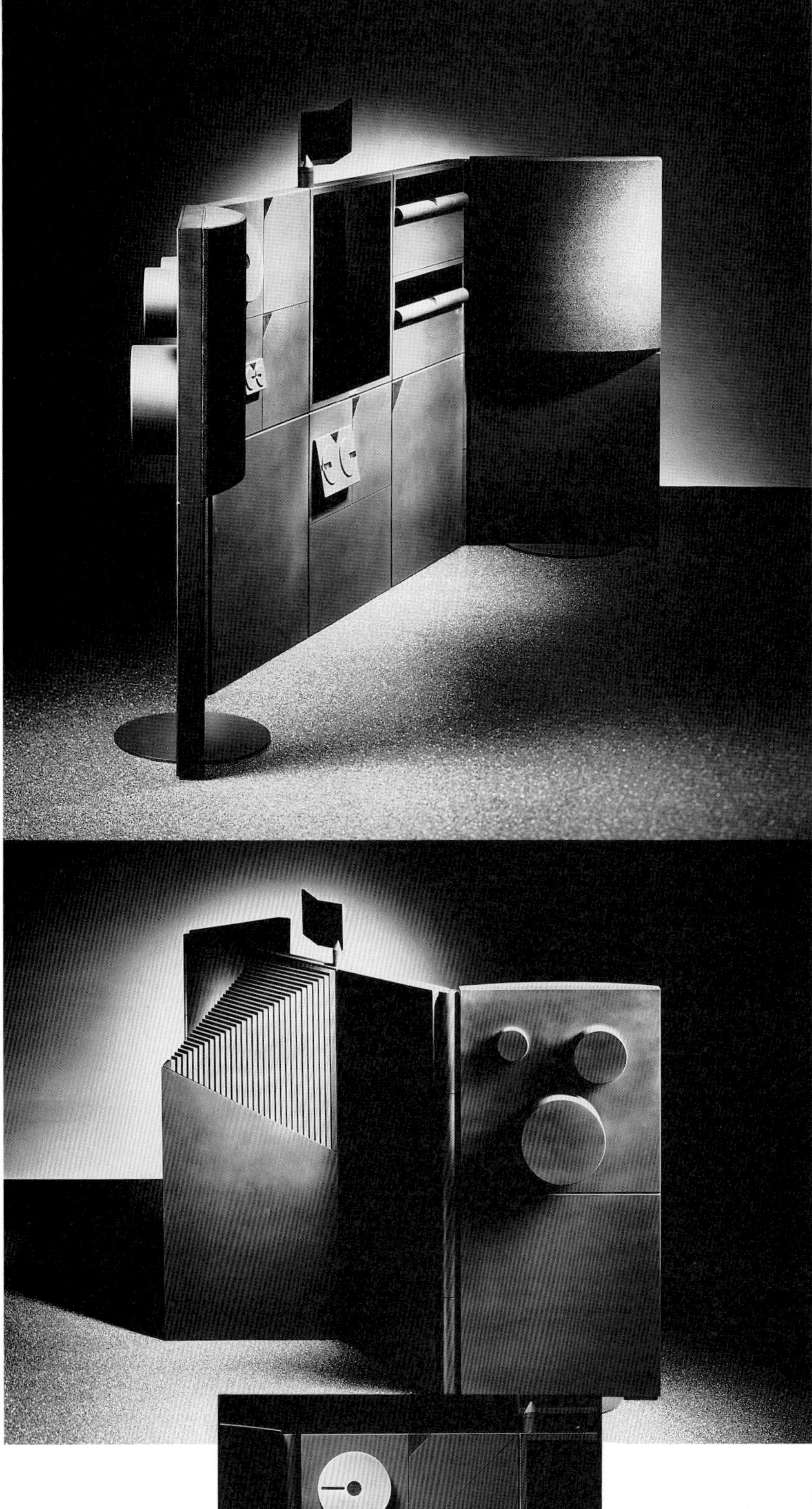

Philips Portable Stereo Model 1987
Michael McCoy and Dale Fahnstrom with David Vanden-Branden, Fahnstrom/McCoy, Chicago, Illinois, designers; N.V. Philips, Eindhoven, The Netherlands, client.
The speaker towers, formed by stacks of discs, are intersected by a soft wall containing the electronics. The top edge of the wall lifts to become a carrying handle.

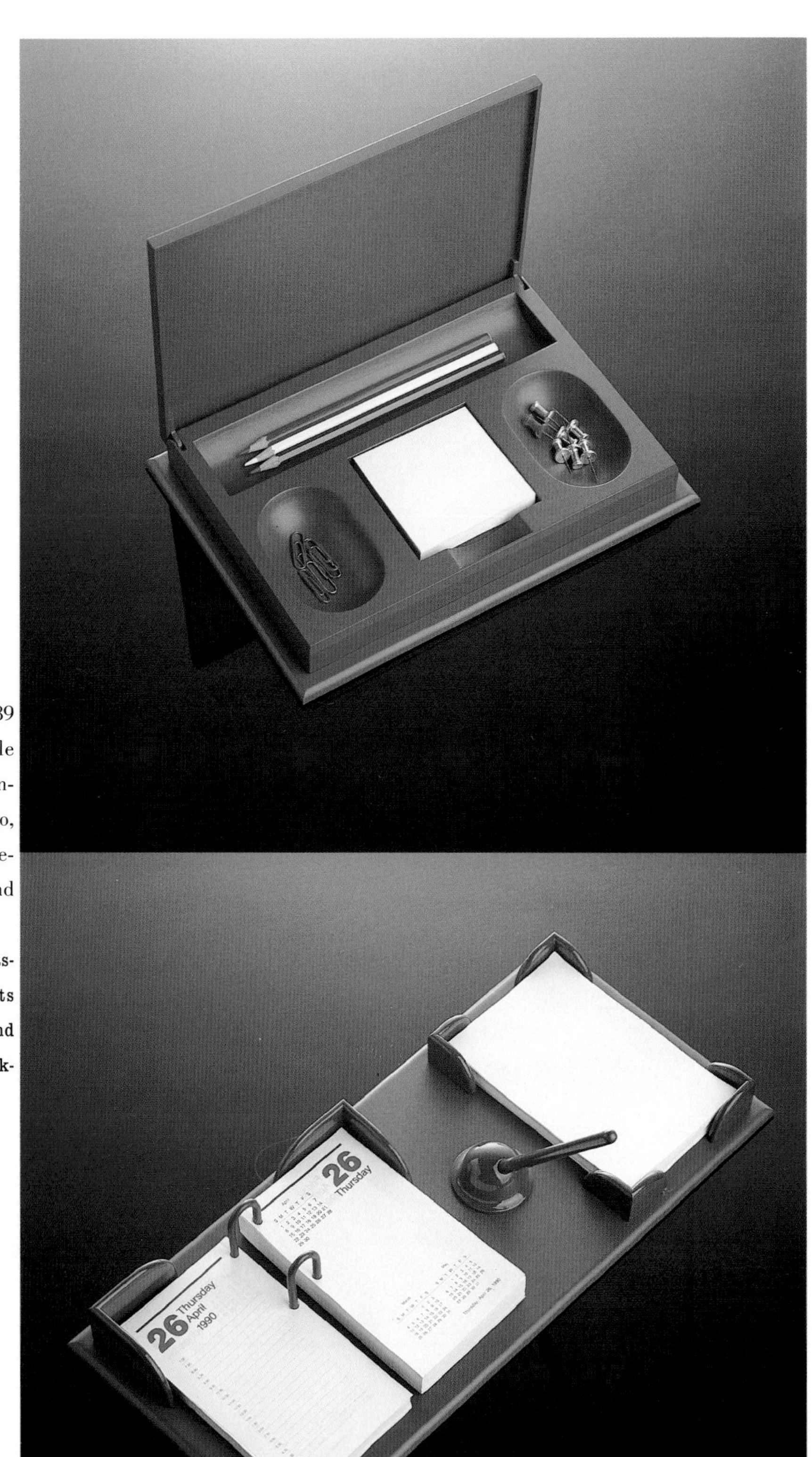

Details Office Accessories 1989
Michael McCoy and Dale Fahnstrom with David Vanden-Branden, F/M Studio, Chicago, Illinois, designers; Steelcase Details, New York, client and manufacturer.

Articulated cast metal and plastic vertical-support elements contrast with stone, metal, and leather base plates in this desktop accessory system.

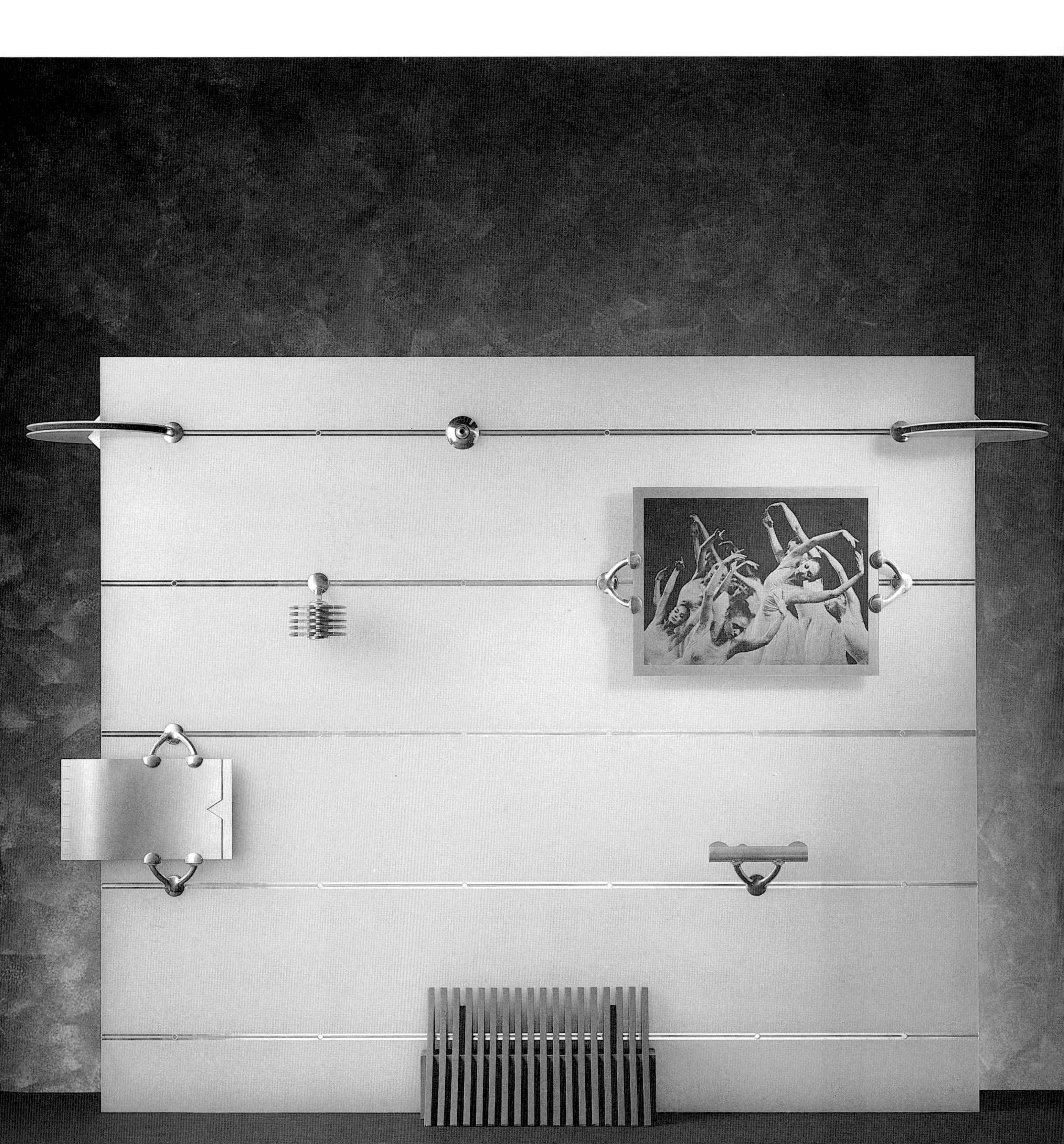

The Electronic Plane Model
1989

Michael McCoy and Dale Fahnstrom with David Vanden-Branden, Fahnstrom/McCoy, Chicago, Illinois, designers.

This home information and entertainment system is comprised of a sheet of glass, six feet by five feet, that contains an imbedded digital network. Video displays, CD players, telephones, printers, video imagers, audio speakers, and other devices are held in place by the aluminum "agents" which connect them, through small holes in the glass, into the network.

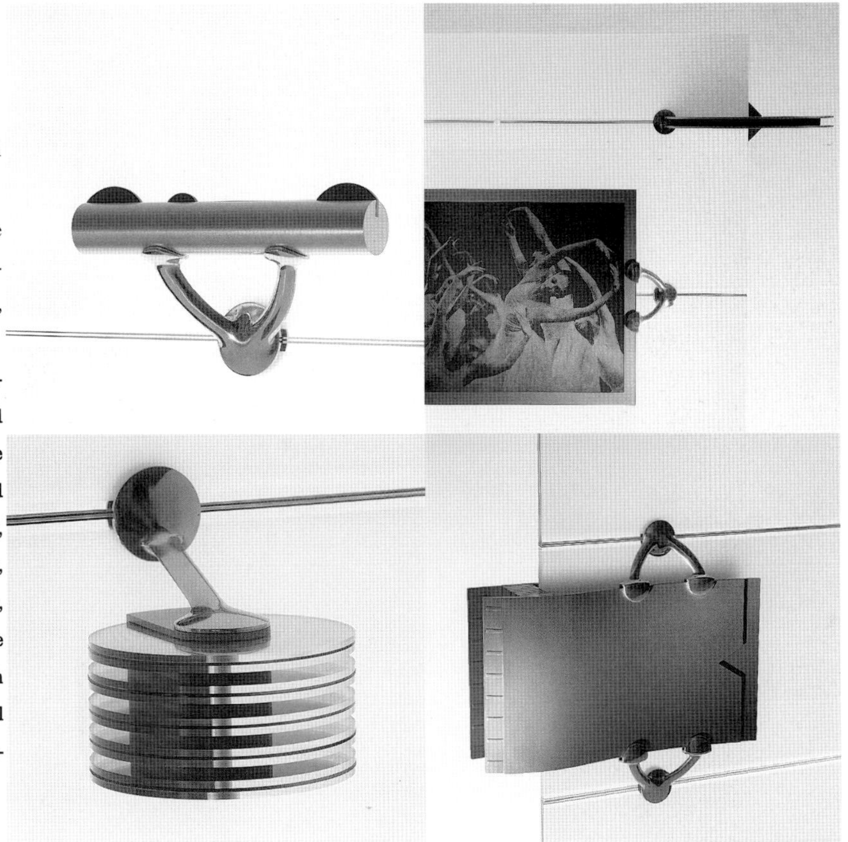

Quadrio Seating 1987
Michael McCoy, McCoy & McCoy, Bloomfield Hills, Michigan, designer; Artifort Company, Maastricht, The Netherlands, client and manufacturer.
A modular sofa that transforms abstract elements of architecture to seating scale. The separation of seat and back presents an ambiguity of structure.

Colorado Seating 1986
Michael McCoy, McCoy & McCoy, Bloomfield Hills, Michigan, designer; Artifort Company, Maastricht, The Netherlands, client and manufacturer.
The spanning structure for this seating, the back, is a sinuous line of continuity in space. The seats are cantilevered forward from the concealed steel beam. (Shown in LaVillette, Cité de Science, Paris).

Planétarium
ouverture

Visitor's Chair 1988

Michael McCoy and Dale Fahnstrom with David Vanden-Branden, F/M Studio, Chicago, Illinois, designers; Brayton International, High Point, North Carolina, client and manufacturer.

Slender and simple curved planes define the seat and back of this side chair. A flexible membrane makes possible an extremely thin profile.

Elizabeth's Rock Table 1989

Bruce Armold, designer; NOOZ, Portland, Oregon, manufacturer.

An inverted pyramid form balances precariously on a massive support structure.

Thylax Chair 1988

Noboru Inuoe, designer; Itoki Company, Tokyo, Japan, client and manufacturer.

An ergonomically designed chair that flexes at the knees to relieve pressure on the thighs when reclining.

D/3 Chair 1988

Dale Fahnstrom and **Michael McCoy** with David Vanden-Branden, F/M Studio, Chicago, Illinois, designers; Vecta Contract, Dallas, Texas, client and manufacturer.

A special D-shaped steel tube, flat on one side and round on the other, is used in three frame configurations, giving this chair an unusual structural profile.

Kobe Chair 1989

Dan Cramer, designer; Tuohy Furniture Company, Minneapolis, Minnesota, manufacturer.

A series of wood chairs that explores the possibility of variations in mass-produced furniture.

Door Chair 1981

Michael McCoy, McCoy & McCoy, Bloomfield Hills, Michigan, designer; Arkitektura, Inc., Princeton, New Jersey, client and manufacturer.

One of a series of furniture projects exploring the relationship of furniture to architecture. The architectural element of door is reduced to furniture scale and shifted in use. The closing action of the door becomes the folding action of the chair.

Bulldog Chairs 1989

Michael McCoy and Dale Fahnstrom with David Vanden-Branden, Fahnstrom/McCoy, Chicago, Illinois, designers; Knoll International, New York, client and manufacturer.

A family of office seating, including adjustable work chairs and a visitor's chair, that presents a sense of comforting place. The work chairs' backs adjust up and down for people of different sizes and proportions, and the chairs tilt forward to provide support when working at the computer.

Index

CONTRIBUTORS

Katherine McCoy has been Cochairman of the Department of Design at Cranbrook Academy of Art since 1971. As partner of McCoy & McCoy Associates, her design practice emphasizes interior design and graphic design for cultural and educational subjects. Recent clients include the Detroit Institute of Arts and Unisys Corporation. She writes frequently on design criticism and history and has coproduced a television documentary on Japanese design. She is past president of the Industrial Designers Society of America and an elected member of the Alliance Graphique Internationale.

Michael McCoy has been Cochairman of the Department of Design at Cranbrook Academy of Art since 1971. As partner of McCoy & McCoy Associates, his design practice emphasizes interior and furniture design. His Chicago partnership of Fahnstrom/McCoy and F/M Studio engages in industrial design and contract-furniture design for clients that include N. V.Philips and Knoll International. He was Chairman of the Industrial Designers Society of America national conference *Forms of Design* and recently coauthored an influential article on interpretive product design and product semantics in *Design Issues.*

Roy Slade is President of Cranbrook Academy of Art and Director of the Academy's art museum. Formerly Director of the Corcoran Gallery of Art and Dean of the Corcoran School of Art, he was educated in the fine arts in Wales and was a professor of painting at Leeds College of Art in England. He lectures frequently on art and design and is a practicing fine artist with numerous exhibitions to his credit. He serves regularly on National Endowment for the Arts panels and has chaired the Design Michigan Advisory Council for the past twelve years.

Niels Diffrient, of Ridgefield, Connecticut, is an alumnus of Cranbrook Academy of Art and is design consultant to international electronics firms and major contract-furniture companies. His office-seating family for Knoll International continues to set a standard for the field. During his twenty-five years with Henry Dreyfus Associates, he became deeply involved in ergonomics research and coauthored the *Humanscale* reference books. He is a Fellow of the Industrial Designers Society of America and serves on the board of the International Design Conference at Aspen.

Lorraine Wild is Director of the Graphic Design Program at California Institute of the Arts in Valencia, California. An alumna of Cranbrook Academy of Art and Yale University, she specializes in the design of books on architecture, fine art, and design for major museums and publishers including Rizzoli International, MIT Press, and the Museum of Contemporary Art in Los Angeles. She lectures and writes frequently on design history, theory, and criticism and contributed a major essay to the book *Graphic Design in America: A Visual Language History* (Abrams, 1989).

Daralice Boles is a freelance journalist and a former senior editor of *Progressive Architecture.*

Hugh Aldersey-Williams, a London-based journalist, frequently writes about design and technology. He is a contributing editor to *International Design* and also writes for several magazines in Europe and in the United States. He is the author of *New American Design* (Rizzoli, 1988).

This book was designed and produced on the Macintosh Computer using Aldus Pagemaker, Aldus Freehand, and Adobe Photoshop software with Bitstream Bodoni Book, Egyptian 710, and Geometric 706 Black type fonts.

Photography credits Ben Altman: p. 131; Joseph Coscia Jr.: p. 188; Chris Eden: pp. 136-137; Allen Hori: pp. 6, 8, 10, 12, 33, 36; Greg Hursley: pp. 132-133; Peter Paige: p. 130; Ray Reiss: p. 140; Francois Robert: pp. 99, 198-199; E.G. Shempf: pp. 134-135; Tim Street-Porter: pp. 128-129; David Vanden-Branden and Dan Machnik: pp. 198-199, 202; Thomas B. Wedell: pp. 48, 66-71, 110, 120-121, 124-125, 127, 138-139, 141, 152-157, 166, 172-175, 196-197; Tom Yee: p. 73.